The
U-Boat War
1914-1918

The
U-Boat War
1914-1918

EDWYN GRAY

LEO COOPER
LONDON

First published in Great Britain in 1972 by Seeley,
Service and Co. Ltd., as *The Killing Time*

Reprinted with corrections in 1994 by
LEO COOPER
190 Shaftesbury Avenue, London, WC2H 8JL

an imprint of
Pen & Sword Books Ltd.,
47 Church Street, Barnsley, South Yorkshire S70 2AS

A CIP catalogue record for this book is available from the British Library

ISBN 0 85052 405 9

Printed and Bound in the USA

CONTENTS

AUTHOR'S NOTE   9
CHAPTER ONE   'The essence of war is violence'   13
CHAPTER TWO   'We could not get over the wonder
                    of it'   24
CHAPTER THREE   'A fine day to sink a ship'   39
CHAPTER FOUR   'We can wound England most
                    seriously'   55
CHAPTER FIVE   'The most fatal weapon in naval
                    warfare'   72
CHAPTER SIX   'This campaign of piracy and
                    pillage'   89
CHAPTER SEVEN   'Proceedings for murder'   104
CHAPTER EIGHT   '. . . and a natural born fisherman to
                    boot'   116
CHAPTER NINE   'No death could be more agonizing'   136
CHAPTER TEN   'Act with the utmost caution'   156
CHAPTER ELEVEN   'We were men hardened by war'   172
CHAPTER TWELVE   'I prayed that I was guessing right'   189
CHAPTER THIRTEEN   'A battleship is enough for one day'   208
CHAPTER FOURTEEN   'One of the luckiest decisions I ever
                    made'   225
CHAPTER FIFTEEN   'We must and we will succeed'   241
CHAPTER SIXTEEN   'Are you absolutely sure of your
                    crew?'   257

APPENDIX ONE   *Equivalent ranks of British and
                    German officers*   267
APPENDIX TWO   *Germany's top twenty U-boat aces*   268

6

APPENDIX THREE *Distribution of U-boats 1914–1918*   269
APPENDIX FOUR   *Main U-boat types*   270
BIBLIOGRAPHY   272

INDEX   274

ILLUSTRATIONS

                                                    facing page
1   *Der Brandtacher*   16
2   *Le Diable-Marin*   16
3   Kapitanleutnant W. Schwieger   17
4   German postcard commemorating the sinking of
      the *Lusitania*   17
5   Lothar von Arnauld de la Perière   32
6   Oberleutnant Steinbauer   32
7   Otto Hersing   32
8   Baron von Spiegel von und zu Peckelsheim   32
9   A garlanded U-Boat   33
10 A U-Boat tows its victims to safety   33
11 MAN blast-injection diesel engines   80
12 A 5·9-inch deck gun   80
13 Schwartzkopff torpedoes   81
14 The business end of *U-62*   81
15 Kapitan Paul Konig   96
16 The submarine freighter *Deutschland*   96
17 *UC-5* in New York   97
18 The mine-chutes of *UC-5*   97
19 Lothar von Arnauld de la Perière   176
20 *U-35* unloading empty shell-cases at Cattaro   176
21 *U-157* holds up a Spanish liner   177
22 Torpedoing a freighter   177
23 *U-35* and *U-42* rendezvous at sea   192
24 A *UC-1* class minelayer   192
25 Lt Blacklock takes over a surrendered U-Boat   193
26 *U-58* surrenders to the US destroyer *Fanning*   193

'... hit your enemy in the belly, and kick him when he is down, and boil his prisoners in oil—if you take any—and torture his women and children. Then people will keep clear of you ... '

Admiral of the Fleet Lord Fisher, speaking at the Hague Peace Conference in 1899.

Author's Note

WHEN A NEW and untried weapon of war brings a mighty empire to the brink of defeat there is always a story worth telling. In 1914 the U-boats were such a weapon and this book tells the story of the Kaiser's attempt to destroy the British Empire by a ruthless campaign of unrestricted submarine warfare. It is a story that begins with Germany's first tentative experiments with submarines in the nineteenth century and ends in the revolutionary ferment of the naval mutiny which brought about the Kaiser's final defeat. In between is a detailed account of the terror campaign which, by April, 1917, brought Great Britain within a hairsbreadth of surrender. It is a savage record of men fighting for their lives below the surface of the sea and of atrocity, piracy, and murder. But it is also a testament to the heroism, compassion, and skilled seamanship of the men who were justly proud to wear the insignia of the *Deutsche Unterseeboots Flotille*.

My interest in this fascinating struggle was first aroused when I chanced upon this passage in William Guy Carr's book, *By Guess and by God*: 'The story of the North Sea operations (was) as much a story of men sealed in unsavoury tin cans, wallowing around the shallow ocean and continually at war with Nature, as it (was) a story of dramatic encounters between craft of opposing navies. In this respect the experiences of German submarine officers and men must have been identical with our own.' The thought that the submariners on both sides endured the same hardships, triumphs, and defeats, decided me to write this account of the U-boat war as a sequel to my previous book on British submarine operations in the Great

9

War, *A Damned Un-English Weapon*. And I have endeavoured to maintain a similarly objective and impartial standpoint throughout.

After the war the American author Lowell Thomas visited Germany to interview a large number of former U-boat captains about their experiences and the results of his painstaking labours were published in *Raiders of the Deep* in 1929. His kind permission to quote extensively from these interviews has enabled me to include many vividly personal comments by the men who actually fought the U-boat war beneath the sea and I hope that these valuable extracts have given my narrative a balance that would have been difficult to obtain in any other way.

As usual I would like to acknowledge my personal debt to the many authors and historians who, since 1918, have unravelled the complex details of the U-boat campaigns and I must also thank Doubleday & Co Inc., New York; Sidgwick & Jackson Ltd., The Estate of the late Sir Henry Newbolt and the Longmans Group Ltd., Hodder & Stoughton Ltd., the Estate of the late Admiral of the Fleet Lord Keyes, B. T. Batsford Ltd., George G. Harrap & Co Ltd., Frederick Muller Ltd., The Hogarth Press Ltd., John Farquharson Ltd., Constable & Co Ltd., The Hutchinson Publishing Group Ltd., Anthony Sheil Associates Ltd., The Hamlyn Publishing Group Ltd., and The Times Newspapers Ltd. for permitting me to use their copyright material. I am grateful, too, to the Librarian and Photo Librarian, and their staffs, of the Imperial War Museum for their willing assistance in tracing document and photographs. My apologies to those other copyright holders from whom I have quoted but have been unable to trace.

Finally I must express my appreciation to A. J. Brown of the Naval Records Club for the information he has supplied me on many occasions.

Any man brave enough to go under the surface of the sea in a submarine is, to me, something of a hero. And although some

U-boat captains were, as Lloyd George once said, 'Pirates and murderers', the majority were decent ordinary men with an unpleasant job to do. It is to the decent ordinary men of both sides that this book is dedicated.

EDWYN GRAY

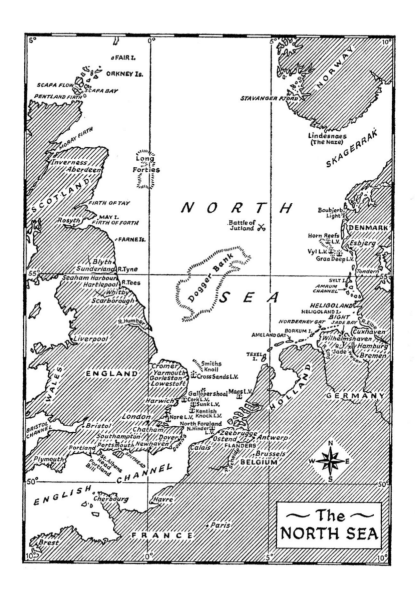

CHAPTER ONE

'The essence of war is violence'

2.20 pm Directly in front of us I sighted four funnels and the masts of a passenger steamer at right angles to our course coming from the SW and going towards Galley Head . . .[1]

IT WAS THE afternoon of 7 May, 1915. As Kapitanleutnant Walther Schwieger entered the sighting report in *U-20*'s log he had no premonition of what the future held—no warning that within the next hour his actions would make him the most hated man in the world. He scribbled his initials against the margin of the log-book entry, glanced quickly at the chart spread out across the control-room table, and snapped his fingers for the periscope to be raised ready for another hurried glimpse of his intended quarry.

U-20 was on her way home to the Fatherland after a marauding cruise along the coast of Ireland. With the overnight fog persisting well into the morning, fuel tanks running dangerously low, and only two torpedoes left in the tubes, Schwieger had decided to call it a day. Ordering the pilot to work out a course for the return to Wilhelmshaven, the U-boat skipper settled himself comfortably into a battered old leather armchair and began reading a book.

The patrol had been dull and unrewarding. True, he had sunk a sailing-ship and two steamers off Waterford, but these were paltry game compared with the achievements of Hersing, Weddigen, Valentiner, and the other great aces of the U-boat

---

[1] From the log of *U-20* (Quoted in *Raiders of the Deep* by Lowell Thomas, Heinemann, 1929.)

14

service. And Walther Schwieger was an ambitious man. A thirty-two year old bachelor from an old and respected Berlin family, he had served in submarines since the earliest pioneer days before the war. Tall and broad-shouldered, with blue eyes and blonde hair, he was every inch an officer of the Imperial German Navy—calm, correct, and coldly efficient. As a fellow captain remarked: 'He knew exactly where he was going—and be damned to anyone who tried to stop him.'[1]

The morning of the 7th had already brought one disappointment. Running submerged at 60 feet to avoid the danger of being rammed accidentally in the fog, Schwieger's attentive ears had caught the sound of powerful propellers churning the surface overhead and he took *U-20* up to investigate.

'I rose to 30 feet to take a look through the periscope. It was a big armoured cruiser. She had passed right over us and was now disappearing at high speed.'[2]

Both ships enjoyed a lucky escape. Had *U-20* been running at periscope depth the steel prow of the cruiser would have sliced through the flimsy hull of the submarine and cut her in half. And, if Schwieger had surfaced just a few minutes earlier, he could have slammed a torpedo into the enemy warship and then vanished into the fog. But it was not to be. Fate had a greater prize in store for the unfortunate Walther Schwieger.

The dense fog which had built up during the night had finally dispersed and the sun was now bright against a clear blue sky. Taking advantage of the improved weather conditions Schwieger had brought *U-20* to the surface and he was standing in the conning-tower enjoying the crisp freshness of the sea air when the unknown passenger ship was first sighted by the look-outs. For a brief moment he thought the forest of masts and funnels on the horizon must belong to a group of ships and he silently cursed the fact that he only had two

[1] *North German Gazette.*
[2] *Raiders of the Deep*, p. 96.

torpedoes left. Then suddenly he realized it was only one ship, one very big ship.

'Dive! Dive! Dive!'

The warning gongs rattled and the men below moved quietly and quickly to their stations. The great diving wheels that controlled the vents to the ballast tanks spun anti-clockwise and disciplined hands pulled the long series of switches and levers that were banked down one side of the cramped control-room. Schwieger slammed the hatch shut, slid down the narrow steel ladder leading from the bridge, and nodded approvingly as the First Officer threw the clutch to disconnect the oil engines.

'Main motors. Full power!'

The electric motors took over and the needles of the ammeters swung into the red discharge segments as a surge of current was sucked out of the batteries. *U-20*'s skipper glanced anxiously at the depth gauges. 10—15—20, down she went. And now, clear of the surface, the submarine stopped pitching and rolling and the soft hum of the electric motors replaced the harsh roar of the main engines. Schwieger checked the chronometer on the wall and moved across to a small table so that he could note his sighting report in the log. The U-boat settled in level trim at 60 feet and her bows swung towards the distant target.

2.25 pm Have advanced eleven metres towards the steamer in hope it will change its course along the Irish coast.'[1]

Returning to the periscope the Kapitanleutnant stared through the Zeiss eye-pieces and found himself almost consciously willing the ship to swing her helm to port. She was making a good 18 knots and opening the range with every passing minute. Groping beneath the surface at less than 5 knots *U-20* was rapidly losing ground.

[1] *U-20*'s log.

But, despite Schwieger's fears, the Master of the passenger ship, Captain Turner, was in no great hurry. He was already in receipt of a general warning signal from the Port Admiral at Queenstown that there had been submarine activity in the area and, just before noon, he received a further message that U-boats were in his immediate vicinity. Swinging in a wide arc to clear the Fastnet, where he thought the enemy might be lying in ambush, Turner pushed on into the St George's Channel. And, as a precaution, he 'had all boats swung when we came into the danger zone.'[1]

As the Old Head of Kinsale came into view he rang down to the engine rooms for a reduction in speed from 21 to 18 knots. As he explained later: 'My reason for going eighteen knots was that I wanted to arrive at Liverpool bar without stopping, and within two or three hours of high water.'[2]

It was a decision based on all known information plus a life-time of deep-sea experience. According to the Admiralty warning signals the U-boats, if there were any, were well astern by now and, in any case, his speed of 18 knots was amply sufficient to outpace any stray submarines he might encounter. Unfortunately the decision, made correctly and in all good faith, was to cost the lives of 1,198 innocent men, women and children.

The great ship changed course again in accordance with the neatly pencilled line which the navigating officer had traced on the charts and Schwieger could scarcely believe his eyes when he saw the target unexpectedly swing towards him.

2.35 pm Steamer turns, takes direction to Queenstown, and thereby makes it possible for us to approach for a shot. We proceed at high speed in order to reach correct firing position.[3]

In the cramped confines of the bow torpedo flat a red

---

[1] Evidence of Captain Turner at *Lusitania* inquest.
[2] Ibid.
[3] *U-20*'s log.

1. Wilhelm Bauer's *Der Brandtacher*, Germany's first "U-boat".

2. A contemporary drawing of Bauer's *Le Diable-Marin*. The orchestra which serenaded Tsar Alexander II from beneath the waters of Kronstadt harbour can be seen at the stern.

3. Kapitanleutnant Walther Schwieger. The man who sank the *Lusitania*.

4. A contemporary German propaganda postcard celebrating Schwieger's attack.

warning light blinked on the bulkhead. The crew turned the wheels that opened the external doors of the torpedo tubes and there was a rush of water as the hollow cylinders admitted the sea.

Hunched over the periscope in the control room Schwieger was entertaining doubts about the old bronze pattern torpedoes that were all *U-20* had left, but he had no choice. Clipped orders passed to the coxswain and the U-boat skipper kept a careful eye on the depth gauges as he closed with the target. His brain ticked like a computer, measuring off angles, ranges and deflection. More instructions passed and his hands closed over the handles of the periscope.

'First tube—fire!'

The torpedo Leutnant pressed the firing button with his thumb and *U-20* lurched slightly as the first torpedo hissed away.

3.10 pm Torpedo shot at distance of 700 metres, going three metres below the surface.[1]

There was a long pause and Schwieger watched the bubbling white track heading straight at the hull of the unsuspecting liner.

Captain Turner was standing on the port side of the liner's bridge when he 'heard the Second Officer, Hefford, call out: "Here's a torpedo". I ran to the other side and saw clearly the wake of a torpedo. Smoke and steam came up between the last two funnels and there was a slight shock. Immediately after the first explosion there was another report, but that might possibly have been internal.

'I at once gave the order to lower the boats down to the rails and I directed that women and children should get into them. I also had the bulkheads closed. I also gave orders to stop the ship, but we found that the engines were out of commission, and so could not reverse screws. It was not safe to

[1] *U-20*'s log.

lower boats until speed was off the vessel. As a matter of fact there was a perceptible headway on her up to the time she went down.'[1]

Glued to his periscope Schwieger watched the explosion through the Zeiss optics as the tragedy unfolded with startling speed. In terse phrases he dictated the entry in *U-20*'s log-book to the pilot.

'Hit steering centre behind bridge. Unusually great detonation with large cloud of smoke and debris shot above funnels. In addition to torpedo, a second explosion must have taken place. The ship stops and very quickly leans over to starboard, at the same time sinking by the bow. It looks as though it will capsize in a short time. There is great confusion on board. Boats are cleared and many of them lowered into the water. Many boats, fully loaded, drop down into the water bow or stern first and capsize. The boats on the port side cannot be made clear because of the heavy list . . .'

Reluctantly dragging himself away from the periscope Schwieger nodded for the pilot to take over. The other officer stared through the eye-piece for a few seconds. His face went white.

'My God,' he gasped, 'It's the *Lusitania*!'

Schwieger almost pushed him aside as he grabbed the 'scope handles. He turned it slowly to the right. And there, on the bows in great gold letters, he read the name for himself.

'It was the most terrible sight I have ever seen,' he told a colleague when he returned to Wilhelmshaven. 'The ship was sinking with unbelievable rapidity and there was a terrible panic on her decks. Desperate people ran helplessly up and down while men and women jumped into the water and tried to swim to empty overturned lifeboats. The scene was too horrible to watch and I gave orders to dive to 20 metres, and away.'

The cold-blooded sinking of the *Lusitania* was the most

[1] Evidence of Captain Turner at *Lusitania* inquest.

publicized tragedy of the First World War and, in the skilled hands of the British propaganda machine, it did much to inflame public opinion in the United States against Germany. Before Schwieger fired that fateful torpedo America's attitude was decidedly pro-German, due, in the main, to the irritations caused by the British blockade of German ports. The underlying reasons for this friction between the two great English-speaking nations will become apparent as the story of the U-boat war unfolds.

There was 'loud exultation' in Germany when the news of the sinking was first received and enterprising publishers sold thousands of *Lusitania* postcards to celebrate the incident—a portrait of Von Tirpitz, father of the German Navy, staring sternly from a garland of laurel leaves in the top left-hand corner of the picture. But, as the German government wilted under a deluge of international protests, the Kaiser and his advisers realized that the destruction of the liner had been a grave political mistake.

Schwieger's action was disowned by the German Emperor though his naval colleagues quickly rallied to his support. They pointed out that *U-20*'s captain had merely carried out orders and should not be held morally responsible for the 1,198 lives, including 128 American citizens, so tragically lost when the *Lusitania* went down. The difficulty, however, lay in the orders themselves which, while authorizing U-boat commanders to sink all British merchant ships in the War Zone, failed to make clear whether such sinkings were to be carried out in accordance with existing international law.

Briefly, in 1914, international law did not countenance the sinking of merchant ships without warning. A warning shot had to be fired whether the attacker was a surface ship or a submarine and the victim must then stop so that her papers could be examined. If, and only if, she was found to be carrying contraband, a very carefully defined commodity, she could be captured and a prize crew put on board or she could be sunk. However, sinking was only permitted if the safety of the crew was not endangered. Weather and sea conditions had to be moderate and lifeboats could not be abandoned to their fate unless they were within pulling distance of land. Any other method of sinking was, of course, unlawful.

But the instructions issued to Schwieger and the other U-boat commanders on 18 February, 1915, merely stated:

'Hostile merchant ships are to be destroyed.'[1]

The starkly-worded order gave no indication whether international law was to be obeyed or not. And, ferreting back through their files, the U-boat captains could find for their guidance only an earlier High Command instruction which had laid down: 'The first consideration is the safety of the U-boat. Consequently rising to the surface in order to examine a ship must be avoided for the sake of the boat's safety.'[2]

It is hardly surprising that many submarine skippers, including Schwieger, interpreted the order of 18 February to mean: sink the enemy without warning.

While politicians in Britain held up their hands in pious horror much naval opinion reflected the German view. When Churchill was asked about the use of submarines to sink merchant shipping he replied: 'I do not believe this would ever be done by a civilized Power.' But on the other hand realists, like Admiral of the Fleet Lord Fisher, First Sea Lord at the time of the *Lusitania* sinking, appeared to endorse German methods:

'There is nothing else the submarine can do except sink her capture, and it must therefore be admitted that (provided it is done, and however barbarious and inhuman it may appear) this submarine menace is a truly terrible one for British commerce and Great Britain alike, for no means can be

[1] *The Most Formidable Thing*, by Rear-Admiral William Jameson (Rupert Hart-Davis, 1965), p. 156.

[2] *The German Submarine War*, by R. H. Gibson and Maurice Prendergast (Constable, 1931), p. 29.

suggested at present of meeting it except by reprisals. All that would be known would be that a certain ship and her crew had disappeared, or some of her boats would be picked up with a few survivors to tell the tale. Such a tale would fill the world with horror, and it is freely acknowledged to be an altogether barbarous method of warfare but . . . the essence of war is violence; moderation in war is imbecility!'[1]

And as the U-boat commander on the spot might not be able to surface and warn his victim the German diplomatic service made vain efforts to circumvent international law by inserting warnings in foreign newspapers. On the day that Cunard announced the sailing schedule of the *Lusitania* the German Embassy placed the following advertisement in all New York newspapers:

NOTICE!

Travellers intending to embark on the Atlantic voyage are reminded that a state of war exists between Germany and her allies and Great Britain and her allies; that the zone of war includes waters adjacent to the British Isles; that, in accordance with formal notice given by the Imperial German Government, vessels flying the flag of Great Britain, or of any of her allies, are liable to destruction in those waters and that travellers sailing in the war zone on ships of Great Britain or her allies do so at their own risk.

IMPERIAL GERMAN EMBASSY
Washington, D.C., 22 April, 1915[2]

The public, stunned by the magnitude of the disaster, turned its venom on the 'baby-killer' U-boat captains. *The Times* referred to 'the atrocious conduct of the Germans' and added that the campaign carried out 'regardless of all considerations of humanity, was a lasting disgrace to the Germans who planned it and carried it into effect.'

[1] Lord Fisher's Memorandum, *The Oil Engine and the Submarine*, June, 1913.
[2] *The Times History of the War*, Vol. 5, p. 276.

The verdict of the Irish inquest jury was even stronger:

'We find that this appalling crime was contrary to international law and the conventions of all civilized nations, and we therefore charge the officers of the said submarine, and the Emperor and Government of Germany, under whose orders they acted, with the crime of wilful and wholesale murder before the tribunal of the civilized world.'[1]

Such was the temper of public opinion in the year 1915. But outraged conscience can degenerate into passive acquiescence with the passage of time. It is chastening to note that, on 9 April 1940, the British Admiralty authorized Royal Navy submarines to sink enemy merchant ships without warning and that the United States Navy carried out unrestricted submarine warfare against the Japanese right from the word 'go'. It is, perhaps, unnecessary to add that unrestricted submarine warfare is *still* outlawed by international law.

Faced with such a barrage of vilification the Germans attempted to justify the sinking. In the official communique drafted by Admiral Behncke they advanced a theory that has been a source of argument and dispute ever since:

'The detonation of the torpedo was followed immediately by a further explosion of extremely strong effect. The second explosion must be traced back to the ignition of quantities of ammunition inside the ship.'[2]

Naturally the charge was immediately denied by both the British and the United States governments and it was publicly stated that the *Lusitania* was only carrying 4,200 clips of .303 rifle ammunition. But there is a strange air of mystery about the exact details of the liner's cargo which, even today, has never been satisfactorily explained. Scraping away the layers of propaganda, Captain Turner's original evidence, given under oath to the inquest jury that the explosion 'may possibly have been internal', suggests that it was no more

[1] *Subs and Submarines*, by Arch Whitehouse (Muller, 1961) p. 71.
[2] Ibid. p. 68.

than the ship's boilers blowing up as the cold sea-water surged into the engine-room.

But the claims and counter-claims continued unabated. In their official note of 9 June, 1915, the United States Government charged that 'Whatever be the other facts regarding the *Lusitania*, the principal fact is that a great steamer, primarily and chiefly a conveyance for passengers, and carrying more than a thousand souls who had no part or lot in the conduct of the war, was torpedoed and sunk without so much as a challenge or a warning, and that men, women and children were sent to their death in circumstances unparalleled in modern warfare.'

By August, 1915, in deference to world opinion, the German government had virtually called off their first attempt to impose a submarine blockade on the British Isles and the Kaiser specifically ordered U-boat commanders not to attack passenger liners. Walther Schwieger's solitary torpedo had brought unexpected and unintended dividends to Britain and her allies.

Although disowned by the German emperor, Schwieger's colleagues rose to support him and began a whitewashing campaign that continued until well after the war had ended. But it *was* only whitewashing; as Schwieger admitted to Zentner, he had fired at the *Lusitania* before he had identified her in any way.

Fortunately Walther Schwieger was by no means typical of the German U-boat captains who, on many occasions, displayed both chivalry and humanity of the highest order to their victims. And, realizing the courage and technical skill needed by the men who command submarines, we may be more merciful in our judgement than the jury at the *Lusitania* inquest.

The U-boat war brought Imperial Germany to the threshold of victory. It was a murderous campaign that destroyed 11,018,865 tons of Allied merchant shipping. It was a conflict that cost the lives of 515 officers and 4,894 men of the U-boat service. It was, for both sides, the Killing Time.

CHAPTER TWO

'We could not get over the wonder of it'

'GERMANY,' ADMIRAL VON TIRPITZ had declared, when he addressed the Reichstag in 1901, 'has no need of submarines.' And, according to an assiduously fostered legend, the Imperial German Navy did not complete its first official *unterseeboot* until December, 1906—well after every other major navy in the world, including even Portugal and Turkey, had added these new underwater vessels to their fleets.

This apparently late start in submarine construction has been seized upon by many German historians, and other kindred apologists for the U-boat campaign, to prove that Germany was forced to build submarines as a measure of self-defence against other and more aggressive powers. But as is so often the case with propaganda the arguments do not match up with the true facts of the case.

The earliest known practical submarine was built by a Dutchman, Cornelis Drebbel, and had been demonstrated on the Thames in 1620 when the inventor and his intrepid crew calmly dived under the water while he 'kept the king and several thousand Londoners in the greatest suspense.' Drebbel's submersible was, however, little more than an open-bottomed rowing boat based upon the same principles as the modern diving-bell and in no way intended as a vessel of war. It is highly doubtful if it could have survived for more than a few minutes in even a moderate seaway.

More than 150 years passed before David Bushnell, an American eccentric of considerable genius, produced the world's next serious submarine. His strange egg-shaped creation, *Turtle*, designed as a vessel of war, was equipped with a primitive screw device with which to clamp a powder charge to the keel of its intended victim. In 1776 *Turtle* actually attacked the English frigate *Eagle* as she lay at anchor off New York but, beset by many unforseen difficulties, not the least being the strength of the tide, her gallant one-man crew, Sergeant Ezra Lee, failed to achieve success.

Bushnell was followed by another American, Robert Fulton, who, after prolonged negotiations with Napoleon, built a copper-sheathed vessel, shaped like a squat cigar, which he called *Nautilus*. Launched on 24 July, 1800, and armed with a spar torpedo, the 21 ft 4 in long submarine was not entirely unsuccessful although both the French and British governments finally decided against buying it—on moral rather than material grounds.

Admiral de Crès told the designer: 'Your invention is good for Algerians and pirates, but learn that France has not yet given up the seas.' Admiral Earl St Vincent, less scornful but even more forthright, said it was 'a mode of warfare which those who commanded the seas did not want, and which, if successful, would deprive them of it.'

Just over a hundred years later when France and Britain were joined as allies the under-lying truths behind these statements were demonstrated by the U-boats, for by 1917 the British government were only too well aware that Germany's submarine campaign was rapidly depriving them of their centuries-old command of the sea.

Next on to the scene was a Bavarian inventor, Wilhelm Bauer, who in 1850 constructed *Der Brandtacher* at Kiel—Germany's first flirtation with underwater warfare and a far cry indeed from the usually quoted 1906 birthdate of the U-boat. Like all early experiments it was primitive in design and inadequate in conception. A mere $26\frac{1}{2}$ feet in length, it weighed 38 tons, and was built of iron sheeting with flat and vulnerable sides. Bauer was no theoretical scientist and he was unaware of the hull stresses which would arise from the pressure of the sea as the primitive craft sank beneath the surface. Like all previous submarine designs there were no engines and motive power was provided by a handwheel geared to a propeller at the stern. A large weight fitted to a threaded bar running almost the full length of the boat was used to control horizontal trim, and ballast tanks, operated by a hand pump, adjusted the vessel's buoyancy. *Der Brandtacher*'s offensive capability comprised two leather 'gloves' which, operated from inside the boat, could be used to fix mines on her victim's keel.

The whole conception was almost ludicrous, yet the mere existence of *Der Brandtacher* was sufficient to scare the wary Danes into moving their blockading fleet away from the German coast—a moral victory for the *unterseeboot* comparable to Jellicoe's evacuation of the Grand Fleet from Scapa Flow to Lough Swilley in 1914.

But Bauer's invention soon met with disaster. On 1 February, 1851, accompanied by two seamen, Witt and Thomsen, he climbed inside the tiny vessel, cast off the mooring ropes, and gently propelled her out across Kiel harbour. At first every-thing went according to plan. The hatches were secured, the valves of the ballast tanks were opened to admit the water and, as the balancing weight moved towards the bows, *Der Brandtacher* dipped slowly and demurely beneath the surface. Then, suddenly and without warning, Bauer lost control and the clumsy little boat angled sharply towards the bottom.

The sides of the submarine yielded to the increasing pressure as she slid down into the depths of the harbour and the sea began pouring in through a dozen leaking seams. The primitive hand pump was unable to cope with the increasingly dangerous situation and, with the vessel's balance upset, the pig-iron ballast in the bilges rushed headlong towards the bows. *Der Brandtacher* dropped like a stone and came to rest in an almost vertical position with her nose buried deep into the mud of the harbour bottom.

There seemed no chance of survival. The forward section of the submarine was flooded and the remaining air was trapped in the stern. But Bauer kept calm and explained how they could escape; by admitting more water the pocket of air in the stern would be compressed and, when pressure had built up sufficiently, it could sweep them to safety through the after-hatch. The two seamen took a good deal of convincing. To admit more water into the already flooded submarine seemed utter madness and Bauer was hoarse with pleading before he finally persuaded them.

Fumbling in the darkness they located the valve wheels and, in obedience to the calm directions of the inventor, they slowly flooded the boat. Soon the increasing air pressure was hurting their ears as, inch by inch, the cold black water crept up their bodies— first reaching their waists, then their chests, until it was lapping around their necks. Bauer positioned them beneath the after hatch and waited as the ice-cold water swirled and gurgled under his chin.

Suddenly, yielding under the immense pressure, the heavy iron hatch burst open and the three gasping survivors were swept to the surface in a giant bubble of air. Their terrifying ordeal trapped beneath the sea had lasted almost five hours.

But *Der Brandtacher* was finished. Completely flooded, she rested on the harbour bed, an abandoned rusting wreck for thirty-six years until, in 1887, she was raised and placed on show in a Berlin museum. Germany's first experiment with the *unterseeboot* had come to an inglorious end.

Undeterred by the disaster Bauer toured the capitals of Europe in search of fresh customers. He found one in the Russian government for whom he built the relatively successful *Diable-Marin* which, on one memorable occasion, shipped a small orchestra on board to play the National Anthem in honour of the Tzar's Coronation while submerged beneath the waters of Kronstadt harbour. Bauer then left Russia and made his way to Paris where he interested Napoleon III in his ideas, but unfortunately none of these later designs got beyond the drawing-board.

The American Civil War produced many revolutionary ideas in the art of warfare the most important of which, in the history of the U-boat, was the *David* design. These vessels were not, at first, true submarines but merely tiny torpedo boats that ran awash with the minimum of superstructure showing above the surface, a necessary precaution since they were powered by a small steam engine. By 1864 the Confederates had produced a proper submersible from the *David* design although it was only capable of running submerged for very short periods. In the process, however, they had to revert to a form of hand propulsion.

The inherent danger to both hunter and hunted was pin-pointed by the first attack when, armed with a spar torpedo, one of the boats, the *Hunley*, sank the Federal frigate *Housatonic* off Charleston on 17 February, 1864, a milestone in the history of submarine warfare. Unfortunately the *Hunley* failed to surface after the attack and was posted 'missing, believed lost'—the first of many *unterseeboots* to perish unseen beneath the sea whilst carrying out a combat mission.

A year earlier France had taken a major step forward by producing the first submarine with mechanical propulsion. *Le Plongeur*, 410 tons and fitted with an 80 hp compressed air engine, gave her designers and crew many unexpected surprises, and the explosive charge which she carried at the end of a long spar projecting from the bows was more of a liability than an asset. But *Le Plongeur* showed beyond doubt that a practical submarine was possible. It required only a talented engineer to act as midwife, and that man, although a less romantic character would be hard to find, was John Phillip Holland, an Irish schoolmaster who had emigrated to the United States in 1873.

Spurred on by the obsession of a vessel capable of travelling beneath the sea the little Irishman, a comic figure with small gold rimmed glasses and a large walrus moustache, persuaded a gullible business acquaintance to part with $6,000 to finance his first essay into submarine construction.

Holland I, completed in 1877, was a pathetic little toy worked by pedal power. So primitive was the design that the pilot had to wear diving-dress because the control compartment flooded each time the boat submerged. By 1883, having formed the John P. Holland Torpedo Boat Co, Holland had progressed to his fifth prototype which boasted not only a small petrol engine but also a pneumatic gun designed and built by Captain Edmund Zalinski. Like the previous designs *Holland V* was no great success but, with dogged perseverance, the little Irish engineer continued his experiments.

Europe, by now, was ablaze with submarine fever. An English clergyman, the Rev G. W. Garrett, built the steam-driven *Resurgam* as a private venture, only to see her sink off Birkenhead on her maiden voyage in 1878. The French Navy, taking a lead it was to hold for several decades, experimented with Gustav Zede's *Gymnote* and also ordered a small two-man submersible from Goubet, while, in 1888, Spain put *her* first submarine into service, a well-built vessel powered by electric motors and fitted with a torpedo tube, based on the plans of a brilliant young naval lieutenant, Isaac Peral.

But it was in the waters of the Baltic that the next important phase in the development of the submarine took place. The world-famous ordnance expert, Thorsten Nordenfelt, had turned his enquiring mind to the problems of underwater warfare and, in 1881, his first submarine was laid down in a Stockholm shipyard. By 1885 it was ready for public trials and the 60 ton boat, powered by steam and equipped with a firing tube for a Whitehead torpedo, was an immediate success. It performed its demonstration tasks with accomplished ease and only Nordenfelt and his intimate associates were aware of the delicate skill necessary to keep it under control. The

Greek Navy snapped it up while Turkey, her age-old rival, promptly ordered *two* similar boats to maintain superiority.

Moving to England Nordenfelt continued his development programme. The two Turkish vessels were built at Barrow and shipped out to Constantinople in sections ready for assembly (an early example of pre-fabrication techniques), while another boat of new and improved design was constructed for the Russian government. And it was at this time, fully ten years before the British Admiralty ordered a single submarine for the Royal Navy, that the Imperial German Navy showed renewed interest in the *unterseeboot*.

Purchasing plans from Nordenfelt, the Germans began building two submarines, *W.1* and *W.2*, one at Kiel and the other at Danzig, in 1890. Both vessels were steam-powered with a surface displacement of 215 tons. Each was 114 feet long and they were capable of 11 knots on the surface and $4\frac{1}{2}$ knots submerged. Shortly afterwards they constructed a smaller submarine at the Howaldt Yard powered entirely by electric motors. And, still experimenting, Krupps also built a French design of 180 tons surface displacement in which, for the first time, petrol engines were used for surface running and electric motors while submerged, a combination that, apart from the substitution of diesel engines for petrol, was to become the standard engineering layout for all non-nuclear submarines of the future. The Nordenfelt boats were assigned to the torpedo flotillas at Kiel and Wilhelmshaven for trials but the official reports on their performances were unimpressive and they were soon removed from service.

But the German Navy had absorbed some interesting experience in underwater warfare, and although they had lost interest in the submarine German shipbuilders had not and, by 1903, the Krupp-Germania shipyard had built a 17 ton experimental model which was purchased by Russia the following year and named *Forelj*. Next came the *Karp* class, a French design by d'Equevilley, of 196 tons driven by paraffin engines. Although private ventures there is little doubt that the German Navy was fully aware of the work and there was no official objection when Russia ordered four of the boats. They were delivered, following an unusual and possibly deliberate delay, in 1907.

Meanwhile John Holland had perfected his Type IX submarine after many difficulties and by 1900 both the Royal Navy and the United States Navy had Holland IXs on order. Holland's latest vessel, and the success of the Krupp-built *Karps*, finally persuaded the ultra-conservative German High Command that the submarine was no longer a temperamental toy but something to be taken seriously. Von Tirpitz had said, 'I refused to throw money away on submarines so long as they could only cruise in home waters,' but the sudden wide-ranging improvements in design in the years immediately after 1900 soon made it apparent that the submarine was no longer a coast-hugging defensive vessel but a fully-fledged seagoing warship with considerable offensive potential. In the 1905–6 Estimates the German Admiralty allocated £73,000 to the 'first' experimental boat, to be built, ironically, to the plans of the French inventor d'Equevilley.

But, as we have seen from this brief account, *Unterseeboot No 1* was most certainly *not* Germany's first submarine. Wilhelm Bauer's *Der Brandtacher* of 1850, having been built primarily as a military submarine, can justly claim to be the first U-boat. The Nordenfelt boats of the '90s, and the *Karps*, were all planned as torpedo-carrying vessels so that, by the time *U-1* was ordered in 1905, both Krupps and the German Navy had a vast store of experience upon which to work. This fact helps to explain why Germany was not plagued by the problems that beset Vickers and the British Navy in the early days. Neither did she suffer the bureaucratic bumblings and political pressures that surrounded the infant submarine service of the Royal Navy.[1]

[1] See *A Damned Un-English Weapon*, by Edwyn Gray (Seeley Service, 1971).

At first progress was slow, the budget for 1906–7 was some £250,000 but this rose consistently and between the years 1912–13 alone, £1,000,000 was spent. The first model, *U-1*, laid down by the Krupp-Germania works at Kiel in August, 1905, was completed on 14 December, 1906. 139 feet in length, with a beam of 12¼ feet, she had a surface displacement of 238 tons, and was broadly comparable with the contemporary British 'A' class. But she had one big advantage over the British boats—surface power was provided by a 400 hp Korting kerosene engine, a far less dangerous animal than the 16 cylinder Wolseley petrol engines fitted in the British submarines whose highly volatile fuel caused a number of fatal accidents. For underwater running *U-1* had electric motors of 400 hp, basically similar to those of other navies.

Her oddly flat appearance contrasted with the high curves of the 'A' class and she was, by comparison, a slow diver. But she was an excellent sea boat and as submarines normally spent most of their time on the surface this was an important asset. Her only weapon was a single torpedo tube in the bows and she carried a total outfit of three 17.7 inch torpedoes.

Even before she had been on trials the German Navy pushed ahead and *U-2*, a new design, was laid down at Danzig dockyard, followed shortly afterwards by *U-3* and *U-4*. Already these new boats were more advanced than their British contemporaries and each carried four torpedo tubes, two in the bows and two in the stern while *U-3* and *U-4* were also fitted with a 37 mm gun that retracted into the hull when submerged.

For some reason, probably no more than good luck, the German Navy escaped the numerous disasters that beset the submarines of the Royal Navy and other countries. In the pre-1914 era only one U-boat was lost, the *U-3* on 17 January, 1911, and even she was salvaged and re-commissioned later. Progress was striking in every field. In 1908 *U-1* successfully completed a 600-mile trip from Heligoland to Kiel, no mean feat in those pioneering days, while *U-3* and *U-4* demonstrated

5. Germany's ace of aces. Lothar von Arnauld de la Perière. Total bag 400,000 tons of Allied shipping.

6. *UB-48's* commander, Steinbauer, who destroyed the Q-ship *Prize*.

7. Otto Hersing used his *U-21* to attack warships. *Pathfinder*, *Majestic*, *Triumph* and *Amiral Charner* were amongst his victims.

8. Baron von Spiegel von und zu Peckelsheim whose book *War Diary of U-202* upset the British propaganda machine.

9. A garlanded U-boat sets out on patrol.

10. Not all were pirates and murderers. A U-boat tows its victims to safety in a ship's lifeboat.

their sea-worthiness by maintaining an average speed of 12 knots in the teeth of an autumnal storm in November, 1910. And in December, 1912, a group of U-boats spent six days moored to buoys in the Heligoland Bight as a demonstration of their endurance. As one captain commented: 'It was considered an incredible achievement and we could not get over the wonder of it.'

The naval manoeuvres of 1912 brought further plaudits. The U-boats were credited with more kills than all of Germany's eighty destroyers put together and, during the Spring manoeuvres of the following year, Otto Weddigen, then only a Lieutenant, 'sank' three battleships with his *U-9*—a boat which put theory firmly into practice when war broke out.

On the technical side the U-boats adopted the diesel engine for surface power some time after Britain despite the fact that the compression-ignition engine was a German invention. Vickers had tried out an experimental diesel power-unit in *A-13* and all the new D class boats were diesel-propelled. But Krupps, although testing a small diesel in 1906 and building a diesel-engined submarine for the Italians in 1912, did not fit this form of propulsion into their own U-boats until 1913.

There is an interesting story about the *U-19*'s engines in Hector Bywater's book *Strange Intelligence*. 'Their construction at the Krupp-Germania works in Kiel would have remained unknown but for the fact that the particular shop where they were being assembled was barricaded off from the others and plastered with notices threatening trespassers with dire penalties. Inevitably it was soon spread about the whole works that something of a highly secret nature was in progress, and as the firm employed 6,000 hands, the news quickly circulated throughout Kiel. Being thus provided with a definite clue, one of our Secret Service men followed it up, and eventually obtained full details of the engine.'[1]

---

[1] *Strange Intelligence*, by H. C. Bywater & H. C. Ferraby (Constable, 1931) p. 91.

But despite the assistance of the Secret Service the Admiralty did not make use of the German designs and our submarines remained at a disadvantage throughout the war. The Krupp-MAN. blast-injection engines were a great improvement on the Admiralty pattern solid-injection units used by the Royal Navy. They were more reliable and had the advantage of producing less smoke—an important detail that led to the destruction of several submarines spotted on the surface. And there were many other significant improvements in the German boats; periscopes were in a class apart thanks to the skills of the great optical firm of Zeiss, their torpedoes were bigger and better (19.69 inch compared with the Standard British 18 inch), while their powerful Telefunken wireless transmitters had a range of at least 140 miles against the British submarine's 40 miles.

Small wonder, then, that the German yards were closely guarded against prying eyes. One British spy travelled on the little ferry steamers running between Danzig and Neufahrwasser to get a glimpse of the building slips but found the U-boats were being constructed on covered slipways roofed with glass. Nevertheless while watching trials at Kiel, 'I discovered, amongst other things, that the German boats were sluggish in diving, and took nearly a minute longer to submerge than ours did ... it was clear that submarine training was being carried out on "safety-first" principles.'[1]

The German Navy may have been cautious but, by 1910, their U-boats could cross the North Sea, carry out a patrol, and then return to Germany without refuelling; while the *U-19* class, completed in 1913, had a range of 5,000 miles at 8 knots. Clearly von Tirpitz's dictum that Germany had no need for coast-defence submarines had been taken very much to heart by the designers at Krupp-Germania.

Yet, despite this apparent emphasis on *offensive* strategy, the Germans lagged well behind the Royal Navy in sheer

[1] *Strange Intelligence*, p. 137.

weight of numbers. In 1910 Britain's 56 submarines were faced by only 8 U-boats and, even in 1914, the situation was not much better. According to *The Times*, in April of that year, Britain had built or was building a total of 98 submarines against Germany's 39, an improvement in ratio but still dangerously behind. In fact, the Fleet Law of 1912 only visualized a total of 72 U-boats by 1920.

The British Admiralty, however, correctly realized that the danger lay not so much in numbers as in offensive capabilities and in 1912 published a memorandum stating:

'No other class of vessel yet designed belongs more naturally to the defensive than the submarine; but the German development of the submarine tends to turn even this weapon of defence into one of offence, by building not the smaller classes which would be useful for the defence of their limited coastline, but large submarines capable of sudden and offensive operation at a distance from their base across the sea.'

Despite the Admiralty's view that the submarine 'belongs more naturally to the defensive', a strategical error that was to bedevil the British submarine service throughout the war, the Royal Navy had, in fact, laid down her first 'overseas' submarine in 1908 and, at the time of the memorandum, was engaged in building the 'E' class boats which were to form the backbone of the British flotillas during the coming conflict. Apart from an understandable apprehension about the offensive power of their potential enemy it is difficult to see why the Admiralty chose to level such charges against Germany when Great Britain was equally guilty.

But, although the British were alarmed, the German Navy itself had a very small opinion of the U-boat arm and it was not until the Kiel Week festivities in June, 1914, when the Kaiser himself personally inspected the despised submarines, that the U-boat crews could feel any outward pride in their chosen profession. The Kaiser boarded several of the submarines, including Weddigen's *U-9*, and was suitably impressed by all he saw. The German Emperor was not the only person to take a close interest in them; the Royal Navy had sent a powerful squadron of her latest warships to participate in the Kiel Week celebrations and the British officers paid more than usual attention to these latest additions to the German fleet. As one U-boat officer noted in his diary: 'Our guests could not gaze for long enough at the low-lying craft.'

The murder of the Archduke Francis Ferdinand at Sarajevo on 28 June brought the festivities to an abrupt close. The gaily coloured bunting decorating the gleaming grey warships was stripped off as bosun's pipes trilled the men to quarters. The four British battleships and their four attendant cruisers moved slowly out of the harbour to farewell sirens and waving arms while a Royal Marine band on the flagship's quarter-deck thumped out a rousing musical selection in honour of their hosts. Everyone, whether they were drawn up in the immaculate ranks lining the rails of the departing squadron or crowded into the cheering throngs on the quay-side, knew that war was inevitable, yet all, or nearly all, still felt that Britain would remain neutral in the coming conflict. It was a sentiment reflected even in the signal flying from the yards of the British flagship:

'Friends in peace, friends for ever.'

In the U-boat flotilla preparations proceeded at almost panic speed and, on 16 July, Weddigen and *U-9* carried out, for the first time, the difficult exercise of reloading torpedo tubes while submerged, a useful tactic when war conditions might keep a submarine under the surface for many hours. Johann Spiess, First Officer of the *U-9*, recalled those final frantic days:

'The practice and manoeuvres of the U-boats now increased to feverish intensity. The dark shadow of war was drawing ever closer, ready to engulf us, and we could not tell how soon those mimic battle operations of diving and torpedoing might become the real thing . . . a surprise attack by the British Fleet was expected hourly.'

But despite all these preparations the ultimate role of the U-boats received scant attention on either side of the North Sea. In Britain the possibility of an all-out attack on commerce was considered and rejected. As we have seen, Churchill was of the opinion that 'this would never be done by a civilized power', and his views were endorsed by the Admiralty professionals. Arguments raged week after week in Whitehall, the clubs of Pall Mall, and the columns of *The Times* on the ethics and practicalities of a submarine campaign, and it is difficult now to understand many of the views expressed by the protagonists after the harsh realities of two World Wars. The general consensus of informed opinion was that attacks against merchant shipping, other than 'prize warfare' conducted by surface cruisers, were impossible within the framework of existing international law, and it was inconceivable that any civilized nation would break that law.

From all available evidence it also seems unlikely that the Kaiser or his intimate naval advisers considered using their U-boats in an offensive war against merchant shipping before 1914. Certainly no documents have been discovered to indicate that such a course was ever seriously mooted. But the restraint of the German government was due not so much to misplaced feelings of humanity—the Clausewitz theory of war was too deeply ingrained in the military mind for such considerations to weigh very heavily—it was due to one simple fact. The German army thought it could crush any enemy in the world without the assistance of the Navy, and it was only after the generals realized that the war was not going to be won by Christmas of 1914 that consideration was given to a U-boat campaign against British trade.

Swimming against the tide as always, Admiral Sir Percy Scott, the father of modern naval gunnery, saw matters with the clear vision of the prophet. In July, 1914, he wrote to *The Times*:

'All war is, of course, barbarous, but in war the purpose of the enemy is to crush his foe; to arrive at this he will attack where his foe is most vulnerable. Our most vulnerable point is our food and oil supply. The submarine has introduced a new method of attacking these supplies. Will feelings of humanity restrain our enemy from using it?'

Sir Percy's question was soon to be answered.

CHAPTER THREE

'A fine day to sink a ship'

THE WATERS OF the Heligoland Bight were ominously
quiet; only the soft slap of the sea against the moored U-boats
and the shrieks of the seagulls wheeling above disturbed the
peaceful atmosphere. Rolling gently on an ebbing tide, with
engines silent and hatches secure, the straggling line of submarines bobbed and pitched while, crouched behind the
canvas screens of their bridges, the officers kept a watchful
eye on the horizon.

It was 2 August, 1914. Germany and Russia had already
been at war for twenty-four hours and the governments of
Europe were taking up their positions in readiness for the
coming conflict. France would enter the fray the following
day and already Belgian neutrality was threatened as the
Kaiser's armies massed on her borders.

Only Britain wavered. She had no formal military alliance
with France and, although she had arrived at an 'understanding'
with the French that she would protect their Channel coast, it
was by no means certain that she would honour her commit-
ments. The British Cabinet was uncertain and Sir Edward
Grey, the Foreign Secretary, was still making desperate last-
minute efforts to avert the crisis and restore peace. Yet although
Russia, the declared enemy, lay to the east and the French
fleet was safely based in the Mediterranean, the U-boat
officers were anxiously searching the *western* horizon.

Perfidious Albion, as every good German knew, was not to
be trusted. Had not Admiral Fisher, the *enfant terrible* of the
Royal Navy, threatened several times within earshot of German
diplomats and officers to Copenhagen the Kaiser's fleet by

executing a powerful strike against it before a formal declaration of war? And was it not well-known that the British Navy had detailed plans to land troops on the island of Borkum and so seal the High Seas Fleet in its base at Wilhelmshaven while English warships imposed a close blockade of the North German sea coast? Well, let them try it, the U-boats were waiting.

At 3 am on 1 August, within hours of the German declaration of war on Russia, the U-boats slipped quietly out of Heligoland harbour, formed up neatly in a single line between the protective flanks of the surface escorts, and set out for their lonely patrol line at the western entrance to the Bight. A row of mooring buoys indicated their position and the surfaced submarines were secured to these floating hulks of iron to form a static, and virtually useless, barrier.

As the sun-set gun boomed out from the fortress ramparts of Heligoland the escorting warships returned to pick up their charges. Engines restarted with a reluctant cough, ropes were cast off from the buoys and the little convoy of U-boats formed up for the short trek back to harbour.

Standing on the bridge of *U-9* Otto Weddigen watched the ruddy glow of sunset spreading over the horizon. It was Nature at its most magnificent and it formed a dramatic backcloth to the sparkling white wakes created by the churning propellors of the ten U-boats.

'Spiess,' he said suddenly to the First Officer at his side on the bridge, 'you see how red the sky is. The whole world seems bathed in blood. Mark my words—England will declare war on us.' Within the next forty-eight hours his prophecy came true.

For the young U-boat commanders it was an inglorious beginning to their high hopes of daring raids deep inside enemy waters and the hours of watching and waiting in the static patrol line were sheer purgatory for their eager spirits. It was, fortunately, a very short-lived phase and, completely reversing their previous tactics, the High Command ordered the U-boats out on an offensive sweep across the North Sea. At dawn on 6 August ten submarines set off from Heligoland in search of the British Grand Fleet.

Once again surface ships escorted them across the Bight but this time the U-boats swept triumphantly past the buoys and pushed out into the open sea.

'Stand by to dive!'

'Open main vents. Clutches out.'

'Dive!'

The hydroplanes tilted, hatches snapped shut, and the U-boats slid slowly, very slowly, beneath the waves. At 10 metres they levelled out and held their depth while the officers carefully checked the hulls for leaks. And then:

'Stand by to surface!'

'Close main vents. Blow all tanks.'

'Surface!'

Compressed air whistled through the tiny hulls, the depth gauge needles began to swing obediently to the left, and ten impatient skippers waited on the steel-runged ladders with their hands gripping the hatch levers. Daylight streamed through the thick glass ports of the conning-tower, the hatch was thrown open, and as the captain hurried up on to the bridge he could hear the routine surfacing orders echoing from down inside the brightly lit interior of the U-boat:

'Switches up. In clutch. Start main engines.'

A belch of black oil smoke erupted from the exhausts as the Korting engines spluttered to life and the submarine began to surge forward. Johann Spiess joined Weddigen on the bridge of *U-9* while, to right and left, the other U-boats wallowed to the surface. Like swimmers testing the temperature of the water they had plunged beneath the sea and now, surfaced and drawn up in line abreast, they were ready for their first war patrol. The great adventure had begun.

Horn Reefs passed on the port side and the crew of the Vyl lightship gave a cheer of encouragement as the U-boats chugged past. Minutes later a signal lamp flickered from the conning-tower of the Senior Officer's boat and the submarines obediently swung north and west—spreading apart gradually until they were covering a band of sea forty miles wide.

Engine defects quickly forced Weddigen's *U-9* to drop out of line and return to base but the remaining nine pushed on until, after nightfall, they separated and went their different ways. By the 8th they were four hundred miles out and probing the waters of the Orkneys. Seven of the boats sighted nothing and returned, dispirited and empty-handed, to Heligoland. The eighth, *U-13*, ran into a minefield after three days out and vanished without trace.

On the same day, 9 August, the remaining submarine, *U-15*, found the Grand Fleet.

Ajax, Monarch, and *Orion,* dreadnought battleships from the Second Battle Squadron, were located at target practice south of Fair Isle. *U-15* stalked her ponderous quarry but, as yet unskilled in the arts of underwater attack, her torpedoes missed. The British battleships scurried back to join the rest of their squadron but their reports of an abortive torpedo attack were dismissed by the Flag Officer on the grounds that 'U-boats could not operate so far from their bases.'

A periscope sighting by the *Iron Duke* the same evening, almost certainly the persistent *U-15* again, confirmed the earlier report but the great leviathans continued to plough westwards to their base at Scapa. John Jellicoe, the Grand Fleet's commander, was well aware of the danger from submarine attack and entertained no illusions about their range and capabilities, but with Scapa Flow devoid of any antisubmarine defences he deemed it safer to keep the fleet at sea. It was a difficult decision for the man who, in Churchill's words, 'could have lost the war in an afternoon', but as the Grand Fleet lost no major warship to U-boat attack in the early months of the war it seemed to have been a wise one in the circumstances.

U-15 clung tenaciously to her quarry through the short summer night and, at 4 am the next morning, the light cruiser *Birmingham* spotted a submarine 'either on the surface or breaking surface in the heavy swell.' Captain Duff swung his ship around like a destroyer as he prepared to ram. The cruiser's bows caught the U-boat at an angle and glanced away, apparently without doing any vital damage, but the impetus of the blow forced up the submarine's bows to reveal the white-painted *U-15* on her prow. For some reason the U-boat remained on the surface—perhaps *Birmingham* had damaged her hydroplanes—and, running at full speed, the cruiser heeled in a tight circle and slammed in again. This time her bows cleaved the thin plating of the submarine's hull just ahead of the conning-tower, and *U-15* was sliced cleanly in half. The two separated parts remained afloat for several minutes but there was no sign of the U-boat's crew. Then, slowly and silently, the two sections slipped beneath the water.

When *Birmingham* reported her success to the main fleet 'a senior admiral thereof immediately categorically denied that the event could have taken place on the grounds that the spot was 450 miles from the nearest German base and no submarine could travel this distance. The fact that (a) dozens of witnesses had seen the end of *U-15* . . . and that (b) the *Birmingham* had to go into dry dock to have her stem repaired and that (c) a large pool of oil had appeared on the sea, was all evidence which apparently meant nothing to the old sea-dog. Some months later his flagship was torpedoed whilst ambling along in full moonlight in the English Channel.'[1]

Fortunately the 'old sea-dog' subsequently became the wiser and later on in the war he commanded the anti-submarine base at Queenstown where his Q-ships and patrol vessels spearheaded a savage offensive which sent many scores of German submarines to the bottom of the Atlantic. But that part of the story will follow in due course.

[1] *My Naval Life*, by Commander S. King Hall (Faber & Faber, 1952) p. 98.

When the men of the U-boat flotilla returned to Heligoland they looked back on their first war patrol with mixed feelings. Ten boats had sailed; only eight had survived. And they had failed to claim a single victim. As one officer observed: 'Our submarine fleet was as good as any in the world—but not very good.'

Meanwhile a second sweep by four U-boats had already left Heligoland a few days earlier for a hit-and-run raid on the crowded troop transports shuttling the BEF from Dover to France. Mechanical failures by the new Krupp-MAN. power units wrecked the plan almost from the outset. Three of the boats crawled back to Germany on stuttering engines and only Otto Hersing with *U-21*, a combination that was later to prove a great thorn in the side of the Allies, succeeded in penetrating the Straits although he, too, failed to achieve results.

By 14 August both *U-19* and *U-22* were back in service and, accompanied by Hersing in *U-21*, the three-boat patrol scouted the bleak waters between Scotland and Norway in search of the British blockade line. Although they sighted a cruiser and a destroyer off the Norwegian coast at 4 am on 16 August and another the following day no useful information about the British blockade was obtained and, once again, the U-boats proved disappointing. Only Hersing added to his laurels by accomplishing a total patrol of 1,600 miles, no mean achievement in those early pioneering months of 1914.

Disheartened by their lack of success the High Command called-off their mass tactics and tried a third line of strategy by sending the U-boats out either singly or in pairs. Quite by chance the Germans had stumbled on the true key to submarine warfare.

For the young and enthusiastic submarine captains it was like being let off the leash and they responded to this new challenge with verve and daring. Periscope sightings along the British coast became a daily occurence and, before long, the Grand

Fleet had been thoroughly infected by U-boat fever. At the beginning of September the stalk of a periscope was spotted by the cruiser *Falmouth* outside the entrance to the Grand Fleet anchorage at Scapa Flow. Firing four rounds rapid she reported 'having probably hit the submarine' and, while the signal was still being passed, the battleship *Vanguard* joined in the fray, lobbing several shells at what she described as 'distinctly a periscope'.

By now the Grand Fleet was in a state of considerable consternation. The 1st Light Cruiser Squadron and the 2nd Destroyer Flotilla were ordered out in search of the elusive U-boat and when, at 6.30 pm, *Drake* reported a 'submarine in sight' Jellicoe promptly ordered the entire fleet to weigh by divisions and leave harbour. The Flow was shrouded in a thick fog that had descended with dusk and it was not until 9 pm, amid scenes of angry confusion, that the Battle Squadrons began to clear the crowded anchorage. By 11 pm all the major units were safely on the open sea while a gaggle of destroyers, minesweeping gunboats, and armed trawlers remained behind searching for the submarine.

But, as was to be repeated on many subsequent occasions, the scare proved a false alarm despite the apparent certainty of the sighting reports. The 'old sea dog' who refused to believe that U-boats could reach as far north as Scapa suffered yet again, for the barge bringing his dinner to the flagship was detailed to join in the mythical submarine hunt and the food was somewhat cold by the time it arrived on his table several hours later.

While the Grand Fleet was engaged in these antics each time an over-enthusiastic lookout sighted a 'periscope', the U-boat crews found their own amusements by landing on the remoter islands of the Orkneys where they hunted wild goats and sea-birds. On a more serious errand both *U-20* and *U-21* probed into the Firth of Forth, although they failed to penetrate to the fleet anchorage above the great bridge.

The continued perseverance of the U-boat captains brought its reward. On 3 September *U-21* had just surfaced off May Island to recharge her depleted batteries when Hersing sighted the light cruiser *Pathfinder* on the horizon. The U-boat slid beneath the surface and gave chase but, unable to rival the cruiser's speed, Hersing watched his prey pull clear and vanish over the horizon. With a shrug of resignation he took *U-21* back to the surface to resume the interrupted battery charging. The weather was getting worse and the tiny submarine was soon rolling uncomfortably in a heavy swell, when suddenly a cry came from the watch officer:

'Smoke bearing Green 2-0-0!'

Hersing's eyes glowed with anticipation when the British warship's three funnels appeared over the rim of the horizon as she doubled back along her patrol leg. Once again *U-21* allowed the sea to swallow her and, this time, the target came squarely towards her. With supreme confidence in his own ability the U-boat skipper fired only one torpedo. Running true, it struck *Pathfinder* behind the bridge and ignited a magazine. There was a tremendous explosion and within four minutes the 2,940 ton cruiser had disappeared leaving 259 shocked and oil-sodden survivors struggling in the water where they were later picked up by British destroyers.

It was the first time in modern warfare that a submarine had sunk a warship and it was an historic moment of which Otto Hersing had every reason to be proud. The Killing Time had begun!

Ten days later the British submarine *E-9* commanded by Max Horton evened up the score by sinking the German cruiser *Hela* six miles south of Heligoland. But, with the bit now firmly in their teeth, the U-boats quickly redressed the balance in a spectacular manner.

The night of 20 September, 1914, found Lieutenant Otto Weddigen and *U-9* off the Dutch coast in a violent storm with the submarine's main navigation aid, the gyro compass, broken. The young naval lieutenant was 'already known as an exceedingly capable submarine man' and his second-in-command, Johann Spiess, left this vivid thumbnail sketch of his legendary captain:

'He was a slender blondish young officer of quiet courteous manner. He was the very reverse of the martinet. Never blindly set on his own opinion, he allowed the officers under him the privileges of initiative and freedom of ideas. You did not feel like a subordinate when you served under Weddigen, but rather like a younger comrade.'

The strength of his character was soon revealed in the action that followed. The storm worsened as darkness fell and, unable to rely on the compass, *U-9*'s captain sent a man down the slippery wave-swept deck to take soundings. The leadsman's line showed seventeen fathoms—the dead reckoning plot on the control-room chart showed them in shoaling waters down to ten fathoms. Clearly they were lost and, worse, further out into the North Sea than they should have been. By now the howling storm was causing physical damage to the little U-boat, by no means in her first flush of youth, and a decision had to be taken—turn back or keep on. For Weddigen there could be but one answer. With superb seamanship he rode out the storm on the surface and, by next day, had located his position from land-marks along the Dutch coast. The patrol continued.

By the following evening, the 21st, the storm had, if anything, worsened and, to escape its rigours, Weddigen took *U-9* down to the bottom. Even so, at a depth of 100 feet, the U-boat still rolled from the effects of the heavy swell on the surface—'bumping' the submarine men called it—and it was not until dawn on the following morning that he dared to bring *U-9* back to the surface.

Johann Spiess continues the story: 'When we rose to the surface in the morning . . . we were agreeably surprised. The light streamed up from the eastern horizon and spread over a cloudless sky. The storm had vanished. Not a cloud was to be seen, the wind was a whisper, and the sea was calm, save for a long swell. Visibility was excellent. The horizon was a sharp clear line where sea and sky met. A fine day to sink a ship. We threw our motors in, to recharge our batteries and replace the energy we had used up while submerged all that night.'

It was Spiess, in fact, who first sighted the cruisers, just three whisps of smoke curling up over the horizon. Weddigen, at breakfast below, was called to the bridge and, at the same time, the kerosene engines were disconnected lest their smoke should warn the enemy of the U-boat's presence. The young skipper stared through his glasses for over a minute intently trying to identify the whispy phantoms. Then came the decision.

'Make ready for diving!'

The lookouts scrambled down the steel ladder into the bowels of the submarine, followed nimbly by Spiess. As the diving orders echoed down the bright interior of the hull, Weddingen closed the dog-catch of the hatch and took his place at the periscope. U-9 was already pushing her nose deep into the water and the sea closed over the U-boat as she disappeared from sight. Even at a depth of 10 metres the heavy surface swell kept the submarine rolling gently and Spiess cocked an anxious eye at the gauges.

'Up!'

It was Spiess's job to operate the lever mechanism which raised and lowered the periscope and, on receiving the order, he ran the steel tube up. Weddigen gripped the handles, swung them slowly towards the bearing on which the enemy had been sighted, and quickly estimated the course and speed of his unsuspecting target.

'Down!'

The 'scope ducked beneath the surface and every man in the control room glanced at the Captain's face hoping that his expression would reveal what he had seen. Discipline sealed the eager question on everyone's lips. Weddigen gave nothing away and they waited.

'Up!'

Again the one-eyed probe rose above the waves while *U-9*'s skipper carefully surveyed his prey. His face, 'drawn and tense', gave no hint of what he could see and almost a minute passed before he broke the tension.

'There are three light cruisers with four funnels—probably Town class boats.'

Revenge for the *U-15*; *Birmingham* had been a Town class cruiser. The men grinned at each other. Spiess broke the silence.

'Torpedoes?'

Weddegen nodded and the orders were repeated up and down the boat for the tubes in the bows and stern to be prepared. Four green lights glowed to show that the initial preparations were completed and *U-9* edged closer to her quarry.

'Make tubes ready.'

'All tubes clear, Herr Leutnant.'

Spiess recalled later, 'I unscrewed the cover of the first tube firing button and held the thumb of my right hand directly over it ready for the order to press it down and make the electrical contact. With my left hand I continued to operate the lever of the elevating device by which the periscope was raised and lowered.'[1]

Weddigen now only dared to snatch brief glimpses through the 'scope for fear of being spotted by an alert lookout on the British cruisers, but they were sufficient to judge the speed, range, course, and firing deflection. *U-9* was only 500 yards away—point-blank range.

Wiping the sweat from the palms of his hands Weddigen told Spiess to take the submarine down to 15 metres as soon as the torpedoes had been fired. The early U-boats had an unfortunate habit of surfacing like a porpoise and he did not intend to take chances. It was exactly 7.20 am Central European Time.

'Out periscope. Stand by first tube.'

[1] *Raiders of the Deep*, p. 19.

Spiess waited as Weddigen watched the target moving into his sights. Co-ordination with the captain was vital for even a fraction of a second's delay would cause the torpedo to miss.

'First tube fire! In periscope.'

Spiess's thumb stabbed obediently. The torpedo hissed away and *U-9* slid down to her new depth. Not a man spoke and all eyes were fastened on the clock. Thirty-one seconds later there was a sharp concussion as the torpedo struck home and, the tension broken, the U-boat men cheered with elation and relief.

Aboukir, hit on the starboard beam, began to heel over as the sea rushed into the gaping hole below the waterline. The officers on the bridges of *Hogue* and *Cressey* saw a fountain of water leap high into the air and assumed their companion had struck a mine, a view shared by *Aboukir*'s own crew. Unaware that a submarine was lurking in ambush the two cruisers moved towards their stricken comrade, braving the suspected mines to take off survivors. It was a gallant action fully in accord with the traditions of the Royal Navy. And it played right into Weddigen's hands.

Aboukir was now 'lying stern-deep in the water. Her bow was high and the ram stuck out above the surface of the sea. Her four funnels were blowing off white steam and lifeboats crowded with men were being lowered.'

Taking advantage of the respite the U-boat crew reloaded the empty tube with a reserve torpedo, repeating the pioneer exercise they had practiced at Kiel in July, 1914. Ten minutes later *U-9* was fully kitted to resume the attack.

But an unexpected crisis intervened. The submarine was approaching too close to her target and, in addition, the heavy surface swell made her pitch up and down. In an effort to bring the boat level Weddigen sent the crew running from one end to the other to act as mobile ballast, a human alternative to Wilhelm Bauer's threaded rod and weight, and pandemonium raged inside the cramped hull.

'All hands aft!'

Every man not required for specific duties joined in the mad headlong rush. The stern settled under their combined weight but the inclometers showed that the bows were rising.

'All hands forward!'

Again the dash down the central companionway which ended with the men, sweating, panting, and cursing, crowded into the bow torpedo flat. *U-9* pitched and tilted like a see-saw but Weddigen pushed ahead with his attack. Ignoring the confusion, he carefully lined his sights on the second cruiser and, at 7.55 am, two more torpedoes streaked from the bow tubes. The range was down to 300 yards.

'Fifteen metres! Motors full astern!'

U-9 executed a bizarre underwater antic as, bows down in a dive, the propellers reversed and dragged her astern so as to avoid ramming her target.

The extricating manoeuvre was not a second too soon. As *U-9* backed away there came two hollow explosions. *Hogue* had been hit, but there was no time for cheering and everything seemed to happen at once. With her bows lightened by the discharge of two torpedoes the U-boat shot out of control and broke surface. Despite her mortal damage *Hogue*'s guns were waiting and opened up on her adversary. Fountains of water erupted around the submarine as she lay exposed on the surface and then, in a flurry of foam, she was gone again.

So, too, was *Aboukir*. Only hundreds of bobbing heads and half empty lifeboats marked her grave. *Hogue* mercifully settled on an even keel and five minutes after *U-9* had dived out of sight her quarter-deck was under water. Ten minutes later she rolled over and plunged to the bottom.

'The batteries are almost discharged, Herr Leutnant.'

Weddigen acknowledged the Chief Engineer's report with a curt nod. They were now almost down to the vital 800 amp-hours needed to restart the Korting engines and the oxygen-starved air inside the little submarine was stale. *U-9*'s captain dismissed the problems with a shrug. There was iron in Weddigen beneath his mild-seeming quietness. Harsh lines were in his face—the expression of relentless will. 'We will continue the attack,' he said serenely.

Only one torpedo was left in reserve and the difficult exercise of re-loading the empty tube while submerged was repeated. Two further torpedoes nestled in the stern tubes and Weddigen decided to use them for the final attack. The U-boat pivoted with one motor reversed and the rudder hard over so that her back was turned on the target.

'Tube three fire!'

'Tube four fire!'

Now fully alerted to the presence of the submarine the lookouts on *Cressey* quickly spotted the foaming wakes of the 'fish' and the cruiser swung away in an effort to 'comb the tracks'. But it was too late. The first torpedo missed by 20 feet, the second slammed into the warship's hull on the starboard side. *Cressey* shuddered under the explosive shock but she remained on an even keel and, gallant to the last, her guns opened fire on *U-9*'s periscope as it poked above the surface.

'We'll make sure,' Weddigen observed grimly. The U-boat turned 180° and the last torpedo shot from the bow tube. It sent up a fountain of water as it struck home.

'The periscope revealed a fearful picture,' Spiess recalled. 'The giant with four funnels turned slowly over to port. Men climbed like ants over her side and then, as she turned turtle completely, they ran about on her broad flat keel until, in a few minutes, she disappeared beneath the waves.'

Spiess and Weddigen watched 'fascinated (but) with a sense of tragic horror. For long minutes we were lost as if in some kind of a trance.'

U-9 had done her job well; she could do no more. Soon a score of avenging destroyers would be in the area picking up survivors and scouring the sea in search of the U-boat. Turning north, Weddigen crawled slowly away, not daring to surface so that he could boost the submarine's exhausted batteries until they were many miles away from the scene. They spent the next night on the bottom, and after an indecisive brush with a British destroyer off the Dutch coast, they steered for Wilhelmshaven.

Stepping ashore to a rapturous welcome Weddigen learned for the first time that he had sunk not, as he thought, three light cruisers, but three armoured cruisers totalling over 36,000 tons, with a loss of 1,460 men, many of them long-service pensioners recalled to the Colours and, more tragically, young cadets scarcely out of training school.

Germany went wild when the news of the victory was confirmed. Weddigen received the Kaiser's personal award of the Iron Cross, 1st and 2nd class, while every man aboard U-9 was given the Iron Cross 2nd class. The U-boat's skipper also became the first Naval officer of the war to win the coveted *Pour le Mérite*, an honour awarded to only thirty other submarine captains between 1914 and 1918.

In Britain there was understandable shock over the loss of the three cruisers. The Admiralty, ever reluctant to give credit where credit was due, insisted that several U-boats had taken part in the attack and quoted the skipper of the Dutch trawler *Flora* who claimed to have observed three conning-towers. But, even when the truth emerged, the Lords of the Admiralty still refused to acknowledge Weddigen's tenacious skill in the official statement issued by the Secretary to the Board:

'The loss of nearly 60 officers and 1400 men would not have been grudged if it had been brought about by gunfire in an open action but it is particularly distressing under the conditions that prevailed.'[1]

Roger Keyes, then Commodore of the British submarine service, also derided the skill and courage of the U-boat crew and observed scornfully:

'In the early days of the war [such a sinking] was about as

[1] *The Times History of the War*, Vol. 2, p. 17.

simple an operation for a submarine captain as the stalking of tame elephants, chained to trees, would be to an experienced big-game hunter, who wished to kill them unseen and unsuspected.'[1]

It seems strange that he did not make a similar condemnation of his own submarine commander, Max Horton, for sinking the cruiser *Hela* a short while earlier. But, as usual, there was one law for the Royal Navy and another for the enemy.

Not everyone in Britain took such a jaundiced view. In a contemporary publication the naval journalist M. F. Wren wrote: 'Weddigen, the best German submarine commander in the early part of the war certainly occasioned heavy loss of life and won a strategic victory.'[2]

One thing was certain. Whether the U-boat captains were murderers, pirates, or just damned good seamen, naval warfare would never be the same again. After 22 September, 1914, the Royal Navy had to take the submarine threat seriously.

[1] *Naval Memoirs*, by Admiral of the Fleet Sir Roger Keyes (Thornton, Butterworth, 1934–5) p. 110.

[2] *Sea Fights of the Great War*, by W. L. Wyllie and M. F. Wren (Cassell, 1918) p. 28.

CHAPTER FOUR

'We can wound England most seriously'

WEDDIGEN'S DAZZLING VICTORY, following so swiftly
after Hersing's success against *Pathfinder*, brought a fresh
impetus to the submarine campaign and, by mid-September,
1914, the U-boats were boldly stalking the British coast in
broad daylight searching for new targets. Hundreds of merchant ships were sighted each day as the submarines crossed
and re-crossed the busy coastal trade routes but not a single
vessel was molested in any way. Germany, at this stage of the
war it seemed, was more concerned in a battle of attrition
against the Royal Navy than a war against what Sir Percy
Scott had called 'our most vulnerable point'—the trade routes.
It was an error of omission they were soon to rectify.

Britain, with the experience of many centuries of bitterly
fought sea-warfare to her credit, suffered no similar blind-
spot. True, she did not sink merchant ships without warning.
She had no need to. But the blockade which she quickly imposed had the same deadly effect on the German economy and
war effort. It was a stranglehold at the throat of her enemy and
it was carried out with efficient expertise by a navy well versed
in the arts of blockade. And, of course, it brought inevitable
friction with the neutrals who objected to the British rights of
search and examination which frequently played havoc with
tightly scheduled sailing times and rigidly applied contracts.

There can be little doubt that the effectiveness of the British
blockade had a strong bearing on the decision to employ the
U-boats in a war against trade and for geographical reasons,
with the British Isles squarely blocking all sea exits from
Germany's major ports, the submarine was the only available

weapon of retaliation. Of greater interest, however, were Germany's frequent allegations of British lawlessness which were used time and time again to justify the U-boat campaign. To understand the German argument it is necessary to consider briefly the legal background to the blockade system.

In 1914, accepted international law permitted certain war materials to be seized or destroyed by a belligerent power if they were destined directly or indirectly for the enemy and the sinking of merchant ships was sanctioned provided that both passengers and crew were placed in a position of safety. 'For this purpose the ship's boats are not regarded as a place of safety unless the safety of the passengers and crew is assured, in the existing sea and weather conditions, by the proximity of land or the presence of another vessel which is in a position to take them aboard.'

It was thus not illegal to sink an enemy merchant vessel if the safety conditions were met although it was implied that the passengers and crew should be taken off *before* the ship was destroyed. As we shall see later there were certain conditions under which an enemy ship could be sunk in defiance of this provision.

Exercising the age-old right of a belligerent to 'stop and search' all ships suspected of carrying war material to the enemy, the Royal Navy quickly set up a blockade system and diverted all suspected ships to various ports for expert examination. Vessels were stopped on the high seas and a boarding-party was sent across to examine her papers. If these suggested the presence of contraband, a prize crew escorted the ship to port for detailed examination and any contraband cargoes found in the holds were seized. The offending ship was subsequently released and, in the majority of cases, the British Government paid compensation to the shippers.

Cargoes, carefully defined by the Treaty of London in 1909, were divided into three separate categories. *Absolute Contraband* covered all war material and made no distinction between goods being carried direct to an enemy port or indirectly, by transhipment, through a neutral country. Under accepted law it was liable to immediate seizure after an appropriate declaration by the Prize Court.

Conditional Contraband, goods with an indirect effect on the enemy war effort such as foodstuffs, fuel, bullion, etc, could, however, only be seized if passing directly to an enemy port. The 'continuous voyage' rule which applied to *Absolute Contraband* could not be used against *Conditional Contraband*.

Everything else came into the third category, *Free Goods*, and a belligerent had no power of seizure or detention of cargoes within this group even though on direct route to the enemy.

The 1856 Declaration of Paris laid down that 'blockades in order to be binding must be real, that is to say, maintained by a force sufficient to prevent access to the coast of the enemy.' Thus any neutral ship carrying *Absolute Contraband* and sailing for blockaded ports was liable to capture. Great Britain and the United States, the two major trading powers, were agreed on this aspect of international law, but difficulties arose when, on 20 August, 1914, the Allies declared that *Conditional Contraband* would receive the same treatment as *Absolute Contraband*. This meant that the 'continuous voyage' concept would apply with the result that goods shipped in neutral bottoms to neutral ports were liable to seizure if the ultimate destination was in enemy territory.

The situation was bedevilled by the fact that the Declaration of London, in 1909, was never ratified by Great Britain for the simple reason that its terms seemed likely to be disadvantageous to her primary interests. And so Britain, not bound by the details of the Declaration, was free to base her blockade regulations on earlier law, in particular the 1856 Declaration of Paris.

Even so, the first list of contraband materials issued under the Royal Proclamation of 4 August, 1914, tallied almost exactly with the items specified under the London Declaration, the only exception being the inclusion of aircraft as absolute rather than conditional contraband. But there was soon a major divergence.

By an Order in Council of 20 August conditional contraband could 'be captured if it were consigned to an agent of the enemy Government, or to any person under (the) control of the authorities of the enemy state.' And on 21 September, 1914, the conditional contraband list was amended to include copper, lead, glycerine, iron ore and rubber. 29 October saw the absolute contraband list extended to include barbed wire, aluminium, and sulphuric acid; and from then onwards the lists were steadily enlarged.

Clearly it was a situation ripe for contention. Germany claimed, naturally, that Britain, by disobeying the terms of the London Declaration and, by imposing her own harsh blockade regulations, was breaking international law. Other countries denied the right of the Royal Navy to stop and examine ships on the high seas and, led by a vociferous body of American opinion, ranted wildly about the 'Freedom of the Seas'. The official view of the United States Government was based on hard reality. As a great trading nation her exports to Europe, especially Germany, formed an important part of her economy and the blockade, by sealing off the Western European ports, was, so they claimed, having a serious impact on American industry.

Sir Edward Grey denied that the blockade was affecting trade and pointed out in a Note that during the first seven months of 1914, before the outbreak of war, American exports showed a decline of $126 million over the corresponding period for 1913, yet, despite the conflict and the blockade, US exports to Europe for Christmas, 1914, exceeded those of the previous year. In fact during the first four months of war American exports had increased by $20 million over the same four months of 1913. Congress grumbled and was not wholly convinced.

The blockade began to bite in real earnest when, in November, 1914, the British Government declared the whole of the North Sea to be a military area with the result that all neutral shipping destined for Norway, the Baltic, Denmark, and Holland had to take the Channel route, thus simplifying the Royal Navy's task of 'search and examination'.

It was a policy thwart with difficulties and, as Admiral Sir Dudley de Chair, Officer Commanding the Northern Blockade Squadron, admitted, there were times 'when the Foreign Office and the Royal Navy seemed to be fighting different enemies.'[1] The Navy, naturally, was concerned only with the defeat of her German enemy; the Foreign Office was equally concerned with placating neutral complaints, especially those of the United States, for fear of driving them into the hands of the Kaiser and his Allies. With Britain apparently making her own rules in defiance of the Declaration of London it was not surprising that considerable friction arose between the various trading powers, a state of affairs which Germany eagerly exploited at every opportunity.

The intricate legalities of international law do not make exciting reading but they play an important part in the story of the U-boat war, for the German Government made skilful use of the British blockade to justify her submarine campaign when the Killing Time began.

Seeking fresh fields to conquer, the U-boats turned their attention southwards towards the Channel and the Straits of Dover and, on 27 September, *U-18* found herself patrolling, submerged, close to the great white cliffs of the Kent coast. Von Hennig steered for Dover Harbour and was rewarded by a fine shot at the scout *Attentive*. But his dreams of glory quickly faded when the torpedo missed, and the U-boat moved out of the area as quickly as possible to escape the horde of destroyers that emerged from the harbour in pursuit. Von Hennig had been unlucky. According to a contemporary

---

[1] *The Sea is Strong*, by Admiral Sir Dudley de Chair (Harrap, 1961).

report of the incident, the torpedo 'ran along the port side of *Attentive*, missing her by inches. Had it not been for Captain Johnson's action (in turning away) we should have undoubtedly lost the cruiser as the torpedo ran beautifully for striking her amidships at the original course and speed.'[1]

The mere threat of a U-boat in the Straits was enough to stir the Admiralty into immediate action and the Navy began laying an extensive minefield in the Channel to protect the vital troopship route between Dover and Calais. Quite by chance it had other benefits. All merchant shipping passing through the Channel was now funnelled into a narrow gap in the minefield and this concentration simplified the task of boarding and examining vessels. When, during the following month, the North Sea was declared a military zone and all shipping was forced to take the Channel route, this tiny gap in the Dover minefield symbolized the tightening stranglehold of the blockade.

Faced by this new threat the Germans reacted immediately. They condemned the minefield as interference with neutral shipping contrary to international law and, for the first time, the inner councils of the Imperial Navy began discussing the possibility of using U-boats in a counter-blockade against British trade routes. Kommodore Bauer, Chief of the U-boat flotillas, prepared a paper on the subject and sent it to Berlin for consideration by the Kaiser's naval advisers. Several months passed before his proposals bore fruit but the seed had been sown.

Turning briefly aside from their main enemy across the North Sea, the U-boats struck next at Russian warships operating in the Baltic. Submarines based at Kiel carried out several offensive patrols and, on 10 October, 1914, an abortive attack was made on a squadron of Tzarist armoured cruisers. *U-26*, commanded by Kapitanleutnant von Berckheim,

---

[1] *Keeping the Seas*, by Captain E. R. G. R. Evans (Sampson Low, 1919) p. 31.

shadowed the warships through the night and, the following afternoon, she struck again. A well-aimed torpedo hit the 7,775 ton cruiser *Pallada* amidships which ignited her magazine. 'All that remained of her and her crew of 600 was her ikon floating on the sea.'[1]

But the main theatre of operations remained the North Sea and on 13 October *U-9* and *U-17* sailed from Wilhelmshaven to reconnoitre the approaches to the Grand Fleet base at Scapa Flow. Two days later Weddigen sighted the 10th Cruiser Squadron off Aberdeen but, despite running *U-9*'s engines until they were almost red-hot, he could not reach a suitable firing-position. Then came an incredible piece of luck.

Watching the fast-moving cruisers through his periscope Weddigen was puzzled as the warships slowed down and began to turn. Suddenly it became 'apparent that they intended to exchange signals, drop a cutter in the water, and deliver mails or orders.' *U-9* steered for the rendezvous point at full speed, as first *Endymion* and then *Hawke* came to a stop; then Weddigen gave the order.

'Second bow tube, fire!'

Hawke was barely 500 yards away. The cruiser had just begun moving forward as the torpedo shot from the submarine's tube and the crew were still hoisting the mail cutter on board as it slammed into the hull abreast of the fore funnel. Within eight minutes she had vanished and, of her 544 man complement, only 52 were picked up by the trawler *Ben Rinnes*. A further 21 survivors were rescued from a raft some time later. With memories of the *Hogue*, *Aboukir*, and *Cressey* disaster still fresh in their minds, the other two cruisers sensibly cleared the danger area and made full speed for the horizon leaving their stricken comrades struggling in the ice-cold water.

Feldkirchner's *U-17* also had a brush with the enemy but the torpedo he aimed at the cruiser *Theseus* missed by a wide margin.

[1] *The Russians at Sea*, by David Woodward (Wm Kimber, 1965) p. 167.

Later *U-9* rashly attempted to attack a group of destroyers steaming at high speed in the Pentland Firth. They were sailing in line abreast, 1000 yards apart, and Weddigen tried a difficult double shot, a torpedo from the bow tubes firing simultaneously with one from the stern as the destroyers passed in front and behind the U-boat's axis. For once he had been too ambitious. He loosed off the bow torpedo and then, in sudden horror, realized that one of the destroyers was out of line, and bearing down on a collision course with the submarine.

The destroyers had acted quickly. The lookouts on *Alarm* had seen the torpedo in time to avoid it while *Nymphe*, spotting the tell-tale feather of spray from *U-9*'s periscope, swung her helm hard over and came in to ram. The U-boat was a notoriously slow diver and she seemed to hang suspended in the water as if reluctant to leave the surface. Every eye in the control room focussed on the depth indicator. It moved with agonizing slowness . . . eight metres . . . nine . . . ten, and in Spiess's words:

'Thirteen metres. At that instant a tremendous roar struck our ears like some overwhelming thunder. The boat rocked as if she would turn over. Through an unscreened port in the rear of the conning-tower I could see a black shadow that loomed and disappeared. The destroyer had charged straight over the top of our conning-tower. We had gone clear by half an inch. A second more and we would have got the full murderous impact of the ram bow.'

Despite *U-9*'s lucky escape the U-boats were having a profound impact on British strategy. Sir John Jellicoe, already concerned by the frequent submarine scares at Scapa Flow, was uncomfortably aware that the main fleet base was almost completely devoid of anti-submarine defences. His margin of superiority over the High Seas Fleet was minimal at this stage of the war, and a determined U-boat assault on the anchorage could easily tip the balance in Germany's favour.

'I decided, therefore,' he wrote afterwards, 'that it was necessary to seek a temporary base which could be used with safety whilst the submarine obstructions at Scapa were being perfected.'[1]

It was an unpalatable decision for a nation accustomed to unchallenged control of the sea. But Jellicoe had the wisdom and courage to face facts. On 17 October, 1914, the Grand Fleet, the mightiest armada of fighting ships the world had ever seen, was ordered to evacuate the Flow and take up temporary bases in Northern Ireland. The feelings of the Fleet were neatly expressed by Admiral Beatty's flag-captain, later Admiral of the Fleet, Lord Chatfield:

'Here was a pretty kettle of fish. The great Fleet was homeless and insecure, like American colonists chased by stealthy Red Indians. We hid in the creeks and bays of the west Scottish coast. Loch-na-Kiel was allotted to the battle-cruisers. Beatty called a meeting. How to improvise our security? Fishing nets and wire hawsers were stretched across the harbour entrance; picket boats were in constant patrol behind them. Admiralty conferences took place. And so the long study of this new and serious problem for the Navy began in earnest.'[2]

It was a tremendous victory for the U-boats. By forcing the enemy fleet to leave its base the submarine was already exercising a profound and unprecedented influence on the war at sea. Yet, so far, Germany's U-boats had scarcely begun to fight.

While Weddigen and his comrades searched the storm-swept waters of the Orkneys other submarine commanders probed southwards. Droescher took *U-20* through the mine-fields of the Dover Straits and was sighted by coast-watchers on the Isle of Wight. The U-boat report caused a wild panic ashore. A large troop convoy was due at Southampton from

[1] *The Grand Fleet*, p. 145.
[2] *The Navy and Defence*, by Admiral of the Fleet Lord Chatfield (Heine-mann, 1942) p. 127.

Canada within the next few hours and the signal wires to London grew red-hot as the news flashed to the Admiralty. The vital convoy was diverted to Plymouth and *U-20* cruised on, blissfully unaware of the commotion she had caused or the prize she had so narrowly missed.

The destroyer patrols and minefields in the Straits had given Droescher plenty to think about and, rather than risk running the gauntlet for a second time, he decided to take *U-20* up the west coast of the British Isles for his return trip to Wilhelmshaven. Off the Hebrides in a violent gale he caught a fleeting glimpse of Jellicoe's ships on the evening of the 17th but heavy seas and an early dusk prevented contact being made. The incident was proof yet again of the Grand Fleet's vulnerability to submarine attack whether it was at sea or anchored in harbour, and served to underline the problems that faced Jellicoe day and night during those early months of the war.

On the following day, a few miles off the German coast, the British submarine *E-3* was engaged on a routine scouting mission. The sea was empty and the submarine was running on the surface to save her batteries. *U-27*, safely submerged and with only her periscope showing above the surface, carefully stalked the unsuspecting British boat as her captain, Wegener, prepared for attack. A torpedo streaked across the sea and *E-3* erupted in a violent explosion, the first submarine to fall victim to one of its own kind. The detonation of *U-27*'s torpedo had exploded, once and for all, the fallacy of Lord Goschen's pronouncement that 'one submarine boat cannot fight another.'

But an even more significant episode occurred two days later on 20 October. Outward bound from Grangemouth to Stavanger with a mixed cargo of coal, iron plates and oil the British merchant ship *Glitra* was sighted by *U-17* fourteen miles off the Norwegian coast. Kapitanleutnant Feldkirchner came to the surface, took his submarine alongside the steamer and ordered the crew to abandon ship. Acting in strict accordance with international law he allowed the British sailors ten minutes grace to collect their belongings and then, as they took to the boats, a prize crew from the submarine climbed on board. The vessel's sea-cocks were opened and she was scuttled, the first merchant ship to be sunk by a U-boat.

Mindful that 'the ship's boats are not regarded as a place of safety' Feldkirchner towed *Glitra*'s lifeboats behind *U-17* for several miles and finally cast them free when they were within easy pulling distance of the Norwegian coast. But, despite the care he had taken in disposing of *Glitra*, the young U-boat captain was very worried about his reception on returning to Wilhelmshaven and thought 'he might get a court-martial for his unauthorized sinking.'

Bauer's suggestion that attacks should be made on merchant shipping had, by now, permeated to the High Command. Supreme power was vested in the hands of the Kaiser and a strangely complicated command structure led to inevitable intrigues between one faction and another, each seeking to influence the 'All Highest'.

Von Ingenohl, C-in-C of the High Sea Fleet, thought the proposal 'uncivilized'. Admiral von Pohl, Chief of Naval Staff with direct access to the Kaiser, showed little interest and added it 'was not yet justified by the infringements of [international] law already committed by England',[1] these infringements, of course, being the British blockade system. Von Tirpitz, Secretary of State for the Naval Department, and von Muller, Chief of the Naval Cabinet, kept their own counsels.

When, however, Britain designated the North Sea as a military area on 2 November, 1914, less than a fortnight after the *Glitra* incident, it was clear that some form of retaliatory action was necessary and Feldkirchner's action provided food for thought. Von Pohl came out strongly in favour of a U-boat war against merchant shipping and a memorandum from the fleet to the Naval Staff indicates the current temper of opinion:

[1] *Der Kreig zur See*, edited by Rear Admiral Arno Spindler.

'As England is trying to destroy our trade it is only fair if we retaliate by carrying on the campaign against her trade by all possible means. Further, as England completely disregards international law in her actions, there is not the least reason why we should exercise any restraint in our conduct of the war. We can wound England most seriously by injuring her trade. By means of the U-boat we should be able to inflict the greatest injury.'[1]

The note went on to point out that U-boats had no alternative but to 'send [the crews] to the bottom with their ships' and pressed for a warning to be issued to all maritime nations that 'all shipping trade with England should cease within a short space of time.' Von Pohl suggested a counter-blockade of Britain to the Chancellor, Bethmann-Hollweg, and the matter was argued for several weeks, the main stumbling-block being both the Chancellor's and the Kaiser's fear of offending neutral opinion. But, while official approval of an all-out U-boat war was withheld, submarine captains were authorized to sink or capture British merchant ships within the framework of international law.

The firing of a warning shot calling upon the vessel to stop so that her papers could be examined was obligatory and she was not to be sunk unless the safety of the crew could be ensured. The sinking of a merchant ship while passengers and crew were still on board was only permitted under international law if there was 'persistent refusal to stop on being summoned, or of active resistance to visit or search.'

Feldkirchner had followed the letter of the law when he sank the *Glitra* but other U-boat captains were to show an unfortunate lack of concern with the small print.

The first example of German ruthlessness occurred on 26 October when *U-24* met up with the French steamer *Amiral Ganteaume* in the Channel. The ship, engaged on an errand of

[1] *Germany's High Seas Fleet in the World War*, by Admiral Sheer (Cassell, 1920).

mercy, was carrying over 2,000 Belgian refugees when Kapitanleutnant Rudolf Schneider torpedoed her without warning. There was wild panic on the decks as she began to sink and a heavy loss of life was only avoided by the quick-thinking of another skipper who ran his ship alongside the listing *Amiral Ganteaume* to take off all but forty of the passengers. Schneider defended his action by claiming mistaken identity—he thought the steamer was a troopship—but his subsequent career suggests that he neither knew nor cared. His target was an enemy ship and that was sufficient.

The other U-boats, meanwhile, were continuing their war of attrition against the Royal Navy. On 31 October *U-27* put two torpedoes into the old cruiser *Hermes* as she was crossing from Dunkirk. Although recently converted into a seaplane carrier and of little military value, the attack demonstrated, yet again, the U-boat's ability to penetrate the Channel defences and there were growing fears for the continued safety of the troop transports. On 11 November the gunboat *Niger* was sunk two miles off Deal and many thousands of people gathered on the cliffs to watch the great column of smoke that rose up over the horizon symbolizing the growing power of the U-boats.

Three days later Otto Hersing was running *U-21* on the surface in heavy mist when he came up with the French steamer *Malachite*. A warning shot was fired across the bows and the ship obediently came to a halt. The sea was running high and Hersing had to cling to a staunchion with one hand as he shouted his instructions.

'Bring me your papers!'

Malachite lowered a boat away and sent the cargo manifest and sailing instructions across to the waiting submarine. Hersing glanced through them. She was carrying contraband from Liverpool to Le Havre. Picking up his megaphone he leaned over the side of the conning-tower and called up to the French captain on the bridge wing.

'Abandon ship!'

The U-boat waited patiently as the crew pulled clear of the doomed vessel and then her 37mm gun opened fire. *Malachite* began to list gently as the shells punctured her waterline and then, with slow grace, she slipped silently beneath the surface. Hersing shouted a course for the lifeboats to follow, rang down for half speed ahead, and the U-boat's diesel engines throbbed to life as she circled away and made off into the swirling mists leaving the crowded boats bobbing awkwardly in the choppy sea.

Three days later Hersing caught the British collier *Primo* in the same area and she, too, joined the Frenchman on the bottom. The new era of 'restricted' warfare had got off to a flying and, reassuringly, legal start.

But it was not all plain sailing. *U-16*, probing into Lerwick harbour on a scouting mission, had a lucky escape when she ran aground in full view of the excited guests at the Queen's Hotel and managed to wriggle free before the Royal Navy had time to close in for the kill. *U-18*, even more daring, pushed into the entrance to Scapa Flow as far as the Hoxa boom only to find the harbour disappointingly bare. Using his periscope to con the U-boat through the tricky shoals and rocky outcrops of South Ronaldshay, von Hennig revealed himself to the patrols and a group of destroyers and trawlers closed in. *U-18* jinked wildly in an effort to escape her tormentors but each time her skipper raised the periscope he was greeted by a barrage of shells. After a series of hairsbreadth escapes, the trawler *Dorothy Grey* cornered and rammed her. *U-18* rolled over violently under the savage impact. Von Hennig, thrown bodily against the side of the control room, groped blindly in the sudden darkness, found the periscope and tried to see what had happened. But it was useless. The trawler's bows had bent the frail tube at right angles making it impossible to see anything. The emergency lighting flickered and then glowed dimly as a string of damage reports filtered through to the captain.

'Steering gear broken.'

'Forward hydroplanes broken.'

Von Hennig hesitated.

'Any leaks?'

'*Nein, Herr Kapitan.* Pressure hull undamaged.'

He walked to the chart and looked down. No joy there. The sea bottom was marked as jagged rocks. He shrugged his shoulders as he made the unwelcome decision.

'Stand by to surface. Close all vents. Blow all tanks. We're going up!'

Like a dying fish floating to the surface of a pond *U-18* began to rise. As she broke into the daylight the destroyer *Garry* swooped forward to ram and, once again, the U-boat lurched under the violent impact. Yet miraculously there was still no vital damage and, as *U-18* sank in a controlled dive, Von Hennig's men fought to save their crippled vessel. But then the sea itself joined in the struggle.

Caught by the powerful currents of the Pentland Firth the submarine was hurled against the sharp rocks of the Skerries and the sea succeeded where the Royal Navy had failed. The pressure hull caved in under the relentless battering and von Hennig knew that the end had come. A makeshift white flag was quickly nailed to a broom handle, the U-boat's secret papers were burned, and for the last time in her life *U-18* swept to the surface as the air was blown from her ballast tanks. She remained on top just long enough for all but one of her crew to escape and then, severely battered by the onslaught of sea and steel, the submarine dropped to her last resting-place on the bottom, while *Garry* scooped the survivors out of the water.

Before the year was out two more of the pioneer U-boats had gone to Valhalla, *U-11* mined in the Straits of Dover on 9 December and *U-5* mined and sunk in the Channel nine days later, making a total of five boats lost in five months of war. It was an encouraging result for both sides. To the Germans it was an acceptable exchange for the losses they had inflicted on the enemy and to Britain it demonstrated that the U-boat, like any other man-made warship, was vulnerable.

But there were other things now in the wind. With most of Belgium under the German yoke, Imperial Navy engineers had moved down into Flanders and set up U-boat bases at Zeebrugge, Bruges and Ostend. These new submarine harbours would cut down the time spent on passage to the enemy trade routes and allow more valuable days in the combat patrol area, a situation repeated by Hitler in World War II when he occupied Norway and the French Atlantic coast. The reduction in passage time was an important consideration for, at the end of 1914, Germany still possessed only twenty operational submarines and most of the new building programme would not be ready for service until 1916. The only hope for rapid reinforcement lay with the tiny *UB* and *UC* classes which, by the use of mass-production methods, might be ready by March, 1915. But being of a completely new design, there could be no certainty that they would prove either sea-worthy or successful until exhaustive trials had been carried out.

Von Tirpitz was optimistic. He told an American journalist that the U-boats could starve Britain into submission 'in a very short space of time', a statement that had whole-hearted support from the German public who were already feeling the effects of the blockade. But in private he was more cautious and advised merely a blockade of the Thames estuary while the Navy set about building U-boats in large numbers. Despite his unique standing as the creator of the Imperial Navy, von Tirpitz had little sway in higher political circles due, in the main, to the Kaiser's refusal to grant him dictatorial control of the Navy in July, 1914 (a situation strangely similar to Admiral Fisher's demands to the Prime Minister in 1915) and to the fact that he despised von Pohl, the Chief of Naval Staff.

The Chancellor, Bethmann-Hollweg, remained concerned at the effect of a trade war on neutral opinion and insisted that unless the Navy could guarantee crippling Britain's trade in a very short period the proposed offensive was not acceptable. Von Pohl's views were becoming stronger with every passing day and, aided by Kommodore Bauer, he continued to press the Kaiser for a decision. But with the two factions straining in opposite directions further consideration of a trade war by the U-boats was deferred.

For the men at sea the argument was academic. They were there to obey orders and that was that. If they were ordered to sink merchant ships they would sink them and if they were told to spare merchant ships they would spare them.

The U-boats celebrated Christmas at sea and many found ways to bring the spirit of the festive season into the cramped confines of their tin-can homes. Rudolf Zentner, at that time Watch Officer of *U-20*, has left an interesting fragment of Christmas, 1914, under the sea. After spending the day on surface patrol the submarine submerged at nightfall and settled snugly on the bottom in sixty feet of water.

'The tiny messroom was decorated in style. A green wreath hung at one end like a Christmas tree. We didn't have any lighted candles as they would have been too risky in the oil-reeking interior of a submarine. The tables were loaded with food. It all came out of cans but we didn't mind that. And all the officers and men had their mess together.'

After the traditional speeches—'Schwieger delivered one and a jolly oration it was'—the ship's band, a violin, mandolin, and a concertina, took over. 'The Berlin Philharmonic does better,' Zentner admitted, 'but our concert was good.'

Five months later these same men sunk the *Lusitania*.

CHAPTER FIVE

'The most fatal weapon in Naval warfare'

KAPITANLEUTNANT RUDOLF SCHNEIDER thought he was dreaming. Rubbing the eye-piece of the periscope with a soft cloth he bent down and peered through the lens again. It seemed that even the impossible could become possible in this crazy war. He passed a curt order to the Watch Officer standing at his side and *U-24* went to action stations.

It was the morning of 31 December, 1914, and the 5th Battle Squadron, flying the flag of Vice-Admiral Sir Lewis Bayly, was proceeding down-Channel for gunnery exercises—eight battleships steaming proudly in line-ahead formation, flanked by two light cruisers, and holding an unswervingly straight course at a steady 10 knots. There was no screen of protective destroyers; they had already been sent back to Harwich in accordance with previous orders as the squadron cleared Folkestone, and in the absence of signals Admiral Bayly assumed 'that there were not thought to be any enemy submarines in the Western half of the Channel',[1] a dangerous assumption to make in wartime.

For Schneider it was sheer purgatory. Slow though it was, the British fleet's speed of 10 knots was too fast for *U-24's* electric motors and, each time he submerged, the ponderous line of warships pulled tantalizingly away into the distance. He played hide-and-seek with the stately column throughout the day but could not produce that extra ounce of speed needed to close up to effective torpedo range. Night fell, the battle-ships extinguished all lights, and vanished into the darkness.

---

[1] *Pull Together*, The Memoirs of Admiral Sir Lewis Bayly (Harrap, 1939) p. 175.

Schneider shrugged away his disappointment and tried to make the best of a bad job.

After a day of submerged high-speed running the batteries were getting dangerously low and *U-24*'s skipper took the submarine to the surface so that the diesel engines could recharge the exhausted cells. It was a moonless night, the glass was falling, and the sea was unpleasantly choppy. Leaning against the periscope standard Schneider could hear the engines throbbing beneath his feet and, lighting a cigar, he wondered idly how far the British ships had gone by now.

'At 7 pm the Fleet was turned 16 points (90°) in accordance with an Admiralty Fleet Order requiring an alteration of course soon after dark in areas where a submarine attack was possible,' Sir Lewis Bayly recorded. 'At 2 am, when near Start Point, the Fleet turned 16 points in succession.'[1]

This second change of course had swung the 5th Battle Squadron completely around so that it was now running on a reversed track towards Portland, and back towards the surfaced *U-24*.

Rudolf Schneider could scarcely believe his eyes when the line of battleships loomed out of the western darkness, and he took the U-boat down fast. There was little need to manoeuvre, just a slight alteration of the helm and, at 1.50 am, he fired his first torpedo. The minutes ticked past in silence, the officers in the control-room exchanged worried frowns, and Schneider knew that he had missed an almost perfect target. Relying on the weather conditions and the absence of moonlight he brought *U-24* boldly to the surface and, using the darkness as cover, he took the submarine around the tail of the squadron, speeded up to overtake it, and fired a second torpedo at 2.25 am. *Formidable*, the last ship in the line, was hit amidships and began to settle immediately. Her boiler rooms flooded and, taking on a heavy list, she pulled out of line.

[1] *Pull Together*, p. 175.

High up on the bridge of the 15,000 ton leviathan Captain Loxley supervised the launching of the boats as the two light cruisers turned to assist, and with disciplined calm the crew went through the routine for abandoning ship. Sea-water reached the dynamos and all the internal lighting flickered and went out but, even in the crowded darkness of narrow passages and tiny compartments, there was no panic. At approximately 3.15 am, Schneider fired his third torpedo and it was now clear to everyone, friend and foe alike, that *Formidable* was doomed. Heavy waves broke over the slanting decks and smashed against staunchions and turrets. A barge being lowered into the water capsized and scattered its occupants into the sea. The end could not be far away.

At 4.45 am the great battleship lurched, rolled over on her beam ends to expose her red belly and giant bronze propellers, and then slipped quietly to the bottom. Only 201 men survived the attack and 547 British sailors, including Captain Loxley who remained on the bridge directing operations to the very last, went down with their ship. The following day, 2 January, 1915, Vice-Admiral Lewis Bayly was ordered to haul down his flag although the Admiralty allowed him to remain on full pay. The U-boats, it seemed, could destroy reputations as easily as they could destroy ships!

The loss of *Formidable* caused considerable dismay in Whitehall. Bayly's request for a court-martial was refused and Admiral Lord Charles Beresford, speaking in the House of Commons, accused the Admiralty of failing to give precise orders to sea-going flag officers that 'no ship should proceed except at speed and with her [destroyer] screens.' That any competent flag-officer should have sufficient initiative to come to such a commonsense conclusion on his own did not, apparently, occur to the valiant Charlie 'B'.

In view of the continuing successes of the U-boats it is interesting to note another passage from the same speech: 'The submarine was considerably over-rated if proper precautions were taken against it, but if such precautions were not taken, it was the most fatal weapon in naval warfare. It was problematical whether a submarine would ever hit a ship going at speed; certainly, it would never hit ships accompanied by their proper quota of destroyers and small craft. These were the two safeguards.'

Jellicoe clearly noted his Lordship's comments and, as the months passed, there were several occasions when the Grand Fleet remained in harbour because there were not sufficient destroyers available to act as an anti-submarine screen. The influence of the U-boats was gaining strength with every passing day.

One immediate result of the *Formidable* disaster was a further strengthening of the Dover defences. Seventeen miles of indicator nets watched by a standing patrol of armed drifters were completed and another minefield, this time off Deal, was laid four weeks later. But the U-boats still wriggled their way through these fresh obstructions and the way to the Channel remained wide open to a determined submarine captain.

On Friday, 13 January, 1915, three U-boats left Wilhelmshaven for a routine patrol: *U-22*, commanded by Kapitanleutnant Bruno Hoppe, *U-31*, by Oberleutnant Siegfried Wachendorff, and *U-32* under Baron von Spiegel. With such an ominous date of departure it is not surprising that tragedy should strike not once, but twice, at the ill-fated trio.

U-31 failed to return from the patrol and was presumed to have struck a mine in the North Sea, a fact confirmed by most official records of the war at sea. Baron von Spiegel, however, told a different story. 'A U-boat above water nosed its way slowly along. Nothing seemed amiss. It looked trim and menacing as if ready to dive and launch a torpedo at any moment. It was drifting before the wind, though, and finally ran ashore on the eastern coast of England. Naval men came hurrying to the scene. They boarded the craft, took her in tow to harbour, and discovered an eerie riddle. It was the same

U-31 that had left port that Friday the 13th six months earlier. And she was in perfect order. She might have been on an active cruise save for one thing. Officers and men were in their bunks and hammocks as if asleep—but they were dead! In the log the last entry was dated six months earlier . . . the record made humdrum reading until it broke off that day six months before. And after that a mysterious blank.'[1]

Spiegel had a theory that the submarine had gone to the bottom for the night and that her sleeping crew had been poisoned by an escape of gas. Over the ensuing months the compressed air had leaked little by little until, ultimately, the tanks had blown. Regaining her buoyancy the U-boat had floated to the surface and then drifted ashore.

It was a good story but, like all old sailor's tales, it should be taken with the proverbial pinch of salt. There is no record of any submarine coming ashore on the English coast in similar circumstances and it must be assumed that the prosaic official account: 'Mined (?) North Sea, January 1915' is more accurate if less romantic.

The hoodoo of Friday the 13th was not yet satisfied. *U-32* returned safely to Wilhelmshaven after an unproductive patrol but as her comrade *U-22* nosed her way into the crowded harbour a few hours later onlookers sensed something wrong. Hoppe, her captain, stepped on to the quay, pale and unsmiling, and walked rapidly to the flotilla chief's office.

'I have to report that I have torpedoed the *U-7*,' he said brokenly. 'There is only one survivor.'

The tragedy was heightened by the fact that Kapitan-leutnant Georg Koenig, skipper of *U-7*, was Hoppe's best friend. They were inseparable companions. As a fellow captain observed: 'They ate together, drank together, and what belonged to one belonged also to the other.' Like so many tragedies at sea it was due to an unavoidable mistake. Hoppe had not been informed that another U-boat was operating in

[1] *Raiders of the Deep*, p. 172-3.

the area and the recognition signals he sent up on sighting *U-7* went unanswered. Assuming that it must therefore be a British submarine *U-22* submerged and fired a single torpedo. Only when the sole survivor was dragged out of the oil-blackened water was it realized that they had sunk a fellow U-boat.

Bruno Hoppe was killed later in the war after an encounter with a Q-boat, but we shall meet *U-32*'s aristocratic raconteur skipper, Adolf Georg Edgar, Baron von Spiegel von und zu Peckelsheim, again before the U-boat story is completed.

The political struggle regarding the projected submarine war against commerce had, by now, reached the Kaiser but Wilhelm disliked the idea of using warships for such a task and quickly sided with von Bethmann-Hollweg. Kommodore Bauer, juggling with statistics, claimed that only seven U-boats were needed on operational patrol at any one time in order to achieve success. Fortunately no one took his figures seriously. Experience later showed that the true total of requirements was over 200!

So, once again, no firm decision was reached and the U-boat captains were left to fend for themselves with scanty orders and no official guidance.

The skipper of *U-19* clearly had his own ideas on the subject. Stopping the steamer *Durward* off the Dutch coast on 21 January, he ordered the crew to abandon ship and then placed time-bombs in the engine room. 'A more effective method of destruction than gunfire,' *The Times* observed with Olympian detachment. Other commanders, however, were not so successful. When a U-boat called on the 4,541 ton steamer *Laertes* to stop in the North Sea her master, Captain W. H. Propert, ignored the warning, clapped on maximum speed, and zigzagged away as hard as he could. The German submarine gave immediate chase and the barrel of its 37mm gun was soon running red hot as it pumped a barrage of shells at its fleeing victim. But not a single direct hit was scored during the sixty minute bombardment and, when the wriggling steamer successfully evaded a torpedo as well, the U-boat admitted defeat and called it a day.

Captain Propert got the DSC from King George V for his stalwart defence. The U-boat commander probably received, in Navy parlance, a 'bottle' from his flotilla chief when he returned to Wilhelmshaven and reported how *Laertes* had escaped. But, despite such incidents, the leading aces of the German submarine service continued to demonstrate an uncanny mastery of the highly skilled techniques demanded in this new field of underwater warfare.

Otto Hersing, who had sunk *Pathfinder* in September, was one such ace. Taking his veteran *U-21* through the new Channel defences on 22 January in search of new victims he found it tricky work although, to his relief, easier than he had anticipated. The marker buoys used to indicate the net defences enabled him to avoid their fatal meshes and an error by the British in laying mines too close to the surface revealed the location of the new fields off Deal. At low tide the ugly black canisters rolled gently on the surface, their upper hemispheres fully exposed, and it required no great skill to move cautiously around them. Once clear of Dover *U-21* steamed defiantly down-Channel, rounded Land's End, nosed her way up the St George's Channel into the Irish Sea, and arrived off the busy shipping route into Liverpool. It was virgin territory for the U-boats and Hersing was determined to make the most of his opportunities.

Finding a small air-field on Walney Island he brought *U-21* to the surface and impudently lobbed a few 37mm shells in the general direction of the sheds and flying-machines. A nearby coastal-battery was surprisingly well awake and replied with a promptness that caused Hersing to have his submarine dive out of the firing-line with considerable haste. The following day *U-21* stopped the 6,000 ton collier *Ben Cruachan* and, after allowing the crew to take to their boats, sank her with time-bombs. Three hours later Hersing met up with, and despatched,

Linda Blanche and he concluded his unexpected foray by sinking the *Kilcuan*.

In every case a warning shot was fired and the crews were given ample time to launch the lifeboats. *U-21*'s captain had certainly read, and obeyed, the fine print, so much so, in fact, that he even roped in a passing trawler to assist the survivors.

Word of a U-boat operating in Liverpool Bay had, by now, reached the ears of the naval authorities and every available destroyer, patrol vessel, and armed trawler, was sent off to hunt down the raider. But Hersing knew that his actions would draw a hornet's nest down on his head and by the time the warships began scouring the danger area *U-21* was already heading safely back towards the St George's Channel on her return trip to Germany. It had been a successful venture and more successful, in fact, than Hersing realized for as a direct result of his presence off Liverpool, the Admiralty had delayed the departure of the 10th Cruiser Squadron for six days, thus leaving a vital gap in their Northern blockade line.

But, while Hersing was proving that strict observance of international law was possible, his colleague Droescher in *U-20* was in the Channel demonstrating the effects of 'German frightfulness'. On 30 January he sank three merchant ships in quick succession without giving any warning and, the following night, fired a torpedo at the Hospital Ship *Asturias* despite the large red crosses painted on her sides and the bright lights illuminating her white hull. The hospital ship escaped on this occasion only to fall victim to another U-boat two years later in March, 1917.

Meanwhile the new submarine bases in Flanders were worrying the British and, as a prelude to the great air-raids on the U-boat pens in the Second World War, the RNAS launched its first bombing attack on Zeebrugge on 23 January. No spectacular results were claimed but it was an indication that Britain had already realized the value of aircraft in the struggle against the U-boats and raids were launched with increasing frequency from then onwards. By 1915 standards they were quite big affairs. An attack on 12 February involved 34 aircraft, followed, four days later, by a 48 bomber raid.

The indecisive Battle of Dogger Bank in which the German High Seas Fleet Scouting Force had to flee in the face of David Beatty's more powerful Battle-cruiser Fleet, losing the armoured cruiser *Blücher* in the process, led to a change in command. The Kaiser was furious that his 'no risks' policy had been flouted by von Ingenohl, especially as the skirmish had brought no glory to the Imperial Navy, and the C-in-C was superceded by Admiral von Pohl with effect from 2 February, 1915.

Von Pohl, of course, was the leading advocate of an unrestricted U-boat campaign against Allied merchant shipping and, before leaving his influential post as Chief of Naval Staff, he was determined to obtain the Kaiser's seal of approval for his policy. The Chancellor had been finally persuaded to agree to the text of an announcement proclaiming British waters as a war zone after repeated assurances that neutral shipping would not be endangered but, as before, von Muller remained obstinately opposed to the campaign. For von Pohl the problem was crystallized in one question. How could he make a direct approach to the Kaiser and circumvent von Muller's opposition when, according to protocol, all avenues to the German Emperor passed through the self-same opponent of a U-boat trade war?

His opportunity came during an inspection of the Fleet at Wilhelmshaven on 2 February. Button-holing the Kaiser while they were crossing the harbour in the C-in-C's barge von Pohl quickly talked Wilhelm into agreeing to his proposed policy. According to von Muller's version the incident occurred when they were returning to the flagship after the inspection was over but Johann Spiesse, by now skipper of Weddigen's old *U-9*, suggests that the decision had been reached before the inspec-

11. The MAN blast-injection diesel units which contributed so much to the success of the Kaiser's U-boats.

12. The big banger! A 5.9-inch deck gun swings into action as the U-boat closes in on its prey.

13. Schwartzkopff torpedoes being checked by submarine crewmen.

14. The business end of *U-62*. Note net cutters and bow torpedo tubes.

tion of the U-boats took place. '[The Kaiser] inspected the naval forces and we were all presented to him. At the conclusion of the ceremony we were informed that the All Highest had signed a proclamation declaring the waters around Great Britain and Ireland a war zone.'

The precise time of the decision was of little consequence. Much more important was the fact that von Pohl's continual agitation for an unrestricted U-boat war had finally succeeded. The Proclamation, dated 5 February, 1915, revealed the ruthless character of his campaign with stark clarity:

'1. All the water surrounding Great Britain and Ireland and all English seas are hereby declared to be a war area. From 18 February all ships of the enemy mercantile marine in these waters will be destroyed, and it will not always be possible to avoid danger to the crews and passengers thereon.

'The shipping route round the north of the Shetlands, in the east of the North Sea, and over a distance of thirty miles along the coast of the Netherlands will not be dangerous. These measures by the German Government are worthy of note by neutral countries as counter-measures against English methods, which are contrary to international law, and they will help to bring neutral shipping into closer touch with Germany.

'The German Government announces its intentions in good time, so that both neutral and enemy shipping can take the necessary steps accordingly.'

The reference to the breaking of international law by England was, as usual, the argument concerning the London Declaration. But, in addition, a second clause to the Proclamation drew specific attention to another German sore-point— the age-old *ruse de guerre* of belligerent ships flying a neutral flag to escape discovery. It was a device adopted by British, French, United States, and Japanese ships on many occasions in the past and had become, almost by tradition, an acceptable form of deceit under international law.

'2. Neutral ships, too, will run a risk in the War Zone, for in view of the misuse of neutral flags by the British Government on 31 January, and owing to the hazards of naval warfare, it may not always be possible to prevent the attacks meant for hostile ships from being directed against neutral ships.'

It was a difficult point and one on which it was possible to sympathize with the German view. A ship was legally permitted to sail under neutral colours so long as no hostile act was committed while the false flag was flying. The Q-ships, or decoy vessels, of the Royal Navy always hauled down their flags of deception at the moment their guns opened fire although the British exploited the law to the limit and, often, the lines that lowered the gun hatches also operated the flag hoists so that the two events took place simultaneously. But in the case of merchant ships no guns were carried and so no hostile act was possible other than an attempt to ram. In such circumstances what alternative did a U-boat commander have when he encountered a 'neutral' in the war zone?

The United States Government had already lodged a protest with Britain over the use of neutral flags but had admitted that flying false colours did not, in itself, constitute an illegal act. Washington, however, requested rather pointedly that the American flag should not be used for the purposes of deception.

The Times in the full flood of patriotic fervour referred to the German Proclamation as 'further deeds of so desperate and abominable a character as to involve the lives of innocent neutrals, the sanctity of the American flag, and the safety of American shipping', completely ignoring the fact that the use of neutral colours by British ships immediately put *all* neutrals at risk.

Even before the campaign had opened the United States sent a firm note to the German Government in which she objected to the Proclamation and referred to the 'indefensible violation of neutral rights'. Washington also threatened to take 'any steps which might be necessary to safeguard American lives and property.' The theme hammered home in this and subsequent notes was that, under international law, ships suspected of flying false colours should be boarded and examined as a prelude to being sunk, a manifest impossibility for submarines operating on a crowded trade route.

There was an unusual Teutonic subtlety about the German reply. They agreed to respect all ships flying the American flag on condition that the United States made an agreement with Great Britain allowing the free importation of food supplies into Germany. They knew full well, of course, that with the blockade now biting in earnest, Britain would never agree and America found herself impotently at the mercy of the two great European powers in their relentless struggle for control of the Channel and the North Sea.

However this fever of diplomatic activity had some effect. When the first orders were issued to the U-boat commanders at the time of the Proclamation they had been given a complete *carte-blanche*:

'Your first consideration is the safety of the U-boat. Consequently rising to the surface in order to examine a ship must be avoided for the sake of the boat's safety, aside from the danger of a possible surprise attack by enemy ships, because there is no guarantee that you are not dealing with an enemy ship even though it bears the distinguishing marks of a neutral. The fact that a steamer flies a neutral flag . . . is no guarantee that it is really a neutral vessel. Its destruction will therefore be justifiable unless other attendant circumstances indicate neutrality.'[1]

But the strong terms of the American note had given pause to the Kaiser's first acceptance of von Pohl's scheme and, on 14 February, revised instructions were hurriedly transmitted to the U-boat flotilla chiefs:

' . . . U-boats (are) not to attack ships flying a neutral flag unless recognized with certainty to be enemies. . . . ' And as a further sign that the Kaiser was getting cold feet the campaign

[1] *Germany's High Seas Fleet in the World War.*

against neutral shipping scheduled to start on 18 February was deferred until instructions were 'received from the All Highest.'[1]

The power struggle between von Muller and von Pohl now began in earnest. On reading the revised instructions the C-in-C immediately protested to the Kaiser, complaining bitterly, 'This order makes success impossible.' Von Muller, standing as he did between the German Emperor and Admiral von Pohl, produced a red herring which he presumably intended to use against his rival at some later and more appropriate time. Acting in the name of the Kaiser he demanded to know 'how far you (von Pohl) can guarantee that within six weeks of the campaign against commerce opening, Great Britain will be forced to lift the blockade.'[2] Although the Kaiser had shown an inclination to agree with his C-in-C's objections to the 14 February message, von Muller had obviously planted a substantial seed of doubt in Wilhelm's mind.

The reply, received next day, was signed by Tirpitz and the new Chief of Naval Staff, Admiral Bachmann, and revealed that they were 'convinced that Great Britain will end the blockade six weeks after the new commercial war begins', a bold statement in the face of the Royal Navy's past history. But like skilled politicians their promise was hedged by a proviso that success could only be achieved if 'it is found possible to employ every kind of warlike resource available for this campaign.' In other words their guarantee of victory depended on the implementation of the Clausewitz theory of total war and terror tactics.

So Tirpitz and the rest of the Navy were now committed to a six week campaign which offered strong hopes of a satisfactory conclusion in the shortest possible space of time. Von Muller had set his trap carefully and his victims had walked into it.

[1] *Der Krieg zur Zee.*
[2] Ibid.

Relying on this assurance of speedy victory a diplomatic reply was sent to the United States stating that American ships would be spared 'so far as they can be recognized as such' and similar assurances were sent to Italy. Bolstered by the promise of early success the months of hesitation and indecision came to an end and Imperial approval was given for von Pohl's campaign to begin on 22 February, 1915. But could these promises be honoured in the reality of the war at sea? The final instructions issued to the U-boat commanders four days before the start of the campaign made it seem unlikely:

'1. The U-boat campaign against commerce is to be prosecuted with all possible vigour.
2. Hostile merchant ships are to be destroyed.
3. Neutral ships are to be spared. A neutral flag or funnel marks of neutral steamship lines are not to be regarded, however, as sufficient guarantee in themselves of neutral nationality. Nor does the possession of further distinguishing neutral marks furnish absolute certainty. The commander must take into account all accompanying circumstances that may enable him to recognise the nationality of the ship; e.g. structure, place of registration, course, and general behaviour.
4. Merchant ships with a neutral flag travelling in convoy are thereby proved neutral.
5. Hospital ships are to be spared. They may only be attacked when they are obviously being used for the transport of troops from England to France.
6. Ships belonging to the Belgian Relief Commission are likewise to be spared.
7. If in spite of the exercise of great care mistakes should be made the commander will not be held responsible.'

Paragraph 7 was the key to the whole matter especially when read in conjunction with earlier instructions regarding the safety of the submarine. And, if the U-boat commander on the spot was not to be held responsible for his actions, *who* was? The implication behind the instructions suggested that the German Government and the Kaiser took full responsibility and that the U-boat captains were to be regarded merely as carrying out orders. This, in fact, was the standard excuse offered by German submarine commanders when faced by accusations of murder and piracy after the war.

One such U-boat captain, Rudolf Zentner, discussing the torpedoing of the *Lusitania* with American journalist Lowell Thomas in 1928, was quite clear in his own mind where responsibility lay: 'Schwieger merely carried out orders. He had been ordered to sink any ship he could in the blockaded waters ... any other U-boat officer would have done the same.' Clearly, in Zentner's view, obedience to orders was sufficient absolution for Schwieger's action.

It was not until the Nuremburg Trials at the end of the Second World War that the principles relating to war crimes were finally clarified and, in the course of the judgements, it was firmly established that obedience to superior orders cannot absolve an individual member of the armed forces from responsibility for 'crimes against humanity' if a moral choice is possible—a legal view subsequently upheld in the Adolf Eichmann case and also by the verdict against Lieutenant William L. Calley in the My Lai massacre court-martial in 1970. But while it is now possible to state that members of the armed forces are only bound to obey lawful and not unlawful orders no such guidance was available to the U-boat commanders in 1915.

In passing judgement it must be remembered that obedience to orders and the lack of personal initiative arising from such blind obedience was commonplace in the armed forces of every nation at the beginning of the twentieth century and while there can be little doubt that a moral choice was offered to each and every submarine captain whenever a merchant ship entered his sights, it is by no means so certain that the officer was aware that the decision to fire was vested in his own conscience.

The concept of humanity in warfare was one that had developed and flourished during the preceding century and by 1914 it was accepted as uncivilized to attack unarmed merchant ships or to kill civilian passengers and crews even though they might be engaged on service vital to the interests of the enemy. Taking a realistic point of view it is difficult to see why a civilian collier carrying coal to the warships of the Grand Fleet at Scapa Flow should be spared from attack or, if sunk according to the rules of war, her crew should be allowed special facilities for escape not granted to the crews of the warships she was succouring.

But further complications cloud the issue for, although even today international law does not permit a merchant ship to be sunk without warning, the German submarine service, in the person of Admiral Karl Dönitz, was absolved from the charge of 'crimes against humanity' by the Nuremburg Tribunal. It was admitted that international law had been broken but an acquittal was granted because both the Royal Navy and the United States Navy had adopted similar sink-on-sight tactics for their own submarines in defiance of the 1936 London Protocol. Two wrongs, it seems, can make a right when the victors are equally guilty.

Bearing this verdict in mind it seems reasonable to conclude that the U-boat captains in the 1914–18 conflict were similarly not guilty of 'unlawful killing' when they sank hostile merchant ships without warning although it must be admitted that, in the Great War, Allied submarines carefully obeyed international law on all occasions.

Attacks on neutral vessels, however, fall into a different category and it cannot be denied that the wholesale destruction of such ships was a crime against humanity. Obedience to orders cannot be offered as an excuse as the U-boat captains had a moral choice but, here again, it is possible to put forward a defence. Without doubt, Britain's persistent use of neutral colours as a *ruse de guerre* gave the U-boat commanders much justified cause for suspicion when they encountered a 'neutral' vessel and, in the white heat of battle, it is scarcely surprising that inevitable and tragic errors were made. The case for a 'moral choice' in such circumstances seems somewhat academic.

That a few, a very few, German submarine captains were guilty of war crimes must be accepted and details of the atrocities which they committed will be found on later pages. But the vast majority of U-boat captains carried out their distasteful task with humanity and chivalry even though, in theory, they were acting contrary to international law.

In arriving at a judgement it is chastening to remember that it was a *British* admiral[1] who said: 'The essence of war is violence, moderation in war is imbecility!' And no one could ever accuse the Germans of being fools when it comes to fighting a war.

[1] Admiral of the Fleet Lord Fisher.

CHAPTER SIX

'This campaign of piracy and pillage'

ALTHOUGH VON POHL'S campaign was not scheduled to begin until 22 February several U-boat captains got off to an early start. Operating off the French coast on the night of 15 February *U-16* demonstrated the new terror tactics by torpedoing the English cargo steamer *Dulwich* without warning and, four nights later, severely damaging the Norwegian tanker *Belridge* outward bound from New Orleans to Amsterdam, a neutral vessel carrying cargo from one neutral country to another. The attack took place at night and, as the tanker was burning her lights, there seemed little likelihood of mistaken identity.

But *U-16*'s marauding patrol was cut short by continuous engine trouble and, with one ship sunk and another damaged, she was forced to return to Heligoland for repairs after only ten days at sea. As *U-16* limped back home her flotilla mate, *U-30*, set out and, after forcing through the defences of the Dover Straits, pushed up into the Irish Sea and took up position on the converging trade routes west of Liverpool.

U-30 had the unenviable reputation of being a hoodoo ship and she lived up to it throughout her short career as a sea-wolf. Later in the war she was accidentally sunk in Emden harbour with all but three of her crew trapped inside. Lying on the bottom in 120 feet of water she defied all attempts to rescue the trapped survivors and, as the other U-boats passed close by, they could hear the pathetic tapping sounds of the imprisoned men beating the iron sides of the submarine with hammers and heavy spanners, an unnerving experience for men who knew they might suffer a similar fate at any second.

The sounds continued for three days, growing weaker with each passing hour until, finally, there was silence. Three months later German salvage teams brought the U-boat to the surface, the dead were lifted reverently out of the hatches, and dockyard workmen began the task of cleaning and overhauling the rusting machinery.

U-30 had left Heligoland on 10 February for her first war patrol but both her captain and her crew seemed to have little enthusiasm for their task. Despite her dominating position astride the main Liverpool shipping route her achievements were small, sinking only the 3,112 ton cargo steamer *Cambrank* by torpedo without warning, and the 337 ton coaster *Downshire* with explosive charges. Then, as if to avoid tempting Fate further, she stole away, rounded the northern tip of Scotland, and returned safely to her base.

As 22 February approached the operational details of the campaign began to take shape. Three main concentration areas were selected: the southern part of the Irish Sea covering routes to both Liverpool and Bristol; the English Channel where there was not only a heavy coasting traffic and main routes to Southampton and London, but also a chance of hitting the troop transports crossing from England to France; and the North-East coast to trap the colliers running south from Newcastle and the important Baltic trade.

Distances, however, weighed heavily against the plans as laid down by the High Command. A U-boat often spent two of its three-week patrol-time travelling to its blockade station and, with only 20 operational submarines in service, the Germans had to be content with restricted success. The continuing air attacks on Zeebrugge already referred to in the previous chapter also had a profound influence on the strategy of the campaign. The proximity of the Flanders bases to the Channel and the Irish Sea reduced passage distance by 250 miles but, following the severe damage to *U-14* during a bombing raid on Zeebrugge early in February, the High

Command ordered the submarines to be quickly withdrawn until the anti-aircraft defences had been strengthened, a decision that militated against maximum deployment of their resources.

On the day the campaign officially opened Kapitanleutnant Alfred Stoss probed for a weak spot in the new Dover defences. His boat, *U-8*, although only launched in March, 1911, was already a veteran and, for surface running, depended on the Korting kerosene engines with their tell-tale black exhaust smoke. Rather than risk being spotted on the surface Stoss took the submarine deep and pushed into the unknown. Suddenly she lurched to a dead stop, her propellers threshing the water in vain, as her bows tangled in a line of indicator nets. The brightly painted buoys on the surface danced wildly as the U-boat struggled to tear free but, before the patrolling drifters could get to the scene with their deadly explosive sweeps, *U-8* had wrenched herself clear and was feeling her way gingerly through the minefields guarding the Straits. It had been a nasty moment and there was an audible sigh of relief from the crew as they felt the submarine get under way again.

Stoss's perseverance was soon rewarded and he quickly bagged a total of five steamers off Beachy Head. All were sunk without warning and all, Stoss claimed, were flying no flags of identity. Three days later four more submarines joined in the fray although one, *U-9*, now under the command of Johann Spiess, had to return to base with defects shortly after leaving the Fatherland. Weddigen, her former captain, had been promoted to command the new *U-29* and was busy preparing her for her first foray against the enemy.

The remaining three submarines, *U-6*, *U-20*, and *U-27*, all had their share of excitement and success. Walther Schwieger, who had taken over *U-20* from Droescher, entered the Bristol Channel where he quickly snapped up a collier and then, heading north, sank another steamer in Liverpool Bay. He returned to Germany via the Channel route after a twenty day patrol. *U-27* also stalked the Irish Sea but had taken the northern route around the tip of Scotland where she had sunk two ships, one of which was an armed merchant cruiser.

It was the veteran *U-6*, however, which produced the real excitement. Submerged off Beachy Head on 28 February she pounced on a 500 ton coaster only to find the tables unexpectedly turned. Captain John Bell, master of the *Thordis*, had already spotted the U-boat's periscope and, calling the crew on deck for safety, he watched *U-6* cross his bows from starboard to port as she took up her firing position. A torpedo streaked from her tubes but Bell skilfully evaded it and, swinging his little ship towards the submerged submarine, moved in to ram. Oberleutnant Reinhold Lepsius tried to escape but *U-6* was old and sluggish and she failed to dive quickly enough. The coaster smashed off one periscope, bent the other at right angles, and severely damaged the conning-tower. Shuddering under the impact the U-boat went deep, leaking oil from her gashed tanks, while the crew of *Thordis*, flushed with victory, headed back to Plymouth convinced that they had sent their opponent to the bottom.

Captain Bell's report of the action was applauded by the press and he was awarded a prize of £500 donated by the newspaper *Syren & Shipping* for being the first British mercantile captain to sink a U-boat, the award being publicly presented by the Lord Mayor of London at the Mansion House on 12 April, 1915.

But, although well deserved, the prize was a trifle premature. Lepsius and his crew had patched up the damaged *U-6* and, steering blind without periscopes, had succeeded in breaching the Dover defences on the return run home. Off the Flanders coast they encountered another U-boat sailing south, ran alongside her, and saved her from imminent destruction by warning her commander, Waldemar Kophamel, that he was heading straight for a new uncharted minefield. Then, having wished his comrade a successful patrol, Lepsius continued to coax his crippled boat back to Wilhelmshaven for repairs. By the time Captain Bell attended the Mansion House banquet *U-6* was safe in dry-dock.

Having returned to Ostend for refuelling and fresh torpedoes Alfred Stoss brought *U-8* back to the Dover Straits in readiness for his second foray against Channel shipping on 4 March. The destroyer *Viking* spotted the U-boat on the surface in swirling mist and opened fire, but Stoss dived quickly to safety and even had the temerity to launch a torpedo at his opponent, although unfortunately for him, it missed. Forced to run submerged, *U-8* inched her way down the Straits and, as on the previous patrol, got entangled in one of the nets again. The drifter *Roburn* saw the indicator buoys bobbing and, in response to her urgent signals, the Dover destroyers came pounding towards the spot. An anti-submarine sweep towed by the *Gurkha* suddenly encountered an obstruction and the contact switch to the detonator closed. A gushing fountain of muddy water erupted as the explosives went up, and the submarine shot to the surface. *Gurkha* and *Maori* opened fire, struck the conning-tower almost immediately and Stoss, accepting the inevitable, stepped up on deck with his hands raised high in surrender.

U-8's crew were taken off and a destroyer tried to tow the prize back to Dover. But, before escaping from the submarine, the Germans had opened the sea-cocks and the stricken U-boat soon developed a heavy list 'for all the world like a great disabled fish' before finally sinking in sixteen fathoms. The captured crew were taken to the depot-ship *Arrogant* at Dover where, that same night, Stoss and his officers were entertained to 'a good dinner on board [while] our own submarine officers, after a few gentlemanly leg-pulls, invited their prisoners to sing the "Hymn of Hate"'. Such was the spirit of war in 1915.

Six days later *U-12* met her end off Aberdeen. Chased by a group of trawlers, she tried to escape by turning south, but was ambushed by three destroyers after a hunt lasting four days and rammed by *Ariel*. Fortunately, as with *U-8*, all of her crew were picked up. Retribution, although slow, was inexorable.

U-12 deserves her own special niche in the annals of naval history as the first submarine to launch an aircraft at sea. This pioneer experiment took place off Zeebrugge on 9 January, 1915, while the U-boat was still under the command of Kapitanleutnant Walther Forstmann. A Friedrichshafen FF-29 seaplane, No 204, piloted by Leutnant Friedrich von Arnauld de la Perière—younger brother of submarine ace Lothar von Arnauld—staggered off the U-boat's bows with the aid of a strong head-wind and a good deal of nerve. Although the flight was successful the High Command was not impressed by the demonstration and the idea was dropped.

Having now fully recovered from a leg injury he had suffered while commanding *U-9*, and with his new *U-29* fuelled and armed for a long patrol, Otto Weddigen set out for a series of operations in the Western Approaches. With the skill expected from Germany's leading submarine ace he dodged through the Dover defences with practised ease and made his way down-Channel. Appearing off the Scilly Isles on 12 March he stopped four ships and, having given the crews adequate time to abandon ship and take to the boats, sank each with a single well-aimed torpedo.

Weddigen's strict observance of international law was becoming well-known and *The Times* dubbed him 'the polite pirate', a nickname he had truly earned. On the 11th he ambushed the *Aden-wen* off the Casquet Rocks and gave her crew ten clear minutes in which to abandon ship, observing: 'We wish no lives to be lost.' Indeed, so great was his concern for the survivors that, when one of *Aden-wen*'s sailors fell into the sea, he personally sent a suit of dry clothes over for the man to put on. Later he stopped and, sank the French steamer *Auguste Conseil* after telling the master of the vessel how sorry he was that he was obliged to sink his ship. Even Roger Keyes, never one to laud the enemy without good reason, referred to Weddigen as 'this intrepid officer'.

Having cleared the area of enemy shipping *U-29* set off on the long northabout route back home, Weddigen apparently not wishing to risk the increasingly dangerous hazards of the Dover defences for the second time in one patrol. By the 17th they had rounded the tip of Scotland and the crew were already beginning to relax and discuss the chances of leave when they got home. Daylight faded into night, *U-29* surfaced to recharge her batteries and then spent a few hours resting on the bottom before resuming her homeward trek at dawn the following morning. But then:

'Action stations! Stand by torpedo tubes! Full speed!'

U-29 quickly took up her attack position.

'It's the Grand Fleet,' he whispered quietly to the Watch Officer standing at his side. 'It's the whole bloody Grand Fleet!'

He selected *Neptune* of the 1st Battle Squadron as his initial target but the battleship's violent zig-zag course upset his careful aim and the torpedo ran wide. Undismayed by the failure he swung the U-boat to starboard and began lining his sights up on the ships of the 4th Battle Squadron following astern. But, confused by the great mass of ships weaving and twisting at 17 knots, and concentrating his whole attention on the target, Weddigen failed to see the looming bulk of the battleship *Dreadnought* approaching from starboard.

It was Lt-Commander Piercy, the Officer of the Watch, who first sighted *U-29*'s periscope one point off the port bow. Captain Alderson reacted promptly to the shouted warning and he handled the 17,900 ton battleship like a destroyer. Her helm spun hard over and the point of her ram bow speared into the submarine's flimsy hull. The U-boat rolled violently under the impact, and the officers on *Dreadnought*'s bridge could see her identification number quite clearly against the dark grey paint. Then, suddenly, she was gone. *Blanche* raced to the spot but found only wreckage, one article of clothing, and 'much oil and bubbles on the surface'. There were no survivors. Otto Weddigen and *U-29* had gone.

By the end of March, 1915, the sixteen U-boats on operational patrol around the coasts of Britain had sunk a total of 28,000 tons of merchant shipping; a small bag by comparison with the peak sinkings of 1917 but a warning of the submarine's ability to impose a ruthless blockade on her island enemy. Yet, for all of Tirpitz's optimistic guarantees, five weeks of the campaign had already elapsed with no sign that it was bringing Britain to her knees. In fact the majority of merchant shipping was still sailing undisturbed. On the other side of the balance sheet Germany had lost three more of her submarines plus her leading U-boat ace. Honours so far, it seemed, were even.

But Britain was learning by experience. Following hard on a suggestion made by Jellicoe after the destruction of *U-29*, details of U-boat losses were no longer made public by the British Government and the German submarine men became the target of an insidious war of nerves as their comrades vanished one by one with no word of explanation to show how they had met their fate. The High Command, too, found the situation disturbing and this cloak of silence forced them to the conclusion that the defences of the Dover Straits were now so formidable that no U-boat could pass through them unscathed.

Their fears were backed by reports from submarine commanders returning from patrols in the Channel. *U-35*, for instance, had been trapped by the indicator nets for several hours before managing to wriggle free while *U-32* also reported various difficulties she had encountered on passing through the Straits two days earlier. Then the new *U-37* failed to return to base, she was sunk by a mine according to post-war records, and orders were quickly issued forbidding U-boats to use the Straits on further operations. It was a serious set-back to the campaign, for the route around Scotland added

15. Kapitan Paul Konig, commander of the *Deutschland* on her first trip to America. Konig was a merchant navy captain *not* an officer of the Imperial German Navy.

16. The submarine freighter *Deutschland* returns to Germany after her first successful Atlantic voyage in September, 1916.

17. Shipped out to New York *UC-5* makes her contribution to Allied victory by advertising the sale of "Liberty Bonds".

18. The mine chutes of *UC-5*.

many days to passage times out and back from operational areas, and resulted in shorter periods of patrol on the vital trade-route concentrations. Plans were sent further awry when von Pohl, now C-in-C High Seas Fleet, insisted on retaining at least six U-boats for defensive patrols in the Heligoland Bight. The six week victory guarantee was beginning to look decidedly doubtful.

Thwarted by Britain's unexpected resistance, the U-boats turned more and more to terror tactics with the obvious intention of frightening merchant ships from the face of the sea. On 28 March *U-28* sank the Dutch steamer *Medea* near Beachy Head. She was carrying a cargo of oranges and tangerines from Valencia to London, scarcely warlike freight, and Freiherr von Forstner, the submarine captain, salved his honour and his conscience by towing the lifeboats for over two hours before inexplicably abandoning them to their fate.

The *Medea* incident produced a first-class row between the Dutch and German governments. A Prize Court at Hamburg exonerated von Forstner and agreed to pay compensation to the ship's owners, but the decision was reversed on appeal. Germany claimed that the London Declaration gave her the right to sink neutral prizes carrying contraband although food, in fact, was only conditional contraband and therefore liable only to seizure. Holland disagreed and argued that the destruction of a neutral prize was an illegal act, an argument soundly based in law. But the Dutch request for the case to be put to international arbitration was rejected by Berlin.

The fast diminishing rights of neutrals were further prejudiced when the British Government again reminded her merchant ship captains that the use of false colours was an accepted and legal disguise in wartime and the situation was made even worse when a definite instruction was issued to transport masters to fly 'neutral flags, preferably American . . . in the Channel approaches.' This latter instruction was promulgated despite the American Note delivered a few weeks earlier and it was becoming clear that both sides were quite prepared to abandon all moral scruples in order to snatch victory. The British government knew that the more they exploited neutral flags the more likely it became that the U-boats would sink *any* ship they sighted, and the more neutral ships that were sunk the greater the propaganda advantage.

Already, since the beginning of the campaign, the Norwegian ships *Regin* and *Nor* had been sunk, the Swedish *Hanna* torpedoed without warning, and the Portuguese steamer *Douro* destroyed in the Bristol Channel. As we have seen there had been several similar incidents in which neutral vessels had been wantonly attacked and sunk in February and March.

Von Forstner struck again on 28 March when, in the entrance to the St George's Channel, he stopped the Elder Dempster liner *Falaba*, gave the passengers and crew five minutes to abandon ship, and then fired a torpedo into her at point-blank range. 101 lives were lost and, at the subsequent inquiry, survivors alleged that *U-28*'s crew had stood on the deck of the submarine jeering at the helpless people struggling in the water. The drowning of an American citizen, Leon C. Thrasher, one of the passengers aboard the *Falaba*, brought yet another angry note from the State Department and the position was acerbated on 1 May, 1915, by *U-30*'s attack on the American tanker *Gulflight*. The damaged ship managed to reach harbour but two American sailors were killed when the torpedo exploded.

'The fundamental error of the German position,' the *New York World* protested in an angry editorial, 'is the assumption that submarines have peculiar rights by reason of their disabilities as commerce destroyers.'

The campaign took a more sinister turn when certain U-boat commanders began to act in defiance of their own instructions. Paragraph 6 of the 18 February Order had laid down in clear and unequivocal terms: 'Ships belonging to the Belgian Relief Commission are likewise to be spared.'[1] But on 10 April, off the North Hinder lightship, the 5,940 ton steamer *Harpalyce* was torpedoed without warning despite flying a white flag and bearing 'Commission for Belgian Relief' painted in large white letters along her side which were visible, so it was claimed, for eight miles. *Harpalyce* sank before her boats could be lowered and 17 members of her 44 man crew were lost.

Yet, while neutral ships were being sent to the bottom one after the other, British merchant vessels often gave as good as they were given. On 27 March the Moss Line steamer *Vosges* was sighted by a U-boat in the Western Approaches 60 miles west of Trevose Head. 'I had always made up my mind to make a fight of it in an emergency,' her master Captain J. R. Green told reporters afterwards. And he proved to be as good as his promise. By turning the stern of his ship to the U-boat he ensured that the German would not waste a torpedo on him and then, pounding eastwards at 14 knots, he tried to outrun the submarine chasing him on the surface. The action lasted ninety minutes and *Vosges*, under continuous fire from the U-boat's deck gun, received several direct hits, one of which killed the Chief Engineer. Tiring of the chase the U-boat finally sheered away and submerged, unaware of the mortal damage she had inflicted on her scurrying victim. Two hours later the defiant British steamer rolled over and sank but, by good fortune, her crew were picked up safely by an armed yacht patrolling in the vicinity. As Captain Green remarked afterwards: 'If only we'd had a gun.'

The campaign continued without respite. In the middle of April *U-22*, having turned north after failing to pierce the Dover defences, sank a Swedish steamer and an English trawler in the North Sea, and her menacing presence off the West Coast of Scotland forced the Admiralty to divert the Grand

[1] See p. 85.

Fleet colliers to the west of Ireland. *U-30*, her hoodoo apparently enjoying a brief rest, located the new route and snapped off four colliers as she cruised south to the Western Approaches. On 1 May she sank her fifth victim and, as noted earlier, also torpedoed the American tanker *Gulflight*. Her murderous foray ended with the destruction of yet another collier, this time off the Wolf Rock, after which she made for home more than satisfied with a highly successful patrol.

U-20, which had left Germany on 30 April, was following only three days behind *U-30* and Walther Schwieger made his first killing off the Old Head of Kinsale, in south-east Ireland, on 5 May when he sank a small sailing-ship. The next morning he put paid to a steamer, failed to catch a White Star liner sighted hull-down on the horizon, and, in the afternoon, polished off another steamer. Heavy fog brought further operations to a halt and for two days *U-20* probed blindly into the mists taunted by the sound of sirens as a number of ships, all hidden by the fog, passed within torpedo range. Several hundreds of miles to the west, running in clear weather, the liner *Lusitania* was steaming hard for Liverpool.

When Schwieger torpedoed the *Lusitania* on 7 May, 1915, he virtually changed the course of history and the attack formed a vital watershed in German-American relations. Until that fateful afternoon the United States, steering a carefully neutral path between the two warring nations, had complained with almost equal bitterness to both belligerents, showing little favour for either. Britain had enraged America by her blockade system, which many claimed was unlawful, and by her continual exploitation of neutral flags; while Germany's unrestricted submarine campaign had shocked a nation which regarded the Freedom of the Seas and the Rights of Neutrals as holy writ. From that moment onwards the United States moved slowly, if reluctantly, into the arms of the Allies and her final entry into the war in 1917 sealed the fate of the German Empire. The *Lusitania* tragedy demonstrated for the first, and by no means the last, time that a single U-boat could change the destiny of nations.

The figures for sinkings in May were a startling 106,293 tons followed, in June, by another 107,188 tons. Although the six week victory promise had been shattered there could be little doubt that the campaign was effective and that Britain had felt those effects.

The potential strength of the U-boat offensive was now being reinforced by the new UB boats operating from Zeebrugge and the other harbours along the Belgian coast. These tiny little submarines, only 92 feet in length and displacing a mere 127 tons on the surface, were ideal vessels for the shoals and narrows of the Thames estuary and the Dover Straits. Despite their limited range and slow speed of $6\frac{1}{2}$ knots they packed a substantial punch in the shape of two 18 inch torpedo tubes and they proved good sea-boats. Built by the Germaniawerft yards at Kiel, they were transported by rail in pre-fabricated sections (a skill based on Nordenfelt's experiences in the 1890's) where they were assembled by trained engineers and, once in service, they took a steady toll of coastal shipping running in and out of London, and were to achieve some remarkable successes in both the North Sea and the Mediterranean as the war progressed.

Development of a small minelaying submarine led, in 1915, to the introduction of the UC types, roughly similar in size and design to the diminutive UBs and fitted with six mine tubes and a complement of twelve mines. The early UC boats were minelayers pure and simple and were fitted with neither torpedo tubes nor guns but they proved a highly successful design on which development continued throughout the war. Built in complete secrecy, they provided an unpleasant surprise for the Admiralty when they began sowing their mines in areas assumed to be safe.

There seemed to be no answer to this new threat; nets, explosive sweeps, moored mines, guns, and ramming tactics were the only anti-submarine weapons available to the Royal Navy and none had proved wholly successful. In the open sea a U-boat had only to dive and she was completely safe from her hunters who, at that period of the war, were without either hydrophones to locate the submerged submarine, or depth-charges to destroy her under water. But what the British lacked in technical know-how they made up for with cunning.

It was Admiral Beatty's secretary, Paymaster-Commander Frank Spickernell, who originally had the idea of using trawlers and submarines as decoy ambush units. The U-boats, early in 1915, had begun to show an interest in the North Sea fishing fleets and Spickernell suggested sending out decoy trawlers which would be towing, not fishing nets, but a submerged submarine. A telephone connected the two ships and, when a U-boat surfaced to attack the trawler with its guns, the submarine would slip its tow and make a torpedo attack on the enemy raider.

U-40 was the first to fall victim to the ruse. Surfacing to attack the trawler *Taranaki* at three bells in the forenoon watch of 23 June, she was unaware that her victim was anything other than an innocent fishing-boat. But, safely submerged and out of sight, the British submarine *C-24* was waiting for just such a moment. A telephone message from the trawler informed Lieutenant Taylor, captain of the submarine, that a U-boat had surfaced fifteen hundred yards away on the port beam. But then everything went wrong.

The tow rope mechanism on the submarine jammed and, unable to slip the hawser, a frantic phone call was put through to *Taranaki* to let go her end. The trawler obeyed and, weighed down by the heavy wire still attached to her nose, *C-24* tilted down at a wild angle as she moved in to the attack. Taylor regained control only to find that the hawser had fouled his propellors. Luck, fortunately, was with the Royal Navy that day and despite the difficulties caused by the towing-wire *C-24* succeeded in reaching an attacking position. At 9.55 am the fatal Whitehead torpedo hissed from her bow tube, struck the *U-40* amidships below the conning-tower, and sent her to the bottom. Only Furbinger, her captain, and one petty-officer were saved from the water and when taken aboard *Taranaki*, were heard to complain 'that they had been the victims of a dirty trick!'[1]

The U-boat service was soon to discover that the British had several more tricks up their sleeves, dirty or otherwise.

[1] *By Guess and By God*, by William Guy Carr (Hutchinson, 1930) p. 152.

CHAPTER SEVEN

'Proceedings for murder'

KAPITANLEUTNANT BERNHARD WEGENER was not displeased with the afternoon's work. Even though she was carrying a consignment of army mules rather than fare-paying passengers, the 6,369 ton steamer would boost his tonnage figures considerably, and there was the added satisfaction that he would not need to waste a torpedo on her. True *Nicosian*'s wireless had been requesting help from the first moment she had sighted *U-27* but Wegener was quite certain he could dispose of her long before any other vessel appeared on the scene.

The crew had already abandoned ship and, as the boats pulled away from the doomed liner, *U-27*'s sailors waited their skipper's order to start shooting. The gun-layer adjusted for elevation and the 37mm quick-firer swivelled smoothly while Wegener tapped his fingers impatiently for the lifeboats to pull clear of the gun's arc of fire.

The first shots hammered into the waterline and *Nicosian* tilted gently as the sea began to gush into her hull. The gun crew took their time, sighted each shot carefully, and pounded away with leisurely efficiency. Wegener joined in the fun. Propping his elbows on the side of the conning-tower he became so engrossed in the sport that he failed to observe a new arrival on the scene, an ancient tramp steamer labouring over the horizon in a cloud of black funnel smoke. He would not have worried unduly if he *had* seen her for she was wearing American colours painted on wooden boards which hung down over her rusty sides. However, somebody on *U-27* finally noticed the interloper and the submarine glided forward as Wegener placed himself between the lifeboats and the oncoming stranger. Then, on second thoughts, he swung towards the intruder with the intention of examining her. For a few moments the listing hulk of the *Nicosian* came between the two vessels so that they lost sight of each other and, by the time *U-27* emerged from behind the liner's bows, the range was down to 600 yards.

It was then, as *Nicosian* passed astern that Wegener suddenly got his first clear view of the 'tramp' steamer. A White Ensign now streamed from her peak, the Stars and Stripes fell away, and a dozen previously hidden 12-pounders opened up on the unsuspecting U-boat. He had come face to face with one of Britain's notorious Q-ships!

Designed with only one function in mind, to hunt and destroy U-boats, these ex-merchant ships were armed with concealed quick-firers and crewed by highly trained Royal Navy veterans. Sailing under neutral colours and changing their appearance frequently they prowled the trade routes trailing their coats to tempt unwary U-boat commanders to the surface where the submarine would be at its most vulnerable. It was a dangerous game calling for skill, patience, and courage for, as we shall see later, the Q-ship was not always the victor and often, in desperation, a decoy vessel would even allow herself to be torpedoed in order to bluff her opponent into surfacing.

Godfrey Herbert, commander of the *Baralong*, and an experienced ex-submariner himself, was in a killing mood. Only a few hours earlier he had received news that the White Star liner *Arabic* had been sunk in cold blood by a U-boat in the immediate area and he felt certain that he had run the culprit to ground. As it happened Herbert was wrong. The man he wanted was Rudolf Schneider. But at that particular moment very little mattered, except that a hated U-boat was squarely in his sights. In the space of as many seconds the *Baralong* let go 34 rounds rapid and *U-27* was literally pulverized. Shell holes peppered her waterline, the ballast tanks were punctured with splinters, and the conning-tower 'went up in the air' as a salvo of shells exploded along its base; in less than a minute the U-boat had disintegrated.

Somehow Wegener and a dozen of U-27's crew got clear of the inferno and, swimming hard for their former victim, they clambered on board via the boat's falls and pilot ladder. Convinced that the Germans intended to scuttle the ship and destroy its valuable cargo of livestock Herbert ordered his men to open fire again. Only four of the German sailors survived the fusilade and, scrambling on to the safety of *Nicosian*'s deck, they quickly vanished into the bowels of the ship. Bernhard Wegener was not one of the four.

By this time *Baralong*'s skipper was certain that the remaining Germans intended mischief and his fears were not allayed when the liner's master warned him that a supply of guns and ammunition were available in the charthouse. There was one only answer to the problem and a party of Marines went across to the crippled steamer in one of *Baralong*'s cutters. They tracked the unfortunate German sailors down into the engine rooms and a quick burst of rifle shots signalled the end of the story. Whether, in fact, the survivors from *U-27* intended to scuttle the liner or whether they were just hiding in fear from the vengeful British marines has never been explained.

Both sides presented their own version of the incident; the Kaiser's government 'took it for granted' that Britain would 'immediately take proceedings for murder' against *Baralong*'s commander and crew, and demanded to know that 'the deed has been punished by a sentence of corresponding severity.'

The British reply, tongue in cheek, noted with satisfaction the sudden concern of the Imperial Government for the principles of civilized warfare and observed that the charges were 'negligible compared with the crimes which seem to have been deliberately committed by German officers ... against combatants and non-combatants!' Both sides raged at each other for several months but in the end nothing concrete emerged despite Germany's portentious threats of unspecified reprisals.

U-27, as it happened, had not been the first enemy submarine to fall victim to the new Q-ships. On the evening of 24 July, *U-36*, having destroyed nine trawlers during a raid on the North Sea fishing grounds, sunk three neutral steamers, and then captured the United States sailing-ship *Pass of Balmaha*, which she had sent back to Germany with a prize crew on board, came up with yet one more disreputable looking tramp.

It was just routine. Kapitanleutnant Ernst Graeff surfaced, fired the obligatory warning shot, and called on her to stop for examination. The 'panic party', a special section of the crew selected to act the part of merchant seamen, abandoned the Q-ship with clumsy haste and, once they were clear, *U-36* began shelling her apparently deserted victim. Suddenly *Prince Charles* ran up a White Ensign, the hatches and deck-houses concealing her guns fell away, and the 12-pounders opened up. Graeff knew quite well he was no match for a surface warship, especially one trained and equipped for the sole purpose of destroying submarines, and he made a wild attempt to dive. The warning gongs clanged and the crew rushed for the conning-tower as *U-36* began pushing her nose into the sea. It was too late. A salvo smashed into the hull just behind the conning-tower and *Prince Charles* closed to 300 yards for a quick kill. The ballast tanks badly punctured and with *Prince Charles* firing at point blank range, the submarine began to slide stern-first beneath the surface. The hatches flew open and the crew struggled to escape as she plunged to the bottom. Only fifteen men were saved from the *U-36*, the first in a long line of victims to fall to the dreaded Q-ships of the Royal Navy.

Meanwhile the trawler-submarine decoy system had also claimed another killing when, on 20 July, Schulthess and *U-23* were snared by *Princess Louise* and her submerged consort

C-27. It was a repeat version of the *U-40* incident but it also proved to be the last. Some repatriated prisoners carried the story back to Germany and U-boat commanders were warned off for the future.

The 'six week campaign' was proving an expensive venture for, in addition to *U-23*, *U-27* and *U-36*, the *U-14* had been rammed and sunk by a trawler in June; Oberleutnant Karl Gross's *UB-4*, surprised by the armed fishing-smack *Inverlyon* off Smith's Knoll buoy on 15 August, had been destroyed by gunfire; and *U-6*, commanded by Reinhold Lepsius, had been stalked and torpedoed by the submarine *E-16* on 24 September. But these individual losses counted for little alongside the accidental sinking of the new coastal minelayer *UC-2* on 2 July, 1915, an incident of major importance in the grand strategy of the U-boat war.

For some months a number of small isolated minefields had sprouted mysteriously along the Kent and East Anglian coasts and the British Admiralty, unaware that Germany possessed minelaying submarines, felt sure they had been sown by neutral fishing boats in the pay of their unscrupulous enemy. A close surface patrol was maintained in vital areas but despite unceasing vigilance fresh fields continued to appear almost every day. Now, as salvage operations on *UC-2* proceeded, the secret of the minefields was revealed. Royal Navy experts found that the tiny 111-foot long submarine housed six vertically inclined discharge chutes containing twelve mines primed and ready for laying. The source of the minefields was a mystery no longer and, with a sigh of relief, counter-measures were quickly put in hand while, at the same time, the Admiralty noted the lesson and some of the British E-class submarines were crudely converted to carry mines in a similar, though more primitive, manner.

Meanwhile the campaign continued unabated with 113 ships totalling 107,188 tons sunk during June and a further 92 ships sent to the bottom the following month. Despite the outcry which followed the *Lusitania* tragedy, U-boat tactics remained unchanged and Schwieger himself showed no change of heart when he torpedoed the Russian steamer *Leo* without warning, with the loss of half of her crew. British ships, however, still tried to outrun the raiders although they were not always successful. The *Caucasian*, challenged by Walther Forstmann's *U-39* near the Scillies, zig-zagged for safety at her maximun speed of 9 knots with the U-boat in pursuit. The chase lasted over an hour until, finally, a shell wrecked the steamer's bridge. The crew were ordered to abandon ship and Forstmann, furious at Captain Robinson's defiant attempt to escape, threatened to sink the lifeboats as a reprisal. But when one of the *Caucasian*'s crew dived into the water to save the ship's pet dog his heart softened and he allowed them to proceed unharmed.

The luckless Von Hennig, taken prisoner when *U-18* was destroyed on 23 November, had by now tired of the confines of his prison camp and with two companions made a daring escape. The party made their way to the Welsh coast, where, using a communication system which still remains a mystery, they arranged to be picked up by a submarine. Max Valentiner was picked for the task and in mid-August *U-38* arrived off a lonely beach north-west of Llandudno to effect a rendezvous.

Nervously aware that the whole affair might be a British trap Max brought the U-boat to the surface at dawn and, while lookouts anxiously scanned the seaward horizon for the enemy, *U-38*'s skipper kept his eyes firmly fixed on the shore as a signaller flashed a pre-arranged code to the fugitives. But there was no sign of life along the barren rocks of the Welsh bay and, after a tense thirty minutes, Valentiner took *U-38* out to sea again where he submerged to await the next day. After two more dawn vigils, neither of which proved successful, he gave up and, with a final glance at the shoreline, he took his boat out to sea for the last time. Yet success had only eluded him by a hairsbreadth. A confusion in locations had led von

Hennig and his companions to another small beach a mile along the coast where, cold and shivering, they huddled behind the rocks for shelter waiting the arrival of their rescuer. A headland, thrusting out to sea separated the two beaches so effectively that neither the prisoners nor the U-boat saw each other although they were less than a mile apart.

Before returning to Germany on 23 August Valentiner avenged his disappointment with a patrol in which he sank no less than 22 steamers, 3 sailing vessels, and 5 fishing boats. This extraordinary score was achieved by the use of the deck gun for which ammunition was plentiful in contrast to the restricted supply of torpedoes. Although he had to risk coming to the surface to destroy his victims his skill was amply rewarded. For von Hennig and his two companions there was no such satisfying end to the adventure. Rounded up by an army patrol he was marched back to the prison camp where he remained until the end of the war.

While Valentiner was scouring the Irish Sea with his gun, Schneider and *U-24* stalked the horizon further north. Coming to the surface off Whitehaven on the 16th he shelled the newly constructed oil works, then, dipping gently beneath the surface, he took *U-24* in search of more excitement.

The 15,801 ton White Star liner *Arabic* had left the Mersey at high water on 19 August and she was already sixty miles out from Liverpool when *U-24* found her. Carefree and relaxed, her 181 passengers were either in the saloons enjoying a quiet drink or sprawled contentedly on the sun-decks in armchairs, chatting and laughing. New York was some eight days ahead and there would be plenty of time to enjoy a pleasant voyage. But, unknown to them, for 44 of the passengers and crew of the ill-fated ship there was very little time left.

Schneider kept *U-24* hidden beneath the waves as the liner approached and only the thin tube of the periscope betrayed his presence. *Arabic* passed squarely across his sights until the mass of her hull filled the lens. Making no attempt to warn his victim Schneider let go a single torpedo. It struck aft and there was a tremendous explosion. Ten minutes later the great ship disappeared from sight. Schneider assuaged his own, and Germany's, conscience by reporting that *Arabic's* zigzag course misled him into thinking he was about to be deliberately rammed. But few believed such a transparent excuse.

The incident rekindled the burning resentment which had inflamed public opinion in the United States after the *Lusitania* affair and which was now, with the passing of time, slowly dying away. Washington immediately issued a strong protest and the sudden stiffening of the American attitude aroused, yet again, the smouldering dispute between naval and diplomatic circles in Germany. Tirpitz, Bachmann, and von Pohl remained convinced that terror tactics were the key to victory at sea. Their view was not based on the use of terror *per se* but followed from a realistic appraisal of the submarine's role in sea warfare. To be effective a U-boat *must* sink without warning; any other tactic reduced the safety factor. Bethmann-Hollweg, backed by the insidious von Muller, maintained a firm stand against the campaign and the latter could not resist reminding all parties of the six *week* victory guarantee which had been made six *months* earlier.

Thoroughly concerned by the American attitude, and strongly influenced by the Chancellor and von Muller, the Kaiser issued orders on 27 August that passenger ships should only be sunk after due and proper warning had been given *and* after both crew and passengers were safely in the lifeboats. The German ambassador in Washington, Count Bernstorff, was instructed to placate the US government and he did so with completely unequivocal assurances. 'Liners will not be sunk by our submarines without warning and without ensuring the safety of the lives of non-combatants,' he pledged solemnly, 'provided that the liners do not try to escape or offer resistance.' The promise did not last long. On 6 September, Schwieger, destroyer of the *Lusitania*, chanced upon the

10,000 ton Allan liner *Hesperian* 80 miles off the Fastnets and fired a torpedo into her. An effort was made to tow her to safety but Schwieger's job had been well executed and she finally rolled over and sank while still some distance from harbour.

Meanwhile von Muller was securing the downfall of his opponents after the failure of the six-week promise. His first victim, Admiral Bachmann, the Chief of Naval Staff, retired as a result of the continual disagreements and was replaced by von Holtzendorff who, by some strange coincidence, was one of von Muller's relatives. Tirpitz and von Pohl also offered their resignations but were too valuable to be spared and the Kaiser refused to accept them. By 27 August the internal disputes had become so violent that an order was issued instructing the U-boats to remain in harbour until the matter was settled, an order apparently emanating from the embittered von Pohl who considered that the operational problems created by the Kaiser's instructions concerning passenger ships physically endangered the lives of the U-boat crews. Even Tirpitz, that staunch royalist, was moved to comment: 'We continued the campaign in a form that could not live and yet, at the same time, could not die.'

With the High Command entertaining such demoralizing thoughts it is not surprising that the fire quickly went out of the campaign. The public disavowal of Schneider after the *Arabic* incident did little to reassure the other U-boat captains and it was almost with relief that they read the Order of 18 September, 1915, instructing them to cease operations in British waters on the 20th. But before the campaign finally closed the U-boats had encountered more troubles.

By the end of 1915 a total of 24 submarines had been lost and the British defences were growing in strength and experience. Mines claimed *UC-9* and navigational hazards led to the loss of her sister-ship, *UC-8*, which was stranded on a mudbank off Terschelling and interned. She was later sold

to the Dutch government and commissioned into the Netherlands Navy as *M-1* where she served alongside a former
British submarine lost in similar circumstances.

Then, in September, the Q-ships struck again. This time the
victim was *U-41* which, a few weeks earlier, had survived a
duel with another decoy ship, *Pearl*, and which was now
operating as a replacement boat to *U-20* in the Western
Approaches. Hansen had already sunk three steamers in the
Fastnet area and was occupied in shelling the *Urbino* on 13
September when an unidentified ship was seen approaching
from the south. Scenting another victim Hansen steamed at
high speed on the surface to cut her off while signalling to her
to stop. Observing neutral colours flying at the stern the
U-boat skipper was slightly off-guard and he allowed the
mystery ship to close dangerously. A boat was launched to
bring the ship's papers to the submarine for inspection and,
as it toiled across, the two vessels drifted even closer to each
other. Suddenly, when the range was down to 700 yards, the
stranger hoisted a White Ensign, unmasked her guns, and
opened fire. It was *Baralong*, already notorious in German
eyes after her destruction of Wegener's *U-27*.

It was too late to escape. Hansen's voice rose above the
noise of the guns as he ordered the submarine down in a crash
dive but there was no time to obey. A shell hit the base of the
conning-tower and exploded. More shots penetrated the
pressure hull at the precise moment the valves opened to
admit the sea into the ballast tanks. Water roared into the
tanks, *U-41* lurched under the additional weight and then,
plunging her bows into the sea, she went to the bottom
leaving only two survivors struggling in the water. *Baralong*
had chalked up her second victim.

The small minelayers of the Flanders Flotilla remained in
action for some weeks after the North Sea U-boats returned to
base and, day after day, isolated minefields mushroomed
unexpectedly along the English coast. The Royal Navy's

resources were strained to the limit in an effort to clear safe channels through the danger areas and although the salvage operations on the *UC-2* had revealed the secret source of the minefields nothing could be done to thwart the furtive movements of the UC-boats. Without an effective underwater anti-submarine weapon the British were powerless to take offensive action against the unseen minelayers and the burden of the task fell upon the minesweepers.

150 mines were sown off Dover, 180 in the area of the Nore, 306 along the approaches to Lowestoft, and 12 in the vicinity of Grimsby. In all, 94 ships fell victim to the scattered minefields including, tragically, the Hospital Ship *Anglia* which encountered a field laid by *UC-5*. And merchant ships were not the only victims. The destroyers *Maori*, *Lightning*, and *Velox* went to the bottom on the Flanders minefields, and the Tribal class destroyer *Mohawk* was seriously damaged. Finally, as if anxious to prove that she was a true submarine *UB-17* torpedoed and sank the French destroyer *Branlebas* on 9 November while returning to Zeebrugge from one of her minelaying missions.

But these were isolated incidents; the six week victory campaign was in all respects over and the Allies could justifiably claim a political, if not a naval, victory. For the Germans the results were disappointing. A total of 166 British steamers and 168 fishing-boats had been destroyed by gunfire or torpedo with a further 28 sunk by mines. Taking into account the vast size of the British mercantile marine it was a meagre total and, in addition, Germany's already small U-boat service had been further depleted by 16 more underwater raiders. Yet the experience gained during the campaign was to stand Germany in good stead for the future and was to cost the Allies dear in 1917.

It was a time for both sides to consider the situation in the light of results. For Britain it meant a continual search for new methods of anti-submarine warfare. For the Germans it meant building U-boats in far greater numbers. Even more important, as the continued struggle between the Imperial Navy and the Kaiser's politicians had shown, it required a combined determination to win, whatever the cost.

CHAPTER EIGHT

'. . . and a natural-born fisherman to boot'

THE DISTANT HILLS of Gallipoli shimmered as the sun climbed to its zenith. Scarred with yellow streaks where exploding shells had torn gaping holes in the soil, and dotted with green patches of scrub, the peninsula stared sullenly across the Straits. Only the small puffs of white smoke and the dull crump of bursting shells interspersed with the chattering machine-guns indicated that two great armies were locked in combat in that otherwise peaceful scene.

At the base of the cliffs, groups of lighters, ship's barges, and small boats, ferried fresh soldiers to the beaches as sacrifices to the Turkish artillery lodged behind the hills to the rear. Englishmen, Frenchmen, Australians and New Zealanders had landed on the beaches of Gallipoli in a vain attempt to push through the Turks and turn the flank of the Kaiser's Europe in a bold dash for Constantinople. If this move proved successful it promised to end the war in a matter of months and sea-power, the trump card of Allied military might, now began to gather in support of the soldiers huddled in shallow trenches only yards from the murderous fire of Turkish machine-guns.

Standing out to sea lay the warships of the Royal Navy, their guns bombarding the Turkish lines as they paraded along the coastline, shuddering each time a salvo of 12 inch shells shrieked over the cliffs and exploded.

The sea itself was smooth as glass, undisturbed by even the slightest breeze, yet no one noticed the periscope that cut the surface. Destroyers and patrol boats were circling around the British battleships but few took the rumoured presence of

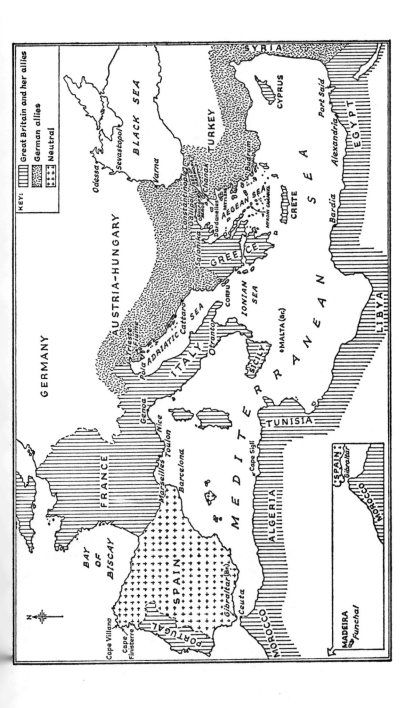

KEY:
Great Britain and her allies
German allies
Neutral

N

GERMANY

FRANCE

BAY OF BISCAY

Cape Villano
Cape Finisterre

PORTUGAL

SPAIN

Barcelona

Marseilles
Toulon
Nice
Genoa

AUSTRIA-HUNGARY

BLACK SEA

Odessa
Sevastopol

Varna

Trieste
Fiume
Pola

ADRIATIC SEA

Cattaro

ITALY

Otranto

CORFU

IONIAN SEA

SICILY

MEDITERRANEAN SEA

Ceuta
Gibraltar (Br.)

MOROCCO

ALGERIA

TUNISIA

Cape Sigli

MALTA (Br.)

GREECE

Salonika

CONSTANTINOPLE

TURKEY

Chanak
Dardanelles
GALLIPOLI

AEGEAN SEA

MYTILENE

Budrum

AFRION CHANNEL

CRETE

CORFU

LIBYA

Bardia

Alexandria

Port Said

EGYPT

SYRIA

CYPRUS

MADEIRA
Funchal

SPAIN
Gibraltar

MOROCCO

enemy submarines seriously, and all eyes were drawn towards the hills to the north.

Kapitanleutnant Otto Hersing lowered *U-21*'s periscope and crept closer to the armada. Every ounce of the skill he had acquired on his hunting expeditions in the North Sea was needed to edge into position without being spotted for the mirror surface of the sea betrayed every ripple. Once again the periscope thrust up above the water for a few seconds as he calculated the bearings and then slid down before it could reveal the U-boat's presence. Only the soft hum of the electric motors disturbed the silence inside the submarine as it crawled closer. Sweating hands spun the diving wheels in obedience to the string of orders from the control room while eyes, heavy with fatigue, watched the flickering ammeters and gauges banked in rows along the sides of the U-boat.

Hersing took a hurried last-minute check through the periscope. The range was closing and, already, the three battleships which he had first spotted had slipped beyond the restricted field of vision of the lens, leaving only one in view, and that was the one the Kapitanleutnant had selected.

'Down periscope . . . 30 metres . . . now!'

The hydroplanes tilted and *U-21* slid deeper into the water as she angled towards the bottom. An unterofficier watched the depth-gauge needles swing down and snapped an order to the men at the diving wheels. The U-boat levelled out.

'30 metres . . . all trim secured, . . . Running level,' he reported back, and Hersing nodded as the Watch Officer relayed the message. *U-21* nosed beneath the circling patrol craft while he watched the second hands of the brass-rimmed chronometers above the helmsman's head. The red arms of the clocks had completed three full revolutions when the U-boat skipper made his decision.

'Take her to 10 metres . . . torpedo tubes stand by . . . bow doors open!'

U-21 began to climb, the hydroplanes tilting as she levelled out at the new depth. The doors of the bow torpedo tubes swung open and the sea quickly filled the hollow cylinders. Turning the handle of a small test cock on the tightly-clamped loading door Gunther watched the water trickle out through the nozzle and nodded to his Chief. A quiet message passed back to the control room that the tubes were flooded and ready.

The periscope inched up, broke surface with a gentle whisper of spray, and swivelled slightly to left and right as Hersing surveyed the scene. '*HMS Triumph* stood in thundering majesty, broadside to us, and only three hundred yards away. Never had a submarine such a target.' He made a rapid last-minute calculation and altered the helm half a degree.

'Torpedo—fire!'

Even Hersing lost his usual calm under the tension of the moment. Instead of immediately lowering the periscope and diving for safety he remained glued to the eye-piece, watching with fascination. 'I saw the telltale streak of white foam darting through the water . . . it headed its way swiftly to the bow of our mammoth adversary. A huge cloud of smoke leaped out of the sea and, in the conning-tower, we heard first a dry metallic concussion, followed by a terrible reverberating explosion.'

Hersing had nearly left it too late. As the torpedo exploded a swarm of angry destroyers and patrol craft rushed in for the kill. The wake of the torpedo was still clearly visible on the calm surface of the sea and every boat made a beeline for its source.

'In periscope . . . dive!'

U-21 ducked down as Hersing forced full power from the dying batteries. The roar of propellers hammered in his ear and he knew that there was only one avenue of escape left for the trapped submarine. He took it without a moment's hesitation.

'Full speed ahead!'

Only *U-21*'s skipper knew they were facing death at that

moment but not a trace of fear showed in his face. 'It was foolhardy,' he admitted later, 'but I had to risk it. Diving as deeply as we dared, we shot right under the sinking battleship. It might have come roaring down on our heads . . . and then the U-boat and its huge prey would have gone down together in an embrace of death. But that crazy manoeuvre saved us.'

Fortune, they say, favours the brave and none can deny that Hersing and his crew were brave men, not for them the slaughter of innocent ships but, as with the torpedoing of the *Pathfinder* in the early days of the war, he preferred the challenge of another warship, pitting his skill and courage against an enemy alert and capable of defending himself. His valour brought its deserving reward. *U-21* streaked beneath the sinking giant, emerged into the safe waters beyond before the battleship had had time to sink and then, swinging in a wide arc to avoid the avenging destroyers, Hersing guided her safely away.

It was the first major success of a German submarine in the Mediterranean and it cast a long shadow over future operations in the area. For a few breathtaking moments Hersing had literally brought the war to an end. A German officer serving with the Turkish army at Gallipoli described the moment of triumph as seen from the battlefield overlooking the scene: '[It] was so tremendous a sight that for a moment war was forgotten. The soldiers in both lines of trenches stood up in plain sight of each other, forgetting everything in their intense excitement. They watched, fascinated, until *Triumph* had taken her last plunge, then jumped back into the trenches and began shooting at each other again.'

The decision to send a U-boat to the Mediterranean was taken almost casually. The original suggestion, in fact, emanated not from the Germans but from the Turks who asked for submarines to be sent as a defence against the vast armada of battleships that Britain and France had assembled for the bombardment of Gallipoli, as a prelude to forcing the Dardanelles. There were hurried meetings and Hersing, who happened to be in harbour at the time, was asked if he would undertake the mission.

It was a momentous operation involving a 4,000 mile voyage without any assistance, from the Ems river to Cattaro in the Adriatic, the Austrian port selected as the most suitable base for offensive action in Turkish waters. No submarine had ever dared to venture so far before. True, three old British 'C' class boats had sailed to Hong Kong before the war, but they had been escorted and towed the entire distance, and even the E-boats, at that time serving in the Gallipoli area, had the advantage of numerous friendly bases en route. But Hersing had faith in *U-21* and the opportunities that such a lone operation offered were too great to resist.

The U-boat nosed her way slowly out of the Ems on 25 April, 1915, and set her bows firmly northwards so that she was running in the opposite direction to her ultimate destination. Anxious that the secret of his goal should not be revealed so early in the game, and with a profound respect for the mine-fields, explosive nets, and eager patrol boats of the Dover Barrage, Hersing took *U-21* on the long and tedious north-about route around the tip of Scotland. For several days a heavy sea fog afforded appropriate cover and it was only when the mists suddenly cleared that Hersing found himself smack-bang in the middle of a British patrol. *U-21* ducked smartly under the surface and pressed on southwards without being spotted. But it had been a close thing.

A week later, off Cape Finisterre, *U-21* rendezvoused with her supply ship, the Hamburg-Amerika steamer *Marzala*, and the two vessels stole into Rio Corcubion for refuelling. Hersing had left Wilhelmshaven with 56 tons of fuel aboard and, already, his oil bunkers were down to 25 tons. The *Marzala*'s supply would ensure *U-21* reaching Cattaro with no risk of running dry on the way. At least, that was how it went in theory. In practice it turned out to be very different. The new oil was thick and glutinous and the diesel engines first spluttered, then coughed, and finally refused to fire at all. The engineers tried to mix the crude oil with the good quality fuel still remaining in *U-21*'s tanks but it was a useless exercise. Sitting quietly in his tiny cabin Hersing considered the position. He had already used 31 tons of oil which meant there was insufficient fuel in the tanks to think of returning to Germany. Yet they were only half-way to the Adriatic which made it just as doubtful whether there was enough to complete the voyage to Cattaro. Which was it to be, forward or back?

For Otto Hersing there could be only one answer and, relying on the 25 tons of good quality oil in his tanks, he set course for Gibraltar. The fuel shortage meant that the remainder of the trip must be made on the surface and, in turn, this meant extra sharp lookouts so that passing ships could be avoided by detours rather than by diving. All went well until they reached Gibraltar but from then on *U-21* ran a gauntlet of chance contacts which forced her beneath the surface and ate up more of her fast-dwindling fuel supply.

Two British torpedo-boats were evaded a few miles from the Rock and, the next day, a large merchant ship forced them to dive for cover. Finally two French destroyers played hide-and-seek with the submerged U-boat for several hours before Hersing succeeded in giving them the slip. But at last, on 13 May, eighteen days after leaving Wilhelmshaven, *U-21* reached the approaches to Cattaro. An Austrian destroyer came out to meet her, a towing hawser was secured to her bows, and the epic voyage was over. Hersing's calculated gamble had come off but it had been a close run thing, there were only 1.8 tons of oil left in the submarine's tanks when she entered the crowded naval base. As her skipper said later: 'I may forget other numbers, my birthday, or my age; but that figure is indelibly fixed in my mind.'

U-21 did not return to harbour after sinking the *Triumph* but lay doggo on the sea bottom for twenty-eight hours waiting for the hue and cry to fade away. Surfacing the next night to recharge her batteries and blow the boat clear of oil fumes and stale air Hersing considered his next move. Intelligence reports at Cattaro indicated that the Russian cruiser *Askold*, nicknamed the 'packet of Woodbines' on account of her five tall funnels, was in the Gallipoli area and, at dawn, the U-boat circled back towards the beaches of the Dardanelles in search of her new prey. The day passed without even a sniff of the elusive Russian and, during the following night, Hersing cruised slowly eastwards to the scene of his earlier success. The glass was falling and a sharp wind whipped the sea into an unpleasantly choppy swell. By morning it was quite rough and Otto was thankful that the disturbed surface would mask the spray from his periscope as he stalked towards the beaches.

Once again his luck was in. Standing off from the gaunt yellow cliffs, and guarded by a swarm of torpedo-boats and small craft, the battleship *Majestic* was covering a fresh landing with her 12 inch guns. It was an opportunity too good to miss and Hersing closed on his quarry with the skill of an experienced hunter. His one big fear was that his torpedo might be wasted by striking one of the numerous small boats protectively circling the great battleship but he decided it was a chance that must be taken. Keeping the periscope raised and relying on the rough sea to hide the tell-tale spray he waited patiently for an opening. Suddenly 'the road was clear' and, in obedience to his crisp word of command, a torpedo hissed away from the starboard bow tube. This time he did not dally to enjoy his triumph. Taking *U-21* down in a steep dive he began to crawl away. The seconds ticked by and then a violent explosion rocked the U-boat. The crew exchanged knowing grins and a quick peek through the 'scope showed the *Majestic* already listing dangerously as the sea flooded through the gaping hole in her keel. Having satisfied himself that the battleship was doomed, Hersing hurried away from the scene before the destroyers ran him to ground. Exactly four minutes later the ironclad capsized and *U-21*'s victory was complete.

Hersing's boat, however, was not the only German submarine operating in the Mediterranean. Using similar techniques to those employed in building up the Flanders Flotilla Germany had sent a number of small UB-type submarines by rail to Pola where the prefabricated sections were assembled and hurried into service.

Heino von Heimburg, skipper of *UB-15*, made a speciality of fratricide by selecting enemy submarines as his main victims. On 10 June, 1915, he sighted the Italian submarine *Medusa* cruising on the surface off Venice. *UB-15*'s torpedo streaked straight towards its target, but von Heimburg's triumph was somewhat upset when the German boat lost trim and leapt to the surface. Even at the moment of success when the torpedo struck home the U-boat's crew were still struggling for control and the majority of the men were cramped into the bow compartments in a wild effort to bring her level. Finally, when he had regained trim and restored some semblance of disciplined order inside his little boat, von Heimburg surfaced and picked up the survivors of the *Medusa* who were floundering helplessly in the water.

Shortly after this initial success *UB-15* snapped up a small Italian torpedo-boat and, the following month, scored a resounding victory by sinking the armoured cruiser *Amalfi* despite a strong protective screen of destroyers. On this occasion Heino and his crew had a narrow escape when the suction created by a passing torpedo-boat dragged the submarine towards the surface. In fact von Heimburg insisted that, had another destroyer been following close behind, *UB-15* could not have escaped being rammed.

A few weeks later the little giant-killer submarine was transferred to the Austro-Hungarian fleet and her former skipper took over *UB-14* with which he scored a number of successes against British transports operating the Gallipoli shuttle service from Mudros. It was von Heimburg, too, who snared the British submarine *E-7* later on during the campaign. On this particular occasion his beloved U-boat was undergoing repairs and he carried out the operation with a *rowing-boat*!

Always a good story-teller, Heino was very fond of this particular tale and the trimmings, like all good fishing stories, grew more ornate with the passing of the years. It seems that while his U-boat was undergoing repairs near Chanak in the Dardanelles he received a report that a British submarine was trapped in the Turkish anti-submarine nets which were strung across the Narrows to bar the passage of enemy vessels trying to force their way up into the Sea of Marmora. Anxious to be in at the kill von Heimburg and his cook, Herzig, set out in a borrowed rowing-boat and worked their way slowly along the line of surface marker buoys indicating the location of the nets below. Heino rowed while his cook, 'a very capable fellow and a natural-born fisherman to boot', sat in the stern carefully casting a plumb-line in search of the man-made fish trapped below.

Herzig soon got a bite and, having located the whereabouts of their victim, the two Germans attached a small mine to a length of cable and lowered it down into the water. A sudden violent explosion nearly capsized the rowing-boat and, seconds later, the dark hulk of the British submarine broke surface. The waiting gunboats opened fire and, as the hatches were thrown open, the crew appeared on deck with their arms raised in surrender. Prodded forward by Herzig who had actually clambered on to the slippery deck of the submarine despite the heavy fire of the Turkish guns the crew were quickly rounded up and transferred to one of the gunboats bare seconds before *E-7* took her final plunge to the bottom. Few other men could claim sinking an enemy submarine with the assistance of a ship's cook, a rowing-boat and a length of rope, and it is not surprising if von Heimburg dined out many times on the story.

As the Cattaro Flotilla expanded so did the scope of operations and, spurred by the exploits of the British submarine aces on their hazardous patrols in the Sea of Marmora, the Germans jealously sought fresh seas to conquer. Anxious to support their Turkish allies their eyes naturally turned in the direction of the Black Sea and Hersing, in the veteran *U-21*, was the first to essay the dangerous passage through the Dardanelles. Having refuelled at a small Turkish harbour after sinking the *Majestic* he set out for the Ottoman capital of Constantinople at the eastern end of the Sea of Marmora on 1 June, 1915. British submarines had to face both the hazards of nature and the Turkish defences when they forced the Straits, while Hersing had only to cope with the natural dangers of navigation; yet even these proved to be more formidable than anticipated.

Near-disaster struck almost as soon as the U-boat had pushed its nose into the Straits. A tremendous whirlpool trapped the submarine and drew it remorselessly towards the vortex. Hersing called for full power but the engines seemed impotent against the giant forces exerted by the swirling water. 'I thought surely we were lost—that we should be dragged down to a depth where the pressure of water would crush the shell of our boat.' The nerve-racking drama of the fight was soon felt by the crew who stared in horror as the dials and gauges of the controls reflected their mortal combat with the sea. Only one man could save them and, unconsciously, every eye fixed on the tall calm figure of the captain as he backed, twisted, and dived the U-boat, to escape the clutches of the whirlpool. 'Inch by inch, struggle as we might, we were hauled down, until we were below 100 feet. Then we were able to hold our own, and presently the grasp that held us was released and we slid ahead.'

For Hersing it had been an experience more fearsome by far than anything he had ever experienced in the face of the enemy and, like most submarine commanders, he readily admitted that the forces of nature were a hundred times more frightening than anything man could devise. Once through the maelstrom it was plain-sailing and *U-21* and her crew were given an heroic welcome on their arrival at Constantinople. German propaganda had ensured that the Turks were aware of Hersing's spectacular achievements off Gallipoli and Enver Pasha himself led the capital in the welcoming celebrations. 'A paladin encased in steel, he had smitten down, under their very eyes two of the great sea-dragons which belched death upon the Turkish soldiery.'

After a month of peaceful relaxation on shore, a holiday necessitated by the repair work required on *U-21*, Otto Hersing set out on the return passage. It was an uneventful trip until, running clear of the Straits, he sighted the transport *Carthage* packed with munitions. A leisurely shot from the bow tubes caught the French steamer amidships and a heavy explosion sealed her doom. Having whetted his appetite the Kapitanleutnant stalked the coast for more victims but the horizon proved disappointingly bare of life and, returning to the strip of coastline where he had won his first victories, he ferreted for more battleships. But, frightened by the sudden upsurge of submarine activity, the enemy capital ships had been withdrawn and the only vessels in sight were two small trawlers.

Lulled by a sense of false confidence after his previous successes Hersing loitered at periscope depth surveying the scene. It was a bad mistake. an alert lookout on one of the trawlers spotted the thin column of the 'scope and he had to crash dive to avoid being rammed. The crew reacted with calm efficiency and the initial danger was soon past but, unknown to Hersing, he had dived *U-21* into the middle of an enemy minefield. There was a sudden explosion at the stern, the lights shattered, and the cramped interior of the U-boat plunged into darkness. It was the moment of truth all submarine men fear. As the officers inspected the hull with torches and the crew carried out emergency checks on the equipment, they could hear the gurgling of water seeping into the boat.

By a miracle *U-21* had sustained no serious damage. The mine had exploded some distance away and not, as they thought in the first moment of panic, directly against the hull. The steel skin was still watertight and the sounds of flooding compartments proved to be no more than the customary trickles and leaks they had lived with for many months magnified a thousand times by fear. Even so the mine had done considerable damage and for a while Hersing thought *U-21* was incapable of diving. But a few hours of strenuous work repaired the main defects and, unwilling to face the hazards of the long trip to Cattaro, Otto took his boat back into the Dardanelles to seek sanctuary at Constantinople again.

Von Heimburg, now commanding *UB-14*, was another early arrival at the Turkish capital. Unlike Hersing he had avoided the navigational snags of the Straits only to run right into a British anti-submarine net which had been slung across the narrow neck of water in an effort to prevent any further U-boats passing up to Constantinople. Completely trapped in the steel meshes and as helpless as a fish snared in a trawl von Heimburg tried every trick he knew to wrench his boat free. Backing away slowly, then smashing forward under full power, he twisted and turned like an eel to escape the net's embrace. The situation was not helped when the British patrol ships on the surface began dropping depth-bombs. Explosions rocked the U-boat, shattering bulbs and sending cork insulation fluttering down like a brown snowstorm, until every man aboard thought they had challenged fate one time too many. But the bombs proved to be *UB-14*'s salvation. The force of the explosions weakened the steel links of the trap and, with one last mighty effort, the U-boat ripped her way through the mesh and, dragging the remnants with her, lurched up the Straits, her trim upset by the heavy weight of the net streaming from her bows.

Grinning widely and none the worse for his adventure von Heimburg brought his damaged craft into the tiny harbour of

Hersingstand, a small fishing village renamed by the Turks in honour of *U-21*'s captain, where they set about repairs before continuing the mission. It was during *UB-14*'s enforced stay at Hersingstand that Heino and his cook commandeered the rowing-boat in which they sank the unfortunate *E-7*.

A short while later the French submarine *Turquoise*, trapped by the Dardanelles nets, surrendered to the Turks and a number of important confidential documents were salved from the wreck. On examination one was found to contain details of a pre-arranged rendezvous with the British submarine *E-20*. It was too good a chance to miss and a few nights later *UB-14* took up position at the point marked on the Frenchman's charts. The British captain, unaware that the secret of his meeting-place was known to the enemy, arrived on time and came to the surface ready to greet his ally. Lying submerged a few hundred yards away with only the baleful single eye of the periscope above water *UB-14* watched and waited as the unsuspecting submarine crept into its sights. Von Heimburg's upraised arm came down, the Watch Officer stabbed the firing-button, and with a slight lurch the torpedo streaked away. *E-20* stood no chance. The torpedo smashed home just below the conning-tower and, with a tremendous explosion, the British submarine disappeared from sight leaving a handful of dazed survivors struggling in the water. Von Heimburg's score of three enemy submarines destroyed, set a record that was never to be surpassed by a single captain in either of the two World Wars.

The newly constituted Black Sea Flotilla was soon up to strength and Hersing's *U-21* and Heimburg's *UB-14* were quickly joined by *UB-7*, *UB-8*, *UC-13*, *UC-14*, and *UC-15*. Ranging freely across Russia's home waters they caused considerable disturbance to civil and military shipping schedules. On 15 September, Werner, with *UB-7*, sank the British steamer *Patagonia* off the port of Odessa and, during the following month, attacked the Russian battleship *Panteleimon* off Varna. But the Germans did not have things all their own way. Kirchner in the minelayer *UC-13* was chased by a group of Russian destroyers and driven ashore on Kerphen Reef where the stranded U-boat was blown-up to prevent capture, while *UB-7* met her end on a mine during October, 1916. *UB-45* and *UC-15* were similarly lost in the Black Sea minefields during the same year.

Impressed by the string of successes achieved by their U-boats in the Mediterranean, the Dardanelles, and the Black Sea—von Heimburg had added to his already commendable score by sinking the 11,117 ton transport *Royal Edward* with the loss of 866 lives on 13 August and damaging the troopship *Southland* the following month—the German High Command despatched reinforcements by both sea and rail. The small *UB* and *UC* boats continued to travel across Central Europe by train for assembly on the coast, but the larger submarines had to face a lengthy and hazardous sea voyage from Wilhelmshaven before they could join the Cattaro Flotilla.

The earliest reinforcements left Germany in August, spear-headed by Rucker's *U-34*, Kophamel in *U-35*, *U-33* skippered by Gansser, and *U-39* under the command of Forstmann. On the outward trip the submarines carried out a number of attacks while *en route* to the Mediterranean, Gansser and Forstmann in particular leaving a trail of havoc in their wake as they cruised down the Algerian coast, while *U-33* enjoyed a narrow escape in the Gibraltar Straits when spotted and fired upon by *Torpedo-boat 95*. Later in the year Max Valentiner, already notorious for his ruthless attacks on unarmed ships, joined the flotilla with *U-38* in which he was to achieve further infamy as the campaign developed.

Kophamel, in search of shipping taking part in the Allied landings at Salonika, met with early success and an efficient copy-book attack during the afternoon of 23 October sent the 7,000 ton troopship *Marquette* to the bottom with a single torpedo. It was a fine achievement in well-guarded waters but

U-35's humanitarian skipper was greatly distressed when he heard later that 10 nurses on board the trooper had lost their lives in the attack.

Switching to Budrum, across the Gulf of Xeros, he next embarked a Turkish army mission and landed them at Bardia where they helped to stir up a revolt by the warlike Senussi sect against the Allies. The partisan war in North Africa kept the U-boats busy on numerous cloak-and-dagger missions and German submarines maintained a regular shuttle service across the Mediterranean. Before his appointment as flotilla commander at Cattaro, Kophamel was a frequent and welcome visitor to North African shores and on one celebrated occasion he brought two large camels back to Pola as a gift to the Kaiser from a wealthy Senussi admirer. How the U-boat men managed to house two awkwardly shaped and ferocious beasts like the camel in the cramped confines of *U-35* has never been revealed, but one story indicates that the smell of the animals so permeated the garments of the crew that sailors from the other U-boats at Pola refused to allow their *U-35* comrades to share the same mess with them.

But apart from acting as a transporter of live cargo Kophamel put his North African trips to good use and, in November, 1915, sank the Armed Boarding Steamer *Tara* during a daring raid in which he penetrated the harbour at Bardia while, a few days later, he disposed of two Egyptian patrol boats further along the coast. The missions to the Senussi tribesmen, however, were only side-shows undertaken solely as a gesture of friendship to Germany's Turkish allies and were not looked upon by the German U-boat commanders as serious military operations, the real work being done in the expanses of the Mediterranean.

Gansser and *U-33* demonstrated a new savagery during an attack on the Clan Line steamer *Clan Macleod*. The British master tried to out-run the raider and there was a two-hour running battle before he finally surrendered to the U-boat.

Gansser took his revenge by firing on the survivors in the lifeboats, an action that killed twelve of the helpless sailors and wounded many more. Max Valentiner, too, showed a ruthless disregard for life. Ignoring the Kaiser's General Order that passenger ships were to be spared, he attacked the P & O liner *Persia* on 30 December, 1915 and torpedoed her without any hesitation or warning. The tragedy became a disaster of the first magnitude when the liner's boilers blew up and she sank like a stone with the loss of 334 passengers and crew. While on the same patrol Valentiner also sank the Japanese liner *Yasaka Maru*, covering his identity on this occasion by flying the Austrian flag although Germany's ally was swift to deny any implication in the attack.

U-38's assault on the troopship *Mercian* as she passed between Gibraltar and Alboran on 4 November was a further example of Valentiner's coldly efficient code of killing. When the submarine was sighted off the port bow the troops were lined up on deck in expectation of a torpedo attack and, on realising this, Max came to the surface and opened fire on the defenceless lines of soldiers with his deck gun. There was a wild panic as shells began bursting and twenty-three men were killed by the first salvoes. Struggling through the hail of splinters, the demoralized soldiers rushed for the lifeboats and in the inevitable confusion several of the boats capsized with the loss of thirty-one more lives. But *Mercian* was determined to sell herself dear. Calling for maximum speed the captain sheered away from the surfaced U-boat and held an erratic zig-zag course as *U-38* speeded up to give chase. Army machine-guns were brought up on deck and a burst of bullets whined over the U-boat as she closed for the kill. Ducking down behind the steel shield of the conning-tower Valentiner ordered the gun's crew back below. He realized that, once submerged, he could not catch the speeding troopship, and unwilling to face the bullets that were being pumped out by the machine-guns, he reluctantly called off the attack and allowed his intended victim to escape. Three days later he worked off his bad temper by sinking the French transport *France IV* which, by good fortune, was running empty. Then he turned his attention on the Italian liner *Ancona*. Making use of his favourite ruse he hoisted the Austrian flag and, standing off from the stationary passenger ship, opened fire in cold-blood on the survivors, killing 208 before his appetite was appeased. By the time he returned to Cattaro at the end of this particular patrol Valentiner had sunk 14 ships, the first steps towards a final total of more than 300,000 tons that ranked him as third top-scoring U-boat commander of the war, and the *most* hated!

Although Germany was fully aware where responsibility lay for these wanton attacks the inevitable American protests were turned aside by bland denials. If a submarine flew the Austrian flag then, *ipso facto*, it was an Austrian submarine. To admit liability would show that the solemn German undertaking not to attack passenger ships without warning had been broken and, as every one knew, the Imperial German Government and its officers did not break promises. The fact that her ally, Austria, was being blamed for German misdeeds had little effect on the Teutonic conscience and it was only when certain U-boat commanders began sinking hospital ships under cover of the Austrian flag that Emperor Franz Josef's government finally put its foot down over the misuse of its national colours. Even so it was not until 1917 that Berlin issued specific orders to the submarine flotillas forbidding the use, or misuse, of the Austrian flag.

The Mediterranean was proving a fruitful area for the U-boats and in the opening months of the campaign success was achieved with minimal losses by a mere handful of skilfully handled submarines. Between the date of *U-21*'s arrival at Cattaro and the end of 1915 a total of 92 merchant ships had been sent to the bottom of which 54, over 50%, were British-owned. In addition U-boat aces, like Hersing, Kophamel, and von Heimburg, had sunk a substantial number of Allied warships including, as was seen earlier, two British battleships.

Germany's prospects of success were made even rosier by the usual organizational disagreements that bedevil most alliances, and the arguments which raged between the Allies played directly into their enemy's hands. To begin with the Mediterranean was divided into a number of separate and distinct areas of control each of which was administered by one of the participating countries and the lack of an overall commander led to acrimonious disputes between the various parties concerned. Even more damaging to the Allied cause was the policy of directing merchant ships into certain well defined routes and U-boat commanders were not slow to exploit the situation that resulted.

In addition, on the political front, the Mediterranean provided less diplomatic problems than the Atlantic and the North Sea *vis-à-vis* the United States. Very few neutral ships sailed the area and the chances of mistaken or careless identification were correspondingly reduced. Although Italy was not at war with Germany she *was* engaged in hostilities with the Austro-Hungarian Empire and the U-boats conveniently regarded themselves as being 'in the service of the allied Navy' whenever an Italian appeared in sight. While Italy was strictly neutral the German submarine commanders felt secure in the knowledge that the nationality of a periscope was a trifle difficult to determine even in good weather conditions and they were never reprimanded for 'illegal' attacks of this nature. For some reason America showed little interest in the Mediterranean and, throughout the war, events in the area provoked very few protests in comparison with similar incidents in the Atlantic.

With the British diverting the bulk of their anti-submarine defences into home waters and with the Western Front mentality that the Mediterranean was little more than a 'side-show' the U-boats reigned supreme until very late in the war and, in the circumstances, it is not surprising that most of the top-scoring commanders made their reputations in this theatre of operations. Perhaps of even more significance was the fact that nearly all the U-boat aces who survived the war came from the Cattaro and Pola Flotillas. Small wonder that they nostalgically referred to it as 'the happy hunting ground' at their post-war reunions.

CHAPTER NINE

'No death could be more agonizing'

WITH THE DANGER of unrestricted submarine warfare removed by the Kaiser's decision to call off the 'six week's campaign' in August 1915, the pendulum of American public opinion, volatile substance at the best of times, began to swing against the British blockade system again. A series of tart diplomatic notes voiced Washington's disapproval of the Royal Navy's contraband control methods and when the Admiralty announced that merchants ships were to be armed with guns as a means of defence against U-boat attacks a distinctly acrimonious tone became apparent in the protests.

Viewed from Berlin the changed situation on the diplomatic front looked encouraging and, with unwarranted optimism, the German Government felt that the American attitude betrayed an inherent hatred of the British which they could turn to advantage. In addition the bloody stalemate on the Western Front and the continuing bite of the blockade was giving serious cause for concern and thoughts again turned to a renewal of the U-boat campaign bolstered, this time, by a false impression that the United States was now so anti-British that she was unlikely to enter the war on the side of Germany's enemies despite the provocations of a renewed campaign.

It was the army's Chief of General Staff, von Falkenhayn, who first mooted the proposal at a top-level conference in Berlin on 30 December, 1915, barely four months after the collapse of the first campaign. Von Holtzendorff, the Chief of Naval Staff, supported the proposal, a move that must have disconcerted von Muller who had placed him in the seat of power with the intention of thwarting any further submarine campaigns, and Tirpitz added his agreement. The conference betrayed an unexpected level of optimism fostered, no doubt, by von Holtzendorff, whose sanguine views were well-known, and while it was felt that America would not be provoked by a renewed campaign the general consensus of opinion amongst the experts was that the hostility of the United States was an acceptable risk.

Matters were left to rest somewhat indecisively after the conference ended although diplomatic soundings in Washington revealed that America would accept a further outbreak of submarine warfare provided due warning was given before an attack was made. The British decision to arm their merchant ships, however, made a mockery of any such promise for few U-boat commanders would endanger their submarines by coming to the surface if their intended victim carried a gun. In consequence of the British action sinking by torpedo without warning remained a basic tactic of German submarine warfare.

A further conference was held on 4 March, at which the military and naval leaders revealed themselves in their true colours. Although the war was going well with both Russia and Serbia virtually written off as serious threats to the Central Powers the economic situation on the home front was growing worse each day as the stranglehold of the blockade tightened. Time, they realized, was *not* on their side. And if victory was to be achieved England, the arch enemy, must be defeated quickly and decisively. Von Holtzendorff put his finger on the key in a memo he wrote after the meeting: 'England can only be injured by war on her trade.' He made it clear, too, that such a trade war must be completely ruthless and unhampered by restrictions of any sort. The army leaders, for once, found themselves in agreement with their naval colleagues and von Falkenhayn, obviously infected by the general atmosphere of optimism, declared: 'Even a state of war with America need not be shunned.'

The Chancellor, Bethmann-Hollweg, remained unconvinced by the arguments advanced by the military and naval experts. He had been caught before and, no doubt influenced by the wild promises made at the beginning of the abortive first campaign, he questioned the highly coloured statistics produced by that eternal optimist von Holtzendorff. He foresaw, too, that any renewal of unrestricted submarine warfare *must* drag America into the conflict and he did not share the conference's views that such a risk was acceptable. But his efforts to postpone the campaign was now meeting opposition from a new source.

Admiral von Pohl, the C-in-C of the High Seas Fleet, had died on 5 February, 1916, and his successor was Admiral Reinhold von Scheer, a staunch advocate of a U-boat trade war. And, of course, as C-in-C he now had control of the majority of Germany's submarines. Making use of his powerful new position Scheer sought the ear of the Kaiser and it did not take him long to persuade his master that victory at sea could be achieved by the U-boats. And so, with his mind already conditioned by the C-in-C's arguments, Wilhelm had little difficulty in accepting the proposals put forward by the conference. He approved the start of the campaign for 1 April, 1916, but, indecisive as ever, he changed his mind two days later, following representations by the Chancellor. A diplomatic offensive was to be launched in Washington designed to persuade the United States to bring pressure to bear on Great Britain to ease the severity of the blockade. It was a forlorn hope but the astute Bethmann-Hollweg knew that the Kaiser's great fear was the possibility of American intervention in the war and he knew that any straw he offered would be eagerly grasped.

As a sop to the militarists, however, Wilhelm agreed that a restricted campaign under the Prize Regulations could begin on 15 March. Once again there were internal political repercussions. The veteran von Tirpitz, disgusted with this continual 'procrastination in the conduct of the war', finally resigned and the unrestricted warfare lobby was weakened by his replacement as Secretary of State by Admiral von Capelle, a known supporter of the cautious Bethmann-Hollweg. The muddle was further heightened by the fact that several submarines had left their bases or were beyond wireless range by the time the Kaiser's revised orders were announced. It was not a good augury for success.

For the U-boat commanders themselves the autumn and winter of 1915–1916 was one of boring routine. Attacks on merchant ships had been forbidden and the opportunities for attacks on warships were few and far between. Otto Steinbrinck, the captain of *UB-18*, told an American journalist that he 'had let forty ships in the Channel go by' which, under unrestricted warfare, he could have sunk. Other commanders voiced similar complaints.

But despite the ban on unrestricted warfare there remained other methods of attack within the framework of international law and Karl von Georg, captain of *U-57*, was not slow to exploit them. Surfacing at night in the North Sea he found himself in the middle of an English fishing fleet. His orders were quite clear; he was not to sink one single vessel without first warning the crew and making provision for their safety. And, equally, as soon as he revealed his presence on the surface the rest of the fleet would scamper away and disappear in the darkness.

During the previous afternoon von Georg had sunk a Norwegian steamer and, in strict observance of the prize warfare regulations, he had taken her master and crew aboard *U-57* for safety. Now, as he stared at the English fishing fleet through his night-glasses, he saw an unexpected opportunity to take advantage of his earlier humanity. Calling the Norwegian skipper into the control room he asked him if he would take the U-boat's dingy to the nearest trawler and order the crew to abandon their vessel without raising the alarm with the rest of the unsuspecting fleet. The Scandinavian captain agreed to co-operate and, ten minutes later, the little rubber boat set out into the darkness. It was a gigantic bluff but, incredibly, it worked. One by one the trawlers were approached and boarded. One by one they listened to the warning and, one by one, they obediently abandoned ship.

'For several hours,' von Georg recalled, 'the splashing of oars resounded on all sides in the darkness. Scores of crowded lifeboats gathered around the black form of the submarine. We gathered the crews aboard one of the trawlers and then set about the work of destruction.' *U-57* destroyed a total of twenty-two fishing boats that night and, having safely transferred the crews to a passing Belgian steamer, von Georg backed his submarine away and disappeared into the dawn mists. 'Without endangering a single life we had polished off a neat batch of potential minelayers and sweepers and anti-submarine craft.'

An even more incredible incident occurred when Ernst Hashagen met up with the steamer *Fritzoe* in the North Sea. The cramped confines of his little *UB-21* prevented him from taking the crew aboard and an inspection of the splintered and weather-worn lifeboats indicated that they were completely unseaworthy. Under the tight restrictions of his operational orders Hashagen seemed to have little alternative but to let his victim go but, like von Georg, he decided to bluff. Calling *Fritzoe*'s captain on board the submarine and wearing his fiercest expression Hashagen offered the ship's master two choices, to sail his boat back to Cuxhaven as a prize of war or to be torpedoed there and then. The captain eagerly accepted the first alternative and gave his solemn word that he would sail direct to Germany and surrender. As a precaution *UB-21*'s commander warned him that the submarine would be following behind at periscope depth and that, if he tried to make a run for it, *Fritzoe* would be sunk without further warning. Thoroughly shaken by the threat the English captain obeyed his orders to the letter although, in fact, the U-boat made no attempt to follow him, and when Hashagen arrived back in Cuxhaven at the end of the patrol he found the English ship safely tied up in harbour as a prize of war. 'That Britisher knew how to play cricket,' *UB-21*'s skipper laughed afterwards. 'All honour to him. His word was his bond.'

Unfortunately the correctness and humanity of von Georg and Ernst Hashagen was not always reflected in the actions of other and more unscrupulous U-boat commanders. On 1 February, 1916, at a time when German submarines were supposed to be operating in strict accordance with international law, *La Belle France* was torpedoed and sunk without warning by an unidentified U-boat. Her crew took to the boats but in the inevitably scramble one of the lifeboats capsized spilling its occupants into the sea. The submarine came to the surface to pick up survivors and called one of the other lifeboats across to take them off. But, by an unfortunate mischance, the rescue attempt ended in murder. Four trawlers were sighted on the horizon and, fearful that they were naval vessels, the U-boat captain ordered his crew below and prepared to dive. In the panic of the moment he forgot the sailors standing on the deck and the submarine slid beneath the surface with them still aboard. Nineteen men were drowned when the U-boat submerged and British newspapers were quick to seize upon the incident as a further example of German brutality on the high seas although, in this instance, the action was more probably one of forgetful panic than cold-blooded murder.

Interspersed with these spasmodic actions at sea the verbal war between Britain and Germany concerning the arming of merchant ships continued with unabated fury. On 11 February, 1916, the *North German Gazette* issued the text of an official memorandum in which it was alleged: 'armed British merchantmen have an official order to treacherously attack German submarines wherever they meet them; that means, to mercilessly wage war against them.' As *The Times* commented in its report, the Germans were protesting 'against merchant ships having any means of defence against submarines, despite the fact that these German instruments of war, contrary to every usage of the law of nations . . . had for months shelled innocent merchant ships without notice or pity.'

Although the *defensive* arming of merchant ships had always been recognized under international law Germany preferred to interpret the British action as hostile and the Memorandum already quoted added: ' . . . enemy merchantmen carrying guns are not entitled to be regarded as peaceful merchantmen. The German naval forces . . . will receive an order to treat such vessels as belligerents.' This, Berlin considered, should at least frighten the neutrals.

Once again it is not difficult to understand the German dilemma. If merchant ships carried guns the attacking submarine was immediately at risk if she dared to surface in order to issue the required warning. And to avoid such a risk firing a torpedo while still submerged seemed the only alternative. The chivalry of the nineteenth century, however laudable, could not cope with the weapons of twentieth century warfare. And whilst it was true that obsolescent guns manned by virtually untrained crews were likely to have little effect against a submarine handled with skill it was understandable that few U-boat commanders were prepared to risk their vessels by surfacing during an attack. Yet, by the same token, Germany could hardly expect the enemy not to hit back.

Armed merchant ships were not the only dangers confronting the U-boats. British anti-submarine defences were a constant headache for submarine captains and to be trapped in a steel-meshed anti-submarine net was an experience that few ever forgot. In January, 1916, Kapitanleutnant Wenninger described the horror of the nets to a Hungarian newspaper correspondent. 'I looked through the periscope and could see a red buoy behind my boat. When, ten minutes later, I looked I saw the buoy again, still at the same distance behind us. I steered to the right and then to the left, but the buoy kept following us. I descended into deep water but still saw the buoy floating on the surface above us. At last I discovered we had caught the chain of the buoy and that we were dragging it along with us.'

The demented wanderings of the tell-tale buoy attracted the attention of British patrols and before long five destroyers were circling the surface directly above the U-boat. Wenninger went deeper. 'At this juncture my boat began to roll in a most incomprehensible manner. We began to rise and sink, the steering gear apparently being out of order.' The U-boat commander knew they were trapped in a net and for the next ninety minutes UB-55 twisted, turned, plunged, and reversed, in a vain effort to tear free. In desperation Wenninger took a further six tons of water into the ballast tanks and, under the increased weight, the U-boat sank to the bottom. 'Suddenly we felt a shock and were clear of the netting.' Taking his boat to ninety feet he remained on the bottom for eighteen hours before he dared to rise to the surface. The compass had failed, leaving the submarine blind and helpless, and the manometer (depth-gauge) was inoperative. When the submarine finally reached the surface it was discovered that the steering gear, too, was not working and Wenninger had to submerge for a further six hours to carry out repairs. Even then, on returning to the surface, he found a destroyer waiting for him and, to avoid being rammed, he dived yet again for a further two hours. In the end Wenninger succeeded in crawling away from the trap, but it had been a terrifying and unnerving experience.

Perhaps the most dramatic example of the horrors endured by U-boat men trapped in the net defences was contained in the report of a Canadian army surgeon, Dr M. S. Inglis, dated 10 February, 1916. He entered the interior of a salvaged U-boat and found the entire crew dead, apparently shot by their commander to avoid the agonies of death by suffocation. Even though such stories were often only mere propaganda inventions (the submarines were rarely identified) they must have exerted a baleful influence on German morale when they filtered back to the U-boat bases and the courage of the German submarine crews in facing the possibilities of such dangers cannot be denied.

The new prize warfare campaign had begun on 15 March and by mid-month U-boats were once again operating in the Western Approaches. Unrestricted warfare, however, remained strictly forbidden on direct orders from the Kaiser himself who remained anxious to avoid any further friction with the United States. But the diplomatic manoeuvres of the German emperor and his advisers were soon shattered by the actions of the U-boat commanders themselves. Although rigidly forbidden to sink passenger ships the submarine captains were instructed that all ships making for the Channel ports at night could be regarded as transports, an open invitation, in fact, to sink all and sundry. And the imprecise nature of these operational orders opened the way to a renewed spate of attacks. It was especially unfortunate that the Channel U-boats, mainly of the small UB-type, were commanded by young and inexperienced junior officers. Impetuous and reckless by reason of their youth they were consumed with a burning anxiety to win honour and glory, and, of course, promotion to the larger ocean-going submarines.

Prime mover in the catastrophe was Oberleutnant Herbert Pustkuchen, captain of *UB-29*. Setting out from the Flanders U-boat base he seemed determined from the very outset to wreck the entire political strategy of the German Government although, undoubtedly, in his own mind he was merely carrying out his duty. He began his marauding cruise by sinking a French ship at anchor and followed this up by torpedoing two neutrals, a Norwegian freighter and a Danish steamer. For the next few days he prowled the narrow seas in search of more victims and on the afternoon of 24 March, he sighted the French cross-Channel packet *Sussex* on her way from Folkestone to Dieppe.

Closing to 1400 yards Pustkuchen let go a torpedo which demolished the steamer's bow section and killed over fifty men, women, and children when it exploded. Fortunately, despite the damage, the ship did not sink and after it had been towed back to Boulogne salvage experts discovered fragments of a German torpedo in the shattered wreckage. Berlin at first denied all responsibility for the tragedy but, faced by the damning evidence of the torpedo fragments, was finally forced to admit that a U-boat had made the attack. But a plausible excuse was quickly manufactured. Pustkuchen, it was explained, had mistaken the steamer for a minelayer and, as visual proof that such mistakes were possible, the German Admiralty even supplied a drawing showing the similarity in appearance. Pustkuchen, meanwhile, unaware of the furore he had caused, continued blithely on his way and sank the British steamer *Salybia* without warning before returning home.

The neutrals, too, were having a hard time. On 28 March the Dutch steamer *Medea* was sunk by *U-28* off Beachy Head and several other Dutch ships were lost during the same period. *Palembang* blew up on 18 March while *Eemdijk* exploded five miles south-west of St Catherine's Point en route from Baltimore to Rotterdam on 6 April. In both cases U-boats were named as culprits although it now seems more probable that German saboteurs in New York, working under the direction of Kapitan Franz von Rintelen, were placing time-bombs on board shipping destined for Europe and these unfortunate ships were two of their victims.

There could be no such doubt about the loss of the Dutch liner *Turbantia* torpedoed off the North Hinder lightship on 16 March outward bound for Buenos Aires. Two witnesses observed the wake of air bubbles left by the torpedo's track and pieces of metal found in the ship's boats were identified as coming from a Schwarzkopf torpedo. Confronted by such evidence the German authorities were hard put for an excuse but an eagle-eyed expert conveniently identified the metal as coming from Torpedo Number *2033* which had been lost during an abortive attack on a British cruiser on 15 March. The *Turbantia*, claimed the Germans, must have struck this drifting torpedo and, obviously satisfied at producing such a brilliant explanation, they refused to discuss the matter further.

But Pustkuchen's attack on the *Sussex* could not be swept under the carpet so easily and American public opinion, for some reason, seemed more shocked by this incident than by the earlier *Lusitania* tragedy. 'How many more Americans must be killed before Wilson declares war?' demanded the *New York Herald* and other newspapers rattled their pens like sabres. The German explanation that the *Sussex* had been mistaken for a minelayer was decisively rejected in an American Note on 18 April:

'The commanders of the Imperial Government's undersea vessels have carried on practices of such ruthless destruction which have made it more and more evident as the months have gone by that the Imperial Government has found it impracticable to put any such restraints upon them as it had hoped and promised to put.'

The note continued in similar strain for several paragraphs and referred to the *Lusitania*, the *Arabic*, and 'mere passenger boats like the *Sussex*' as evidence of Germany's destructive policy on the high seas. Then, having recited the facts, Washington set out its solemn warning: 'Unless the Imperial Government should now immediately declare and effect an abandonment of its present methods of submarine warfare against passenger and freight carrying vessels, the Government of the United States can have no choice but to sever diplomatic relations with the Central Empires altogether.'

President Wilson's dire threat had an immediate response in Berlin. The optimistic claims of Scheer and von Holtzendorff suddenly faded in the face of America's warning and, for a while, Bethmann-Hollweg's less aggressive policy won through. Although complaining that the British blockade was driving German women and children to starvation and was just as great a crime against humanity as the U-boat campaign, orders were promptly issued that no more merchant ships were to be sunk without warning.

While the diplomats had been arguing, however, the U-boats continued to wage a relentless 'restricted' war against all and sundry. In March Wagenfuhr's *U-44* had sunk 29,500 tons of shipping in the Irish Sea although, having learned from Schwieger's mistakes, he had sufficient sense to allow the giant liner *Mauretania* to pass unharmed. During April *U-66* destroyed 20,000 tons and in a short five day patrol *U-69* despatched a further 21,000 tons to the bottom. Weisbach's *U-19* accounted for another 19,000 tons and, emulating the cloak and dagger exploits of the Mediterranean submarines, landed the traitor Roger Casement in Tralee Bay on 20 April as part of the German plan to create a civil war in Ireland.

Admiral Scheer, thoroughly annoyed by the way his Government had backed down in the face of American threats, retaliated by recalling all U-boats to their bases. If they could not fight *his* way he did not intend them to fight at all. In a strange way the German reactions to the American Note of 18 April was to lead to that great clash of battle fleets off the Jutland Bank a few weeks later for, with the submarines firmly under his personal control, Scheer began to evolve the plans that led eventually to the Battle of Jutland.

Although forbidden to attack merchant ships the U-boat captains were by no means dismayed and the more enterprising set out to find more legitimate naval targets. Few succeeded but, on 25 April, Otto Steinbrinck in *UB-18* met up with four British submarines a few miles from Yarmouth. It could have been a dangerous moment but his luck was in for *UB-18* was snugly out of sight below the sea at periscope depth while all four British boats were running in full view on the surface. Steinbrinck fired at the leading submarine, but at the last moment the British captain sighted the German periscope, swung his helm hard over, and turned to ram his attacker. *E-22*'s last-minute swerve saved her and the torpedo shaved her stern by little more than inches as she swung on to her new course. Realizing that the tables had been unexpectedly turned *UB-18* went deep as Steinbrinck took avoiding action and the U-boat passed directly beneath the British boat, so close, in fact, that her net-cutters struck the underside of *E-22*'s hull with a resounding clatter. Otto brought the U-boat up and snatched another quick glance through the periscope just in time to see the British boat turning to ram again.

Steinbrinck snapped an order to the helmsman and, as *UB-18* swung around to face her adversary, he fired both bow tubes. It was a gesture of defiance rather than hope. The first torpedo splayed to starboard missing the enemy by yards but the second held an unswerving course. There was a violent explosion and *E-22* vanished in a billowing cloud of black smoke leaving only two dazed survivors struggling in the water. As if taking the explosion as their cue the three remaining submarines submerged with the intention of ambushing the U-boat and Steinbrinck knew he was in deadly trouble. With odds of three-to-one he stood no chance at all.

But his next move took everyone by surprise. Ordering *UB-18* to surface, he shouted for flank speed and steered for the spot where *E-22* had gone down, taking care at the same time to keep his stern towards the three submerged submarines in order to reduce their target area. Reaching the oil slick that marked his victim's grave he slowed down for a moment while a couple of German sailors ran down the deck. Leaning over the side of the U-boat they grabbed the two survivors, hauled them aboard, and then hurried them to the conning-tower hatch. Once secured Steinbrinck wasted no further time. *UB-18* dipped swiftly below the surface and headed for home while his crew rubbed the two Englishmen down with hot towels and revived them with Schnapps. Having out-distanced the submerged submarines by his quick dash on the surface Steinbrinck was now quite safe from attack and, after checking the condition of his prisoners, he set course back to his Zeebrugge base.

Kapitanleutnant Bruno Hoppe, the skipper who had accidentally sunk his flotilla mate *U-7* in 1914, experienced the other side of the coin some weeks before Steinbrinck's escapade. His U-boat had been cruising off Belfast in dense fog when a British warship sighted her on the surface. Ernst Hashagen, at that time serving as Second Officer shortly before promotion to command of *UB-21*, was on watch and as the enemy cruiser opened fire he ordered the submarine down in a crash-dive.

U-22 tilted violently as the diving planes angled down and the rush of water into the ballast tanks roared like thunder inside the boat. Hashagen had given orders to level out at 50 feet but, due to an unexpected fault in the depth rudder, the U-boat plunged below the 50 feet mark and kept falling. 'She tilted up and down like a rocking-horse, sinking now by the head and then by the stern—but always sinking.' Hoppe rushed into the control room but with the British cruiser lying in wait on the surface he did not dare to blow the ballast tanks and *U-22* was at the mercy of her broken rudder. When the submarine reached 200 feet the situation was fast becoming serious for, at that depth, the pressure of the sea would crush the steel hull like a matchbox. Already the metal was groaning under the strain, the steel support beams were beginning to buckle and tiny beads of water glistened around unseated rivets. But something even more terrifying was happening in the cramped confines of the battery compartment.

'Everything else lost its importance ... I caught the acrid smell of chlorine gas and everyone was coughing, spluttering, and choking,' Hashagen recalled. Sea water, forcing its way through the seams, had mixed with the sulphuric acid of the batteries and was sending off clouds of greenish-yellow vapour.

'I don't think there is anything that will strike such fear in a submarine man as the thought of being trapped in the iron hull while choking gas seeps from the batteries bit by bit. No death could be more agonizing.' Faced by the lethal vapour which was now billowing and swirling through the boat Bruno Hoppe, like Steinbrinck, decided to stake all on a desperate gamble. His orders were calm and precise and his face did not betray the fear he felt in his heart. The ballast tanks were blown and U-22 swept to the surface like a cork. All thoughts of the British cruiser had gone in the face of the crying need for air. As Hashagen remarked: 'Better to be shot to pieces and drown in a quiet way than this death by choking torment.'

The fog was still thick when they broke surface and although only a few hundred yards away the enemy warship failed to notice the U-boat rolling gently in the swell with her hatches thrown open as the life-giving fresh air was sucked down into her hull. There was a tense interval while U-22 cleared her lungs of gas and then, using the electric motors, Hoppe crept silently away into the mist leaving his powerful adversary unaware that its prey had escaped from under its very nose.

But, no matter what the U-boats achieved, the strangling grip of the British blockade remained around Germany's throat. No surface ship could get through the iron cordon and submarine designers began turning their minds to a new concept: monster freight-carrying U-boats which would be capable of breaking the blockade by running as submerged merchant ships. It was a dazzling idea worthy of Jules Verne and Germany's first-class team of designers and scientists proved more than capable of turning the idea into a practical form. The first of these submarines, *Deutschland*, was launched on 28 March, 1916. Built by the Germaniawerft at Kiel, the hull being completed at Flensburg, she measured 213 feet in length and displaced 1,575 tons on the surface with an underwater speed of nearly seven knots.

The new blockade-runner left Kiel on 23 June, 1916, with a

cargo of dyes, precious stones, and mail, arriving at Baltimore on 2 August. Commanded by a merchant navy skipper, Kapitan Paul König, she returned to Bremen exactly three weeks later bringing a return cargo of zinc, silver, copper and nickel which were all urgently needed war materials for Germany's blockade-starved armaments industry. It was a successful venture and was repeated later the same year when *Deutschland* called at New London, Connecticut, the following November. Her sister-ship *Bremen*, however, engaged on a similar mercantile mission never arrived at her destination. Serious damage from a mine explosion forced her to return to Germany although one account claims she was struck by a torpedo from the British submarine *G-13* at the phenomenal range of 7000 yards![1] After repairs she finished her days as a surface vessel.

Germany naturally obtained the greatest possible publicity for her underwater blockade runners and, as propaganda, they were a great success. But their cargo capacity was too small and they proved to be a commercial failure and were later converted into combat submarines for long-range raiding operations. With an armament of two 5.9 inch guns, two 3.4 inch guns, and two 20 inch torpedo tubes they were, indeed, veritable underwater cruisers.

Admiral Scheer's interests, however, lay nearer home and for the moment he dismissed the giant submarine cruisers as little more than experimental playthings. He had bigger and better fish to fry. A firm believer in the proposition that attack was better than defence, the C-in-C was still anxious to bring about a battle between the High Seas Fleet and an isolated portion of the Grand Fleet. With the U-boats recalled from their commerce war and available solely for naval purposes a grand strategy began to form in Scheer's fertile brain. A bombardment of Sunderland would undoubtedly bring Jellicoe's ships pounding south in full cry and, aided by

[1] See *A Damned Un-English Weapon*, pp. 218-9.

Zeppelin reconnaissance, it seemed possible to give battle under terms most advantageous to Germany.

As part of his master plan Scheer sent the North Sea U-boats into Scottish waters to lie in ambush for the Grand Fleet as it left its various bases and to signal vital information on British movements. Three submarine cordons were set up: at Scapa Flow itself, at the Moray Firth and at the Firth of Forth; sixteen U-boats which took up their positions on 23 May. Bad weather, however, upset Scheer's careful planning by making air reconnaissance impossible and, unable to delay the sortie beyond the date set by the endurance of the scouting U-boats, he formulated an alternative plan to raid shipping in the Skaggerak to lure Jellicoe's fleet to sea.

The High Seas Fleet sailed at 3 am on 31 May and two hours later the first U-boat reports were coming in. At 5.37 *U-32* radioed that she had sighted two dreadnoughts, two cruisers, and a group of destroyers 60 miles east of the Firth of Forth, course bearing south east. A few minutes later *U-66*, of the Moray Firth cordon, reported seeing eight battleships with supporting cruisers and destroyers east of Peterhead. And then silence.

The interweaving of submarines into the grand strategy of battle proved as disappointing to the Germans as it had to the British in the early days of the war. The destroyer *Trident* was attacked by an unknown submarine on the 30th but succeeded in evading the torpedo which was fired at her and the sloop *Gentian* avoided attack under similar circumstances off the Pentland Skerries. Apart from these two isolated incidents the grandiose plan to ambush the Grand Fleet was a dismal failure and the U-boats played no part in the battle itself although many British warships claimed to have sighted periscopes. Not a single submarine was present when the great fleets finally clashed although it is only fair to add that Jellicoe's decision to turn away, rather than follow when the High Seas Fleet reversed course at a crucial stage of the battle, was due almost entirely to his fear that Scheer was leading him into a U-boat trap.

But there was one unexpected result from Scheer's U-boat tactics at Jutland, a result that was to rob Britain of her most famous war leader.

U-75 was one of the submarines making up the cordon around the exits to the Scapa Flow. Passing the Orkneys her commander, Kapitanleutnant Kurt Beitzen, began speculating on the probable passage of the Grand Fleet and, recalling his own observations on previous scouting missions in the area, he concluded that *some* units might pass close inshore before turning eastwards into the North Sea. U-75 was a minelayer, one of a class known as the Sisters of Sorrow, and so there was no necessity for Beitzen to remain in the area for a torpedo attack as his deadly cargo of 38 mines was equally effective whether the submarine was present or not. Having weighed up the situation U-75's captain made his fateful decision and the crew swung into their practiced routine as his orders passed down the boat.

At 6 am on 29 May the first of the horned cylinders drifted astern as it was discharged from the aft minelaying tubes. The rest followed one by one in an irregular north-west, south-east line, each set to float at a depth of 30 feet. By 8.30 am the operation was completed. Beitzen noted the position of the field on his charts, wrote up the log-book entry, and turned back for home before the weather worsened. The glass was already beginning to fall and he felt in his bones that a storm was coming. Chances were that the mines would snap their mooring cables and float with the wind and tide, still deadly if encountered but no longer in the vital position that U-75's commander had so carefully plotted. He shrugged. Given just a small piece of luck he might snatch a destroyer prowling the area or, perhaps, some fat lumbering freighter heading north for Archangel.

The imminent collapse of the Russian Empire and the

subsequent release of more German troops for the Western Front had been worrying the Allies for several months and, in a last vain effort to stop the rot, it was decided to send a high-powered military mission to north Russia for discussions. Field Marshal Lord Kitchener led the party and Jellicoe's Grand Fleet was entrusted with the care of Britain's greatest and most respected military leader. The cruiser *Hampshire* was delegated to take the party and all was ready by Monday, 5 June.

Jellicoe originally planned to send the cruiser on a route to the east of the island of South Ronaldsay but the north-easterly gale which Beitzen had noticed developing a few days earlier meant that the weather was unsuitable for a destroyer escort and, in addition, there had been reports of a U-boat lurking in the area. An alternative route westwards and then north to longitude 5°W was also discarded because early morning signals had indicated another U-boat skulking near Cape Wrath. After further discussions with his staff Jellicoe picked on a third route, the regular commercial channel up the west coast of the Orkneys, which had the advantage of running close inshore to gain protection from the easterly gales.

At 4.45 pm precisely *Hampshire* weighed anchor, steered through the Hoxa Gate protecting the Scapa Flow base, and turned west into the storm-tossed waters of the Pentland Firth. Her destroyer escort joined up and the little group altered course to the north west. Entering the open waters of the Hoy Sound they swung north and pounded into the gale which had, by now, veered to the north west. *Hampshire* drove ahead at 19 knots, her armoured bows plunging deep into the foam-flecked waves, sending a wall of green water smashing against her bridge. The conditions proved too much for the destroyers and the cruiser's skipper, Captain Savill, signalled them to return to base to avoid serious damage.

Even *Hampshire* was finding it tough going and in an effort to provide a smoother passage for his distinguished guests Savill reduced speed. Hidden by the wind-lashed sea Marwick Head lay some ten miles to starboard and they had, by now, been running into the teeth of the gale for nearly three hours. But at least the weather afforded them complete protection from U-boat attack and that, in itself, was cause for thankfulness.

At 7.40 pm a tremendous explosion ripped the cruiser apart as she ran full tilt into the minefield which Kurt Beitzen had laid almost a week earlier. The heavy seas destroyed any chance there may have been to save the ship and within minutes she had vanished completely. Only fourteen members of her crew reached the shore, everyone else was lost. Despite an intensive search no trace was ever found of Kitchener or any member of his staff. Britain's greatest army leader, a legend in his own lifetime, had fallen victim to the U-boats, his mission unaccomplished. Nothing could now save Russia from revolution and surrender.

U-75, without being present or firing a single shot, had made her momentous contribution to the pages of world history.

CHAPTER TEN

'Act with the utmost caution'

DESPITE THE KAISER'S bombastic claim that 'the gigantic fleet of Albion, ruler of the seas which, since Trafalgar, for a hundred years has imposed on the whole world a bond of sea tyranny [had been] beaten'[1] Admiral Scheer knew the bitter truth of Jutland. While he had inflicted more damage than he had received and had extracted his ships from certain disaster by a display of dazzling skill, he was under no illusion that the Grand Fleet could be beaten in straight battle.

After Wilhelm had concluded his fiery oration to the crews of the High Seas Fleet at Wilhelmshaven on 5 June the Commander-in-Chief drew the All Highest to one side and renewed his proposals for another unrestricted U-boat campaign. Von Muller, as usual, opposed Scheer's basic proposition although even he, by now, was admitting acceptance of 'a successful submarine war to the knife.' Scheer contended that by giving pause to an all-out U-boat war the inevitable adoption of unrestricted submarine warfare at a later date would become that much more difficult while von Muller, comfortably perched upon two stools, urged the C-in-C to moderate his plans although he assured him that 'we were forced, with rage in our hearts, to make concessions to America.' Then, wielding the big stick, he threatened to transfer the North Sea U-boats to the Mediterranean if Scheer did not reconcile himself to the realities of diplomacy. The reasons behind von Muller's threat were simple. During the previous March and April the Mediterranean submarines had sunk 180,000 tons of Allied shipping and in some naval quarters it seemed preferable

[1] *Jutland, An Eye-Witness Account*, by Stuart Legg (Hart-Davis, 1966) p. 137.

to operate in an area where a high rate of sinkings could be achieved without the danger of embarrassing incidents with the United States.

A short while later the Chancellor informed the Commander-in-Chief that he, too, remained completely opposed to a renewal of the unrestricted campaign which, he said, 'would place the fate of the German Empire in the hands of a U-boat commander.' And, on 4 July, the Kaiser, obviously influenced by von Muller's more moderate line, told Scheer that he could not agree to 'a more ruthless' campaign at present.

Foiled for the moment Scheer bent his energies on another confrontation with Jellicoe's Grand Fleet. This time his surface ships were to act as bait for a U-boat ambush and he revived his earlier Sunderland scheme. It was an ambitious operation and included fifteen submarines from the fleet flotillas and a further nine boats from the Flanders command. Kommodore Bauer, the U-boat's leader, embarked on a battleship to exercise direct control over the flotillas and on 18 August the High Seas Fleet set out to bombard Sunderland which, it was confidently expected, would lure Jellicoe southwards from Scapa Flow in opposition.

The U-boats were spread out on five patrol lines ahead and behind the German fleet's projected course and were supported by two Zeppelin scouting groups. As Scheer had expected Jellicoe responded to the challenge and by dawn on 19 August the Grand Fleet was running south in full cry with decks cleared for action. At 7 am the light cruiser screen of Beatty's Battle-cruiser Fleet passed through the U-boat line off the Farne Islands and Kapitanleutnant Hans at the periscope of *U-52* drew a fast bead on the light cruiser *Nottingham*. Three torpedoes shot from the bow tubes and two slammed into the cruiser's hull. Unaware of the ambush the British thought they had strayed into an uncharted minefield and circled cautiously away from their stricken comrade. Then, having decided that the attack had been made by an isolated U-boat

Dublin was sent to protect the listing *Nottingham* and cruised up and down at high speed to keep the submarine submerged. At 6.26 am a fourth torpedo from *U-52* completed the work of destruction and at 7.10 am the cruiser sank beneath the surface. Hans remained in the vicinity, however, and Jellicoe records that 'several torpedoes were fired at *Dublin* and the two destroyers during their work of rescue but all fortunately missed.'[1]

A U-boat attack on the flagship *Iron Duke* had been avoided the previous evening and although one torpedo had been seen no one in the Grand Fleet suspected Scheer's underwater ambush. But on receipt of Beatty's signal about the *Nottingham* there were second thoughts and the Grand Fleet swung north to await clarification of the position. Only when, three hours later, Admiralty reports confirmed the presence of Scheer's ships in the mid North Sea, did the Grand Fleet head south again. But by now it was too late. At one time only 40 miles separated the two great fleets but they were destined never to meet.

It was a U-boat signal that saved Scheer from disaster. Kapitanleutnant Rose of *U-53* sighted 'a great pall of smoke', realized it was the full might of the Grand Fleet, and sent an urgent wireless message to Kommodore Bauer. Scheer did not hesitate. The High Seas Fleet immediately turned for home while Jellicoe, unaware that the enemy had been within his grasp, continued to dash south with battle ensigns streaming and guns secured for action.

U-53's signal had been received by Scheer at 1.15 pm and he had turned away almost at once. At 1.23 pm *Minotaur*, in the van of the Grand Fleet, sighted a U-boat and, fifteen minutes later, the light cruiser *Boadicea* spotted another. Jellicoe changed course slightly and then continued in search of his elusive enemy. But he was now thoroughly uneasy about the extent of the submarines lying in wait. 'It seemed fairly certain to me

[1] *The Grand Fleet*, p. 439.

that the enemy would leave a trap behind him in the shape of mines or submarines, or both; and indeed numerous submarines already sighted made it probable that the trap was extensive.'[1] Events were to prove the correctness of his surmise.

At 3.20 pm the 3rd Light Cruiser Squadron reported yet another U-boat and ten minutes later Jellicoe turned the fleet away for the last time. He was almost too late. *U-66*, commanded by von Bothmer, swung into an attack position and at 4.52 pm two of his torpedoes struck the cruiser *Falmouth* causing serious damage. A determined depth-charge attack drove *U-66* off and discouraged *U-49* from following up the assault and the destroyer *Pelican* narrowly missed ramming one of the submarines as it scuttled for shelter. *Falmouth* was taken in tow and, aided by tugs, headed for Flamborough Head at 5 knots. Almost within sight of home Otto Schulze in *U-63* put two more torpedoes into the crippled cruiser and sent her to the bottom. The destroyer *Porpoise* claimed to have rammed and sunk the U-boat responsible but, in fact, Schulze escaped and *U-63* survived to the end of the war in one piece.

The Grand Fleet ran the gauntlet of numerous U-boat attacks on its return to Scapa although, in every case, no hits were obtained. Jellicoe, however, was impressed and noted: 'The enemy's submarine commanders were no doubt increasing in efficiency, and risks which we could afford to run earlier in the war were now unjustifiable.'

Scheer's trap had almost succeeded and was, indeed, one of the few occasions in naval history when submarines operating in conjunction with surface ships met with success. But he had narrowly escaped disaster himself and only *U-53*'s urgent report saved him from another and more decisive Jutland. Thwarted in his plans his mind turned yet again to a commerce war by the U-boats. Unbeknown to the German C-in-C he had, in fact, achieved a greater success than he realized for, in

[1] *The Grand Fleet*, p. 443.

appraising the results of the U-boat ambush, Jellicoe decided
the game was not worth the candle and, on 13 September,
1916, he restricted the Grand Fleet to the north-east corner of
the North Sea unless exceptional conditions made a strike
southwards worthwhile. In coming to his decision Jellicoe was
prepared to leave the East Coast towns virtually unprotected
from future tip-and-run bombardment raids and, once again,
the influence of the U-boat on naval strategy had produced
repercussions which few could have foreseen in 1914.

Losses by the U-boats during the first eight months of 1916
had remained encouragingly small when set against their
achievements. *U-68* had fallen victim to the Q-ship *Farnborough* on 22 March and the following month saw the loss of
UB-26, sunk in the harbour defences at Le Havre, *UB-13*,
mined off Walcheren, and *UC-5*, captured intact by the
British. The surrender of *UC-5* and her subsequent public
display as a trophy of war gave rise to a splendid story.[1]

The submarine had apparently penetrated a British harbour
to lay its cargo of mines and was resting on the bottom to await
dusk when the crew became aware of a ghostly tapping on the
outer surface of the hull. At first they suspected some new
secret weapon but, listening carefully, they realized that the
mysterious sounds were the long and short symbols of the
morse code. *UC-5*'s commander, who spoke fluent English,
picked up a signal pad and began jotting down the coded
letters until he had the complete message scrawled on the
paper.

'Surface and surrender or depth charges will be exploded
against your hull.'

A puzzled expression crossed the skipper's face and one of
the junior officers wanted to know how the British were able
to transmit messages underwater. He was quickly silenced as
the ghostly tapping began again and a further signal was
scribbled, letter by letter, on the pad.

[1] This account is based on the story in *Subs and Submarines*, pp. 59–61.

'Depth charge has been wired and lowered.'

By now the source of the mysterious signals was academic. Something obviously had to be done, and quickly. Faced with surrender or certain death the U-boat skipper made his decision without hesitation.

'Close main vents. Blow all tanks. Stand by to surface!'

The submarine came to the surface in a lather of foam to find an armed naval trawler anchored 100 yards off her beam. The trawler crew seemed equally surprised to see a U-boat in their midst but, with commendable promptitude, manned their solitary 12-pdr gun and sent a warning shot whining over the enemy's bow, following this up with a direct hit on the conning-tower. A white flag fluttered from the U-boat and, minutes later, the crew were being herded on board the trawler as prisoners of war. And then the source of the mysterious signals revealed itself.

A stream of bubbles erupted alongside the fishing-boat and the copper helmet of a deep-sea diver glinted in the sun as it broke surface. When the helmet had been removed the diver explained that he had been responsible. Spotting the submerged submarine lying on the harbour bottom he had made his way across to it and tapped out his ultimatum with the aid of the hammer he carried in his belt.

The story undoubtedly derived from an imaginative matelot who guided visitors over the captured submarine during its propaganda tour along the coast. And a great many people, including journalists and naval writers, believed it. In fact UC-5's fate was far less romantic. She had simply got stuck on a mudbank off Harwich during a minelaying patrol and had been captured, without fuss or bother, by the destroyer *Firedrake*.

27 May, 1916 witnessed the end of three more U-boats. U-10, sister-ship to Weddigen's U-9, was mined and sunk in the Baltic, while U-74 and UC-3 were both lost in the North Sea, UC-3 in a minefield and U-74 sunk by four naval trawlers.

No submarines were lost in June but July claimed *UC-7*, *U-77*, and *U-51*, followed in August, by the torpedoing of *UC-10* by the British submarine *E-54* off Schouwen. Even so, in comparison with the successes obtained in the same period, it was not a gloomy balance sheet and the German High Command were well aware that the Royal Navy had still found no real solution to the U-boat threat.

The stalemate caused by the cancellation of the Spring campaign and the relative failure of operations in conjunction with the surface fleet was worrying Admiral Scheer who hated to see the war-winning potential of his submarines locked up in harbour by the fears of the diplomats and politicians. The strangling effect of the Allied blockade and the continuing lack of progress on the Western Front was causing concern in other circles as well and, on 30 August, 1916, a conference was convened at Pless at which the Chief of Naval Staff, Admiral Holtzendorff, once again proposed a renewal of the U-boat campaign against merchant shipping. Von Jagow, the Foreign Minister, and Secretary of State Helfferich continued to oppose the plan prophesying realistically that 'Germany will be treated like a mad dog' if the U-boats were unleashed on the world's shipping routes. The Chancellor once again voiced his opinion that a renewed terror campaign would bring America and other neutrals into the war on the side of Germany's enemies. The army, too, in the person of Ludendorff, were none too happy about the Navy's proposals and feared the creation of a second front by Holland and Denmark if their ships were sunk in any numbers by the U-boats. Von Hindenburg, now Chief of the General Staff, did not object to the campaign on moral grounds, he was too good a Prussian to be deterred by humanitarian sentiments, but felt that it was too much of a gamble while the military situation on the Western Front remained in the melting pot.

In the end, as at all previous meetings, no decision was taken although at least some thought was given to the future by the approval of a building programme for a further twenty-one submarines. It was a hopelessly inadequate number and there can be little doubt that the wavering indecision of the first Pless conference was a major contributory factor in the final failure of the 1917 and 1918 campaigns.

The Chancellor's hand was strengthened, too, by reports from the German ambassador in Washington indicating that public opinion in the United States was still firmly opposed to the British blockade which was considered to be 'a means of destroying American commerce and securing America's customers for herself.'[1] In such an atmosphere it is not difficult to see why the Kaiser and his political advisers continued to resist the pressure of the militarists for an all-out U-boat war. The stakes were high and there was much to gain by holding their hand. As Hindenburg remarked at the time, 'first weigh, then wager.' The politicians had weighed. But the important question was: could they stop the naval and military hawks from wagering?

Admiral Scheer soon made it clear that the politicians were going to have a difficult task. Aware that the British had posted a number of warships off the American coast in an attempt to trap the cargo submarine *Deutschland* on one of her commercial voyages to the United States, he sent Kapitanleutnant Hans Rose and *U-53* across the Atlantic to attack the assembled patrols. The weather was bad and, riding low in the water due to the weight of extra fuel, the U-boat endured an unpleasantly rough crossing. But she made it and, on 7 October, entered Newport harbour for a brief rest and overhaul. Within 24 hours she was standing out to sea again only to find that her main quarry had vanished. Deferring to American protests the British patrols had dispersed, leaving the U-boat with only merchant ships as targets. Rose, however, was undismayed and began searching for prey along the New England coastal routes, although he took the greatest care to operate just outside

[1] *Life and Letters of Walter H. Page*, Vol. 2, p. 184.

the limits of United States territorial waters. Acting in full accordance with international law he sank five merchant ships, three British, a Norwegian, and a Dutchman, before setting back across the Atlantic. But despite his careful precautions Rose had not counted on the psychological effect of his attacks on America's ocean doorstep and there was a violent outcry of protest when news of the sinkings appeared in the newspapers. What probably annoyed Americans more than anything was the fact that United States Navy destroyers were present, silent and impotent, during each attack. To a virile nation impotence was an insult that only blood could avenge and Wilson, soon to be re-elected for another term as President, warned the German ambassador that such attacks must not be repeated.

Although hamstrung by the tight restrictions placed upon their operations the U-boat commanders continued to achieve the maximum results and, as the politicians had feared, there were signs that the more ruthless submarine captains were breaking free from the restraints placed upon them.

The authority for a renewed campaign was issued in October, 1916, and great stress was laid on the necessity for observing the formalities of international law. Once again the safety of the victim's crew became paramount and U-boats were ordered to surface and examine intended targets before sinking them. 'Incidents which may lead to well-founded claims by neutrals ... are to be avoided,' the Naval Staff chided Scheer, and the U-boat commanders were enjoined to 'act with the utmost caution and conscientiousness.' As a final safety precaution submarine captains were advised that 'in case of doubt the ship is to be allowed to pass.'[1]

But no matter how stern the advice it was difficult to restrain U-boat commanders once they took the bit between their teeth and there were soon many instances of ships, both enemy and neutral, being attacked and sunk without warning. By

Der Krieg zur Zee.

December a total of 63 U-boats were operating around Britain and merchant shipping losses began to mount to an alarming average of 300,000 tons per month. *U-49* and *U-50*, for example, destroyed 19 ships totalling 58,364 tons in a single cruise during November into the Bay of Biscay. Pushing northwards three more U-boats scoured the Arctic trade routes in search of Allied shipping en route for Archangel. Penetrating the Barents Sea they scooped up 48,111 tons for the loss of only one submarine, *U-56*, and the Royal Navy's anti-submarine patrols were stretched to the limit by the continued expansion of the U-boat's operational areas. By January, 1917, there were no fewer than 111 U-boats on patrol and the four winter months of the new 'restricted campaign' cost the Allies $1\frac{1}{4}$ million tons of merchant shipping. There could be little doubt that, with U-boats probing as far south as the Canary Islands and as far west as *U-53*'s American foray, the Royal Navy would be powerless should an all-out terror war develop.

In theory the U-boats were still operating within the restrictions of prize warfare but there were plenty of signs that many commanders were blatantly disregarding their orders. On 27 November, 1916, the Ellerman liner *City of Birmingham* carrying 170 passengers, including 90 women and children, was torpedoed without warning in heavy seas 126 miles from the nearest land. The torpedo struck the after hold and the ship began sinking immediately. There was no panic and within ten minutes all boats had been launched, the women even singing as the lifeboats pulled away from the doomed liner. A hospital ship picked them up three hours later and, by good fortune, only four members of the crew lost their lives.

Another liner, the Furness-Withy *Rappahannock*, was sunk in October while outward bound for Halifax. The unfortunate ship was apparently destroyed in mid-ocean and no survivors were ever found. An Admiralty statement roundly condemned the attack. 'If the crew were forced to take to the boats in the ordinary way it is clear that this must have occurred so far from land, or in such weather conditions, that there was no probability of their reaching the shore. The German pledge not to sink vessels "without saving human lives" has thus once more been disregarded, and another of their submarines has been guilty of destructive murder on the high seas.'

Feelings were undoubtedly running high as reports of more and more cold-blooded attacks appeared in British newspapers and it was becoming increasingly clear that some U-boat commanders were now operating in total disregard of their orders. Neutrals, too, were discovering the bitter truths of the war at sea. On 22 December the Danish steamer *Hroptotz* was torpedoed in heavy seas. As the boats were being lowered the U-boat came close alongside and struck one of the lifeboats, hurling it against the steamer's side. 'The captain was crushed to death against the hull, his head being severed from his body, and a sailor was so badly injured that he died.'[1] The culprit was identified as *U-18* but the witnesses were mistaken for *U-18* had met her end two years earlier when von Hennig scuttled her off Scapa Flow.

Another Danish ship sunk during the same period, the *Naesborg*, was torpedoed at dusk during a violent storm. The crew scrambled into the lifeboats and begged the U-boat to tow them to safety. But their pleas were ignored and they were left to their fate. The list of atrocities grew with each passing day and it became clear that there were several submarine commanders who did not believe in 'acting with the utmost caution.'

On occasions the pendulum of fate swung the other way and in October the most hated U-boat in the world, *U-20*, the killer of the *Lusitania*, was lost off the coast of Denmark. Her last voyage had begun ominously enough on Friday the 13th and, to make matters worse, she became entangled with the hoodoo submarine *U-30* which had been accidentally sunk and

[1] *The Times History of the War*, Vol. 13, p. 64.

then salvaged in 1915. *U-30*'s temperamental diesel engines had broken down and, when Schwieger met up with her, she was crawling home at 3 knots. *U-20* took station on her beam and the two submarines made their way south. The morning mists thickened into dense fog and Schwieger was soon huddled forward over the conning-tower bridge straining his eyes to keep *U-30* in sight. A sudden lurch nearly threw him into the sea as *U-20* ploughed into an unexpected mudbank and, judging by the shouts he could hear echoing through the fog, *U-30* had apparently met with a similar fate.

There was a mad scramble to lighten the submarines and *U-30*, with typical contrariness and despite her crippled engines, succeeded in sliding back into deep water. *U-20*, however, remained stuck fast. Realizing the propaganda value to the Allies if they could capture the killer of the *Lusitania* intact Schwieger broke wireless silence and sent out an urgent distress call. It was picked up and, a few hours later, a large force including four capital ships left the Jade on a rescue mission. The squadron, led by Admiral Scheer personally, took the luckless *U-30* in tow but, despite repeated efforts, *U-20* refused to be dislodged from her mudbank. The rescue attempt was abandoned and the squadron started back for Wilhelmshaven.

The British submarine *J-1* was lying in wait close to the Horn Reefs as the German squadron headed for home and Noel Laurence, her skipper, fired a spread of four torpedoes as the enemy ships passed across his sights. Two torpedoes struck home, one on the *Kronprinz* the other on the *Grosser-Kurfürst*, and Scheer found himself with two badly damaged battleships in exchange for a U-boat that nobody wanted. When he heard the news the Kaiser vented his rage on the Commander-in-Chief for daring to risk his beloved battleships. 'To risk a squadron, and by so doing nearly to lose two armoured ships in order to save two U-boats, is disproportionate, and must not be attempted again,' he informed

Scheer curtly. It was apparent from the rebuke that the German emperor attached little importance to his submarines.

Walther Schwieger was given command of the new Danzig-built *U-88* but it never brought him the notoriety or success of *U-20*. On his third patrol he met up with the Q-ship *Stonecrop* and, unaware of her identity, Schwieger opened fire with his 4.1 inch deck gun as his victim turned away in pretended flight. To entice the U-boat closer the decoy ship began transmitting SOS signals adding, for good measure, *en clair*, 'Hurry up or I shall have to abandon ship.' Convinced that he had his victim on a plate Schwieger closed for the kill.

U-88's crew, however, were by no means as efficient as the men of *U-20*, and Commander Blackwood, the skipper of *Stonecrop*, found himself in difficulties in his efforts to ambush the U-boats because not a single one of her shells had scored a hit! Resourceful as ever, the Q-ship's captain gave orders for the smoke apparatus to be lit and within minutes the steamer appeared to be on fire. The 'Panic party' abandoned ship in accordance with the carefully rehearsed plan, and Schwieger, certain that he had crippled his prey, submerged and came in closer to inspect the burning ship. He made a complete circle and, satisfied that he was in no danger, came to the surface 600 yards off *Stonecrop*'s starboard beam. Hidden by the dummy bulwarks Blackwood watched and waited for three long minutes before ordering his guns to open fire.

'... the fourth shot hit the base of the conning-tower, causing a large explosion and splitting (it) in two. The fifth shot got her just above the waterline under the foremost gun, the sixth struck between that gun and the conning-tower, the seventh hit 30 feet from the end of the hull, the eighth got her just at the angle of the conning-tower and deck, the ninth and tenth shells came whizzing on to the waterline between the after gun and the conning-tower, whilst the eleventh hit the deck just abaft the conning-tower and tearing it up.'[1]

[1] *Q-Ships and Their Story*, p. 244.

U-88 sank stern first but rose to the surface again seconds later with a heavy list to starboard. With the conning-tower hatch jammed no one inside could escape and, after rolling gently in the oil-covered swell for a minute or so, she sank to the bottom with her crew entombed inside. Walther Schwieger had paid the ultimate price. The man who had sunk the *Lusitania* now lay on the bottom of the sea alongside his own innocent victims.

Revenge in the killing time was ruthlessly swift. The following day *Stonecrop*, herself, fell victim to a U-boat's torpedo although, fortunately Blackwood and most of the crew were saved.

Mercantile losses were now rising alarmingly and from October, 1916, to January, 1917, sinkings were running in excess of 300,000 tons per month. Anti-submarine measures were hopelessly inadequate to cope with the rising tide of attack and the shortage of destroyers and patrol craft militated against the introduction of a convoy system, even if the British admirals concerned could have been persuaded to adopt it.

Some of the schemes devised to hunt the U-boats were so ludicrous that it is difficult to believe they were ever taken seriously. In his autobiography Stephen King-Hall has quoted two examples: one gentleman arrived at *HMS Vernon* with a tank of performing seals which, so he claimed, could be trained to locate submarines by associating the sound of their propellors with fish; the other was an adventurer who said he could pinpoint oil underwater with the aid of a phosphor-bronze fork. His first demonstration was quite sensational but discreet enquiries revealed that 'the men who had sunk the first oil drums had been got at by the oil diviner and bribed to give him the location.' Another suggestion actually investigated by the Board of Invention and Research involved training seagulls to follow periscopes, and an elderly lady, who claimed to be psychic, volunteered to locate the whereabouts of

U-boats on a chart with the aid of a needle and a length of cotton.

On the more practical side there was the ram, the gun, and the anti-submarine net. All had proved successful on occasions but the first two were useless if the submarine remained submerged and the latter could only be employed in narrow waters like the Dover Straits and the Straits of Otranto. Mines undoubtedly constituted the greatest hazard to the U-boats but Jellicoe stated after the war that, in April, 1917, of the 20,000 mines available for use, only 1,500 were effective. And at one time, in desperation, picket boats were even issued with hammers so that their crews could smash the lenses of enemy periscopes and force the U-boats to the surface for attack by gun fire and ramming!

Spurred by the increased rate of sinkings scientists were following new ideas. Hydrophones, listening devices that could detect the presence of underwater vessels with reasonable accuracy, were being developed and the invention of the depth-charge, a cylinder containing 300 lbs of explosive which could be detonated underwater by means of a pre-set hydro-static valve, held promise of eventual mastery over a submerged submarine. Production, however, was scandalously slow and although the ultimate weapon had been found it was not produced in sufficient quantities to be of any use. Even in July, 1917, the output of depth-charges was only 140 per week although this was increased to 800 by December of the same year.

Jellicoe, watching the rising graph of merchant ship losses from his isolated eyrie at Scapa Flow, was seriously worried and wrote to the Admiralty pointing out 'the ever increasing menace of the enemy's submarine attack on our trade.' But Their Lordships seemed unconcerned. 'No conclusive answer had yet been found to this form of warfare,' they replied, 'perhaps no conclusive answer ever will be found. We must for the present be content with palliation.'[1]

[1] *British Sea Power*, by Vice-Admiral B. B. Schofield (Batsford, 1967) p. 53.

But the chill wind of change was blowing through the ancient corridors of the Admiralty. Jellicoe was appointed First Sea Lord on 3 December, 1916, with specific instructions to defeat the U-boat menace and, four days later, Lloyd George succeeded Asquith as Prime Minister. One of his first actions was to dismiss Balfour as First Lord and to replace him by Sir Edward Carson and the new team of Jellicoe and Carson set up an anti-submarine division under Rear-Admiral Duff to concentrate the Royal Navy's best brains into the fight against the U-boats.

Germany, too, was changing direction. The Allied blockade had reduced the population to near starvation and the anti-German attitude of Wilson and the United States government made it obvious that America's entry into the war would not be long delayed. Pressure for an unrestricted campaign mounted and Admiral von Holtzendorff was, as usual, well to the fore. His statistics showed that an average rate of sinkings of 600,000 tons a month was possible and, more importantly, if this could be maintained for five months Britain would have to sue for peace. 'I have come to the conclusion,' he wrote, 'that we must have recourse to unrestricted U-boat warfare, even at the risk of war with America, so long as the U-boat campaign is begun early enough to ensure peace before the next harvest, that is, before 1 August.'[1]

A further conference was called at Pless on 8 January and von Bethmann-Hollweg finally bowed to the inevitable. On January, 1917, the Kaiser issued the fateful edict:

'I order the unrestricted submarine campaign to begin on 1 February with the utmost energy.'[2]

[1] *British Sea Power*, p. 56.
[2] *The Most Formidable Thing*, p. 209.

CHAPTER ELEVEN

'We were men hardened by war'

ALREADY WARMED TO their task of wholesale slaughter the U-boats wasted little time on receiving the Kaiser's order. Despite the restrictions of the Prize Regulations they had already sunk 282,000 tons of British shipping in January, 1917, and a further 464,000 tons in the following month. Now, freed from restraints of any kind, they unleashed their full potential. 211 ships totalling 507,000 tons were destroyed in the first full month of the new terror campaign and, in April, no fewer than 354 ships went down to U-boat attacks setting a new record of 834,549 tons lost in a single month. But cold statistics tell only half the story. In human terms the ferocity of the slaughter plumbed new depths.

Douglas Duff, fourth officer of the British steamer *Thracia*, torpedoed on 27 April, gave reporters a vivid account of German brutality when he was landed at L'Orient. The attack had taken place on a pitch dark night and the U-boat surfaced alongside one of the lifeboats to ascertain the name of her victim and details of her cargo and destination. Duff answered all the questions that were put to him only to find that the submarine captain had pulled a Luger automatic from his belt and was pointing the gun at his head. 'He (the U-boat commander) said "I am going to shoot you." I told him to shoot away. He then said "I don't waste powder on any pig of an Englishman" and left me in the boat.'[1] The U-boat then put on speed, circled away, and disappeared into the darkness, leaving *Thracia*'s cold and hungry survivors to their fate.

Other incidents reported in British newspapers showed a

[1] *The Times History of the War*, Vol. 13, p. 58.

similar contempt for human life. Six survivors of the steamship *Jupiter*, attacked and sunk on 21 May, were informed by the U-boat captain responsible: 'You've no home now but there's room for you below!' And, five days later, a Dutch trawler carrying the crew of a torpedoed Norwegian barque was stopped by a German submarine and told not to pick up any more survivors. 'It is quite unnecessary to save them,' the U-boat commander explained suavely. Another Dutch ship stopped off the Hinder Lightship in July was told: 'You have brought condensed milk to France instead of Germany. You shall sink for that even if you were in neutral waters. We missed you last trip.'

German counter-propaganda naturally painted a totally different picture of their submarine crews. Baron von Spiegel, commander of *U-93*, told how he had surfaced after sinking the steamer *Horsa* and found a lifeboat floating upside down with survivors clinging to it. 'We came alongside and dragged them aboard. Some had arms and legs broken by the force with which they had been knocked down when the torpedo hit . . . We were men hardened by war. Incessant danger and the sight of death had dulled our sensibility to horror. And yet my men were naturally kindhearted. The sight of those poor fellows battered and broken on our deck touched them sharply. They held a veritable competition of doing things for them. They put splints on legs and arms and administered drugs from our medicine chest. Some gave up their bunks to our injured prisoners.'[1]

While the survivors were being dragged on board *U-93* someone heard a knocking sound coming from inside the upturned lifeboat and the U-boat sailors tried to turn the boat over to rescue the men trapped underneath. When this failed 'one fellow tied a rope around his waist, dived and, swimming below water, made his way under the boat. There he took hold of the two men (trapped inside) and dragged them out.'

[1] *Raiders of the Deep*, p. 179.

Von Spiegel's account forms a strange contrast from the harsh brutalities of the *Jupiter* and *Thracia* incidents. But the stresses and dangers of war are often capable of producing such paradoxes.

When the U-boats began the practice of taking prisoners it brought a fresh zest to the newspaper atrocity stories and a certain Captain Pennewell of Philadelphia claimed that 'German submarine commanders had added kidnapping to their other crimes.' He went on to reveal, with great circumstantial detail, that the wife and daughter of a merchant captain had been taken on board a U-boat after their steamer had been sunk off Gibraltar and the implications of their fate were easy to guess from the undertones of the story. In this particular instance neither submarine nor merchant ship was identified but a reliable report exists concerning the Norwegian sailing-vessel *Thor II* which was torpedoed off the coast of Ireland in early February. The vessel's captain, Isak Jacobsen, his wife and their six-year-old daughter were taken on board *U-45* and remained as unwilling guests for the rest of its eight day patrol, during which time a further three ships were destroyed. They were well-treated throughout the voyage and were repatriated to Norway immediately on their return to Germany. In Jacobsen's case it seems probable that the U-boat commander, Kapitanleutnant Erich Sittenfeld, acted on humanitarian grounds and chose to take the young woman and her child on board the submarine where they would be warm and safe rather than leave them adrift in an open boat.

Judging by contemporary British newspaper reports, however, when U-boat captains abandoned women in open boats they were, apparently, as guilty of war atrocities as the 'kidnappers'. On 11 February the Norwegian steamship *Dalmata* was attacked by a German submarine and the crew, including the captain's newly married wife, were cast adrift in four lifeboats. 'The sea was extremely heavy, it was piercingly cold, and my two coats and blanket were soaked as the result of sea washing over the boats,' the woman told a reporter from the Scandinavian newspaper *Afterposten*. The food and water failed after three days and during the next night one of the men died from exposure. 'I lay down in the bottom of our boat prepared to die. My arms and legs were like sticks and my eyes bloodshot from staring.' By good fortune their terrible ordeal was not prolonged and the next day the survivors, including the captain's wife, were picked up by a schooner and taken to Queenstown.

Some of the incidents were little short of cold-blooded murder. In May a steward and his wife from the Norwegian steamer *Fjeldi* were ordered aboard a U-boat as its commander wanted to use their lifeboat to ferry bombs across to another victim he had stopped close by. The steward was cross-examined about shipping movements out of Bergen and when he refused to give any information he and his wife were ordered back on to the deck of the U-boat without their lifebelts. The hatches were closed and the submarine started to dive. 'Both of them were drawn down a considerable distance by the suction but on coming to the surface they happily found themselves close to one of the lifeboats.' On this occasion outright murder had been averted—but only by the narrowest of margins.

That the U-boat men themselves were affected by the brutalities they witnessed was apparent from their private letters. The following extract, written by a sailor serving on *U-39*, was typical. 'It was an extremely sad day for me . . . in the morning I saw dead on the deck two poor Norwegians who had unhappily fallen victim to our gunfire . . . the day will be engraved on my memory in letters of blood.'

The subordinate officers, too, had no illusions. A boarding-officer examining the cargo manifest of a Dutch freighter told her captain: 'You may think yourselves lucky indeed that I was sent to examine your papers. We have a wild young commander, only 22 years of age, who usually sinks without

enquiry. Whatever kind of ship he meets down she goes!'
Many others felt a similar distaste for the excesses of their
captains.

Statistics show that more than one U-boat skipper had the
same ruthless attitude to his victims as this 'wild young
commander'. In 1915 only 21% of ships attacked by U-boats
were sunk without warning and by 1916 the figure had only
increased to 29%. But in 1917 the number of ships sunk
without warning rocketed to 64% for, as anti-submarine
defences improved, the U-boats had no choice but to sink or
be sunk. Surprise attacks became commonplace routine. *Spurlos
versenkt*, sunk without trace, became the watchword of the sea.

The campaign developed hesitatingly at first as if the submarine commanders were unwilling to unleash the full
ferocity of their potential. *U-45*, for example, pirated drums of
oil from an American tanker but allowed the ship itself to
pass unharmed and, a short while later, permitted a Norwegian vessel to proceed after examining her papers. Kapitanleutnant Sittenfeld, *U-45*'s skipper, also continued to surface
and warn his victims before sinking them with gunfire
although, on two occasions, defensively armed British steamers
drove him off, the *Saturnia* on 3 February and the *Tresillian*
the following day.

Other commanders were equally uncertain. Hans Rose,
whose *U-53* had earlier scoured the American east coast
trading routes, allowed the French steamer *Anna Maria* to
escape unscathed on discovering that her lifeboats were
unseaworthy and later permitted a Norwegian vessel to
continue her voyage after satisfying himself that she was not
carrying contraband. His attack on the American freighter
Housatonic on 3 February, however, was a remarkable demonstration of both ruthlessness and humanity. The ship was
carrying grain to England and, in accordance with law, her
cargo was liable to be taken as prize. Seizure, of course, was an
impractical task for a submarine with its limited resources and

19. Lothar von Arnauld de la Perière.

20. *U-35*'s crew unload empty shell cases at Cattaro at the end of another successful cruise.

21. Max Valentiner's *U-157* holds up the Spanish liner *Infanta Isabel de Bourbon* on 28 March 1918.

22. The Killing Time! A dramatic action photograph of a freighter being torpedoed.

Rose compromised by scuttling the steamer after allowing the crew time to take to the boats. Then, taking the lifeboats in tow, he led them towards Land's End and only cast them off when rescue, in the shape of an armed patrol yacht, appeared on the horizon.

Although the U-boats suffered only minor losses in the early months of the campaign there were more than sufficient narrow escapes. *U-67*, sighted and depth-charged by the decoy ship *Q-15*, escaped from the trap undamaged and both *U-81* and *U-60* were attacked by patrol craft, the latter being slightly damaged by a depth-charge explosion. Also, early in February, *U-43* received a glancing blow from the bows of the steamer *Kerry Range* which thoroughly unnerved the U-boat's commander, Jurst, although the submarine was barely scratched by the impact.

The Q-boats, too, were now taking exceptional risks in their efforts to lure enemy submarines to the surface. Gordon Campbell made an heroic sacrifice by allowing his *Q-5*, alias *Farnborough*, to be torpedoed in order to entice the U-boat into the open so that he could sink her with his guns. Acting as the bait for its own trap the decoy ship was struck without warning on the morning of 17 February while patrolling Campbell's favourite hunting-ground south-west of Ireland. In accordance with their much-practiced routine the 'panic party' scrambled for the boats while the hidden gun crews waited expectantly behind their weapons with the ship sinking beneath their feet. Pulling away from the crippled decoy the 'Panic party' found themselves being surveyed by the glassy eye of *U-83*'s periscope and unexpected humour lightened the tense drama of the situation when Campbell, watching through an observation slit on *Q-5*'s bridge, saw one of the men point to the questing stalk of the periscope and shout to his mates: 'Don't talk so loud, he'll hear you!'[1]

[1] *My Mystery Ships*, by Rear Admiral Gordon Campbell, VC (Hodder & Stoughton, 1928) p. 180.

U-83's captain, Bruno Hoppe, an experienced veteran of pre-war days, was taking no chances. Circling cautiously around the sinking Q-ship he remained just below the surface and Campbell said later that the U-boat was so close he could 'see the whole of his hull under water.' At 10.05 am, with *Farnborough* clearly sinking by the stern, Hoppe came to the surface some 300 yards off her port bow while Campbell waited patiently for his chance to strike. Then luck turned against the German. *U-83* sidled even closer until she was directly on Campbell's beam with only 100 yards separating the two vessels. The conning-tower hatch opened and Hoppe clambered out to inspect his victim. It was the last thing he ever did.

A White Ensign broke from the masthead, the dummy hatches folded down, and *Farnborough* opened fire. The first shot landed square on the conning-tower and *U-83* was doomed. 'It seemed almost brutal to open fire at such range,' Campbell admitted, but he did not let his sporting instincts curb his judgement. 'Forty-five shells were fired in all, practically everyone being a hit, so that she finally sank with the conning-tower shattered and open, the crew pouring out as hard as they could. About eight men were seen in the water which was bitterly cold and thick with oil. I ordered the boats to their assistance and they were just in time to rescue one officer and one man.'

Despite the near fatal damage done by *U-83*'s torpedo Campbell succeeded in getting his crippled ship back to Berehaven and on the way home, when things looked helpless he wirelessed a farewell message to his C-in-C: 'Q-5, slowly sinking, respectfully wishes you goodbye.'

Gordon Campbell was awarded the VC for his gallant work against the U-boats, an award referred to at the time by British newspapers as 'the mystery VC' because the Admiralty refused to publish any details that might reveal the secrets of the deadly Q-ships. That their caution was justified was apparent two days after the *Farnborough* incident when *Q-18* ambushed and sank *UC-18* in similar circumstances.

U-84 succeeded in avoiding the same fate when she encountered the decoy ship *Penshurst* on 22 February but was so badly damaged that her skipper, Kapitanleutnant Rohr, was forced to return to harbour on the surface because shell damage to the ballast tanks had made it impossible to submerge. And, on 12 March, *Privet* (*Q-19*) fought a savage forty-minute gun-battle with *U-85* which sent the submarine to the bottom stern-first. As in the case of *Q-5*, the decoy vessel was herself badly damaged in the hotly contested action and, after a gallant effort to save her, she foundered as she was entering Plymouth Sound. But despite this apparent end to her career *Privet*'s part in the U-boat war was not yet over.

Decoy ships were not the U-boat's only enemies. The destroyer *Thrasher* caught *UC-39* red-handed while attacking the collier *Hornsey* on the surface. Oberleutnant Ehrentrant dived for cover but the destroyer dropped her single depth-charge with such unexpected accuracy that the damaged U-boat was forced to the surface. Ehrentrant scrambled out through the conning-tower hatch but, before he could make his intentions clear, was killed by a direct hit from *Thrasher*'s guns. *UC-39*'s crew seemed stunned by the loss of their skipper and the situation was only saved by a British prisoner-of-war, the captain of the *Hanna Larsen*, who braved the shells and waved a white flag of surrender, in this case his pocket handkerchief. Seventeen members of the crew were saved but the U-boat itself sank while being towed back to England. On the same day Oberleutnant Moecke's *UC-46* was rammed and sunk by the Dover Patrol destroyer *Liberty*.

The Flanders Flotilla, in particular, were having a very unhappy time. On 23 February *UC-32* had blown up on one of her own mines while laying her lethal cargo off Sunderland and two days later *UB-30* stranded herself on a mudbank off Walcheren Island and was interned by the Dutch, although she was released four months later. And, to add to their cup of bitterness, *UC-26* collided accidentally with the paddle-steamer *Mona Queen* near Le Havre but managed to crawl back to base with her outer casing ripped open by the paddle-wheel.

As the lessons of experience were absorbed by the Royal Navy their anti-submarine patrols began taking a steady if unspectacular toll of the sea-wolves. On 10 March, the submarine *G-13* succeeded in torpedoing Sebelin's *UC-43* while the U-boat was engaged on a minelaying patrol in the Scapa Flow area and *UC-18* was lost following the premature detonation of her own mines in the Channel. *UB-6*, like *UB-30*, ran aground off the Dutch coast and was interned on 13 March while *UB-25* was accidentally lost six days later when she was rammed by the German destroyer *V-26* in Kiel harbour. In addition there were numerous near-misses and the stresses and strains of constant vigilance and danger began to be seen in the crews. Baron von Spiegel recalled that 'submarine men were likely to break down with nerve strain of some kind or other and were constantly being sent away to recuperate. The ordeal of life aboard the U-boats, with the constant stress of peril and terror, was too much for human flesh to bear for long stretches. Some men went mad. Others, after periods of rest and medication, came around and were, or perhaps were not, fit for undersea service again. All felt the grinding pressure.'[1]

The crews of the merchant ships endured a similar strain and casualties continued to climb as the U-boats ranged the seas in search of further victims. 15 men lost their lives when the RMSP liner *Drina* was torpedoed off Skokholm Island on 1 March and 46 seamen were drowned when the 9,196 ton *Narragansett* sank off south-west Ireland. Lives were lost in nearly every attack and, in some incidents, the numbers reached the proportions of tragedy.

When the Union Castle liner *Alnwick Castle* was torpedoed

[1] *Raiders of the Deep*, p. 174.

without warning 510 miles out into the Atlantic on 19 March the crew and 139 passengers managed to escape from the sinking ship into the lifeboats. The weather was bitterly cold and the Atlantic was still rolling under the wintry gales. Nine days later the first of the lifeboats crawled into a Spanish harbour with eight men dead and twenty-one barely alive. Another had five dead while the third had four. Two boats vanished completely and all the survivors were either delirious from thirst and exposure, or too weak to move. It was a horrifying example of the human suffering which resulted from U-boat attack and was repeated, on a smaller scale, hundreds of times every month. In March alone 630 merchant seamen lost their lives at the hands of German submarines and a further 51 died when their ships were mined.

As if the routine toll of war was not sufficient, some U-boat commanders exhibited a savagery that defies belief. Kapitanleutnant Wilhelm Werner, listed as a War Criminal by the British Government, showed neither mercy nor compassion for his unfortunate victims. When *U-55* sank the steamer *Torrington* on 8 April, 150 miles south-west of the Scillies, he took the ship's master on board as prisoner and then forced the crew to line up on the deck of the U-boat while he submerged. 34 men lost their lives as a result of Werner's infamous action and, as if to prove it was not just an isolated accident, he murdered the crew of the *Toro* in the same manner four days later.

April, 1917 was, indeed, the peak of the Killing Time. Amongst the 354 ships sent to the bottom by the sea-wolves were the Leyland liner *Canadian* on the 5th; the 6,117 ton *Powhatan* with the loss of 36 lives on the 6th; the *Vine Branch* on the same day sunk without trace with her entire crew of 44 officers and men; and the Elder-Dempster steamer *Abosso* on the 24th when 65 seamen were drowned.

The Allies had so far failed to find an answer to the U-boat menace and, even though the United States had finally entered the war on 6 April, the outlook did not inspire confidence. Vice-Admiral W. S. Sims, USN, on being shown the top-secret statistics of the U-boat war, advised his Government that German submarines were winning the war, an opinion endorsed by Ambassador Walter Page who wrote: 'What we are witnessing is the defeat of Britain.' Food reserves fell to a dangerous level and rationing was introduced. With ships being sunk faster than they could be built the Admiralty made a coldly calculated forecast that the war would be lost in November if some means of defeating the U-boats was not found.

Jellicoe, in a memorandum to the War Cabinet on 23 April, warned that 'the situation calls for immediate action' but continued to find many reasons why a convoy system could not be adopted. In his book *The Submarine Peril* he wrote: 'We frequently discussed the possibility of instituting a convoy system. We visualized the losses which might occur were an inadequately protected convoy successfully attacked and the prospects we had of providing sufficient protection to make the system reasonably safe.' As Lord Fisher was fond of remarking in similar situations, we were striving at the gnat of perfection.

In fact convoys were already operating successfully on a small scale. The cross-channel French coal trade was escorted and groups of merchant ships were convoyed to both Scandinavia and Holland. But it was basically the shortage of suitable ships that delayed the general introduction of the convoy system despite Lloyd George's oft-repeated assertion that his visit to the Admiralty on 30 April, 1917, brought the admirals to their senses. In point of fact the decision to adopt the convoy system, based on the proposals of Admiral Duff, was approved by Jellicoe three full days before the Prime Minister's celebrated visit to Whitehall.

Eighty-six U-boats were now operating from bases in Germany or Belgium and the carnage showed little sign of abating. The sinkings in May fell to 549,987 tons but this was due, as the Admiralty realized, to the U-boats returning to their bases for re-fuelling and fresh torpedoes. It was, and could only be, a momentary lull in the storm.

A new and ugly note had entered the conflict when the U-boats began turning their attention to hospital ships, vessels of mercy granted absolute protection under international law. On 20 March the 12,002 ton *Asturias*, running at 14 knots with all lights burning and carrying the internationally recognized emblems of the Red Cross, was torpedoed without warning while on her way to Southampton. She was struck in the stern but, by good fortune, the damage was not too serious and it proved possible to salvage her. Just over a week later, on the 30th, the Hospital Ship *Gloucester Castle* was attacked by a submerged U-boat off the Isle of Wight. The seas were rough and she was carrying 400 stretcher cases but, with the aid of skilled seamanship, all were safely transferred to the *Karnak* and the destroyer *Beagle* without harm. Thanks to the expertise of the Royal Navy only two members of the crew were lost and only one patient died after rescue.

These wanton attacks brought forth various reprisals which showed, sadly, that the Allies were equally capable of terror tactics when aroused. On 14 April bombers raided Frieburg in the Black Forest in an attack that killed civilians 'as a measure of reprisal' and the French Navy began carrying German officer hostages aboard their hospital ships to prevent further attacks. Never loath to exploit terror the Germans responded by exposing triple the number of French officer prisoners in the firing-line on the Western Front. Apart from propaganda the reprisals achieved nothing and, after a while, both sides appear to have come to a tacit understanding and the tit-for-tat policies ceased.

The attacks on hospital ships petered out during 1917 although not before the *Lanfranc* had been torpedoed in the Channel by an unidentified submarine. On this occasion the U-boat commander had miscalculated for amongst the casualties were fifteen wounded German soldiers who were being shipped back to England for hospital treatment. The German excuse for these wanton attacks was not only simple but was also difficult to challenge. They claimed that the British were using hospital ships to carry troops, guns, and ammunition and were, in fact, little more than thinly disguised transports. On several occasions they alleged that khaki clad figures had been observed on deck and, with constant repetition, the lies began to sound convincing in many neutral ears.

One account that did more damage than any other was contained in a book entitled *War Diary of U-202* written by Kapitanleutnant Baron Spiegel von und zu Peckelsheim—the commander of *U-32* and *U-93*, whose activities have already been featured in earlier chapters—and which was widely distributed in the United States. In a chapter headed 'England's Respect for the Red Cross' von Spiegel claimed that he had seen, with his own eyes, a British hospital ship 'laden with guns right fore and aft, and an army of soldiers and horses was packed between the guns and their mountings.' His statement was supported by *U-32*'s First Officer, Leutnant Gröning, and the account had all the hallmarks of a true eye-witness report. It was dangerous material to have circulated in a neutral country where the word of a German was no less believable than the word of an Englishman, and British Intelligence spent many weeks trying to kill the story without success.

However, at the end of April, Baron von Spiegel's career came to an abrupt end and the *War Diary of U-202* had an unexpected sequel. On the evening of the 30th his submarine came up with an innocent looking three-masted topsail schooner and, surfacing, *U-93* began firing on her. The sun was already slipping behind the horizon and von Spiegel was anxious to deal the death blow before dusk made further action impossible.

'Hit her at the waterline and sink her,' he ordered the gun

crews and, holding his binoculars to his eyes, he watched to see what effect his shells were having. 'As our first shell hit . . . there was a loud whistle aboard the schooner. The white war ensign of Great Britain ran up the mast. A moveable gun platform slid into view. A roar and rattling and 7.5 cm guns opened up at us, and machine-guns, too. We offered a fair broadside target. One shell put our fore gun out of commission and wounded several of the gun crew. Another crashed into the hull.'

U-93 jerked as the shells exploded and the Baron realized, too late, that he had tangled with one of the dreaded Q-ships. Another direct hit stopped the main engines and the submarine began drifting helplessly with the wind as the *Prize* closed the range. Von Spiegel ordered his men to the aft gun and, anxious to supervise their fire, he ran down the slippery steel deck behind them. They succeeded in scoring numerous hits on the schooner until, with a searing yellow flash, a 4 inch shell struck the barrel of the gun and exploded in their faces. The petty-officer gunlayer's head was blown off and the Baron and the other two members of the gun crew staggered back stunned and blinded by the blast.

'Then I felt a cold sensation about my legs. We were up to our knees in water. A moment later we were swimming in the Atlantic [and] the *U-93* had sunk beneath us. A dreadful pang of anguish shot through me at the thought of my fine new boat and my crew going down to their last port on the cold silent bottom of the sea, and a touch of ironic pity for those five [British] captains who, skippers of prosaic freighters, had never signed articles about making a last voyage in an iron coffin.'[1]

Prize quickly launched a boat and the three numbed survivors were dragged out of the sea and taken back to the safety of their erstwhile victim. But, as they were soon to discover, their troubles were by no means over. While von Spiegel was

[1] *Raiders of the Deep*, p. 183.

drying off in the commander's cabin a petty officer entered to report that the schooner was sinking. *U-93*'s shells had riddled her like a colander and the crew were making frantic efforts to pump her clear of water and block up the gaping holes in her hull. Then one of the auxiliary diesel engines caught fire and there was a mad rush for extinguishers and hoses. Sitting alone in the diminutive mess room von Spiegel reflected gloomily on the fate of his men trapped in the stricken U-boat.

'I couldn't forget my crew, my friends going down out there, drowned like rats in a trap, with some perhaps left to die of slow suffocation. I could imagine how some might even now be alive in the strong torpedo compartments, lying in the darkness, hopeless, waiting for the air to thicken and finally smother them.' It was not a pleasant picture but it served to emphasize that the U-boat crews, at the moment of truth, faced the same extreme hardships and dangers as the crews of the merchant ships they often so mercilessly sank without warning. *Spurlos versenkt* could be a double-edged weapon.

There was a certain irony in the situation when the captured U-boat men were enlisted to save the very ship they had tried so hard to sink. Drifting helplessly before the wind the only hope of survival lay in restarting the damaged diesel engines but the task was apparently too great for the limited technical skill of the schooner's engineers and Lieutenant Sanders, *Prize*'s captain, asked von Spiegel if his men could help. The Baron agreed and a few minutes later Deppe, *U-93*'s machinist's mate and an expert on recalcitrant diesel engines, began to tinker with the mechanism. Tools and spanners were eagerly lent by the British and, despite Deppe's pungent comments on the obsolete design, he soon coaxed the diesel back to life. There were smiles all round and, with the pumps working overtime to keep the ship afloat, *Prize* set course eastwards towards Queenstown. There was a momentary scare when

Ernst Hashagen's *U-62* was sighted on the surface at close range but the unexpected appearance of a destroyer flotilla discouraged him from pressing home an attack. When the U-boat submerged von Spiegel recalled that he did not enjoy the feeling of being on 'this side of the fence' as he waited for the shuddering jar of an exploding torpedo. But there were no more alarms and, a few hours later, the little schooner and her prisoners tied up alongside the jetty at Queenstown.

As soon as Naval Intelligence in Whitehall learned that one of the prisoners was Baron von Spiegel, the author of '*U-202*', an urgent message was sent directing that he should be brought back to London without delay for interrogation. The interview was conducted by Admiral Sir Reginald Hall, the Chief of Naval Intelligence, and it was not long before von Spiegel admitted that he had not witnessed the hospital ship incident himself but had relied on second-hand accounts from other U-boat captains. A shorthand writer took the retraction down verbatim and, a few hours later, it was released to the world's press. The damage done to neutral opinion by the allegations in the *War Diary of U-202* was swiftly repaired by the admissions of its author and another round in the ceaseless propaganda battle had been fought and won.

The Baron spent the rest of the war in the POW camp at Donnington Castle. His career as a sea wolf was over but his conscience was clear and he had nothing to regret for he had, at all times, shown respect for the law and a great humanity towards his victims. In fact, on landing at Queenstown, he was greeted by the captain of the *Horsa* who shook him by the hand saying: 'I have wanted to meet the man who rescued and took care of my crew as you and your men did.' There were very few U-boat captains who could expect, or deserve, such gratitude from their victims.

Although von Spiegel was safely esconced in his prison camp the captain and crew of the *Prize* were soon back at sea again. Lieutenant W. E. Sanders, her commander, was awarded the

Victoria Cross for his gallantry in the *U-93* action but, unfortunately, he did not live long to enjoy the glory. On the night of 13 August *Prize* was torpedoed by Steinbauer's *UB-48* and sank with all hands.

CHAPTER TWELVE

'I prayed that I was guessing right'

U-93's FIRST OFFICER, Wilhelm Ziegner, was standing on the bridge when *Prize* scored the vital direct hit on the after gun and the blast threw him into a huddled heap on the deck. Stunned by the explosion he dragged himself upright and clung to the combing of the conning-tower. Another shell exploded almost at his feet and splinters of steel shrieked past his face as he peered into the darkness searching for von Spiegel. Looking towards the stern he could see the decapitated corpse of the gunlayer but no sign of either Deppe or Knappe, the other members of the gun's crew, or of the skipper, whom Ziegner had last seen running aft to help direct their fire.

The bows of the submarine yawed wildly and she began to broach in the heavy seas. She was already listing 14° to starboard and lay half-submerged as the shells from the Q-ship burst alongside throwing up columns of water. Ziegner staggered across to the conning-tower hatch and shouted steering directions to the men below. A few moments later he felt the U-boat sluggishly responding to the helm and there was a moment's respite from the shelling as *Prize*'s gunlayers adjusted their sights.

'Where is the captain?' Leutnant Usedom yelled up from inside the control room. Ziegner's eyes swept the bare steel decks.

'He must be below with you somewhere.'

Another salvo of shells exploded and the crippled U-boat shuddered violently. Vivid gun flashes turned the night into day as further salvoes followed and U-93 was bracketed by bursting shells. It was Ziegner's first operational patrol yet, in the absence of the captain, he stood next in the chain of command. His instincts cried out to submerge but the discipline acquired from long months of arduous training made him pause. He surveyed the situation calmly. The U-boat's hull had been pierced at least a dozen times, oil was pouring from the punctured fuel tanks, at least five men were wounded, and both periscopes had been blown away. It was patently obvious that if *U-93* dived she would never rise to the surface again.

The darkness deepened and, as the smoke of battle drifted across the sea, the British ship stopped firing. No submarine, Sanders considered, could possibly survive the point-blank battering *U-93* had received and he was satisfied that he had made a kill. Von Spiegel, sitting alone in his cabin, agreed and he reflected mournfully on the loss of his comrades.

But the submarine was not finished yet. Although it seemed an impossible task Ziegner was determined to get his crippled command back to Germany even though it meant running the entire way on the surface. Sliding down the companionway into the control room he told the U-boat's crew that their captain had been killed and announced his plan. Not a soul voiced any objection.

While Ziegner turned the submarine north on to a course that would avoid the main shipping lanes the crew set to work to locate and repair what damage they could. They had five wounded on board: Bay, the Bosun's mate, cut to pieces by the same shell splinters that had miraculously missed the First Officer, two petty officers with severely damaged legs, and two seamen. All were carefully laid on bunks while the boat's elementary first-aid kit was brought into action. Usedom was deputed to administer the morphine.

'There I stood with a bottle of morphine in one hand and a hypodermic needle in the other, without any idea as to how much I dared give them. I prayed that I was guessing right.'

Petty Officer Bay died during the night and was buried next morning with full naval honours, his body draped in the Imperial German war ensign, while Ziegner read prayers to the bare-headed crew lined up on deck. Then, their grim duty to a dead comrade accomplished, they returned to the job of saving their boat. Shell-fire had damaged the fresh-water tanks and it was necessary to impose a strict system of rationing —no shaving, no washing, no cooking water, and just a meagre cupful to make coffee. Fuel, too, was short and threatened to run dry before the trip was finished. In his anxiety to avoid contact with Allied patrols Ziegner had charted a course that would take the U-boat high into the Arctic Circle, east of Iceland, and the additional distance threatened to deplete their exhausted oil reserves even further.

The weather worsened, making it necessary to blow the leaking ballast tanks every thirty minutes, and *U-93* presented a forlorn sight as she chugged through the heavy seas with her stern section awash and her bows high out of the water. Leaking gases inside the boat led to an order forbidding smoking and the men had to pass their time playing gramophone records or reading dog-eared books from the submarine's tiny library. There was a momentary flurry of excitement when they met up with a patrol flotilla but *U-93* was lying too deep in the water to be spotted in the swirling snow squalls and they succeeded in passing clear without being sighted. The bad weather grew even worse and the seas breaking over the crippled U-boat were so heavy that the look-outs on the bridge had to be lashed to the conning-tower rails to save them being washed overboard, but, with dogged determination, Ziegner held his course.

A spare periscope was lashed into position to help observation and the first time Ziegner used it he found himself looking straight at a British destroyer. More warships appeared on the horizon and *U-93* tried to make a run for it. But she had been spotted and a three-funnelled destroyer peeled out of line in pursuit. Explosive charges were prepared ready to scuttle the submarine when surrender became inevitable and, in the final minutes, Ziegner went through the drill for abandoning ship with the crew so that all knew what to do. Then another providential squall came to their rescue, and hail and snow, whipped by a strong wind, battered the surfaced U-boat. But by the time it had passed the enemy ships had disappeared and Ziegner was able to stand down his weary crew and resume course for Heligoland.

They rounded the north of Scotland and chugged into the North Sea without further incident although floating mines caused a momentary scare a short distance from home. But they finally made it and Ziegner was justifiably elated when he moored alongside a German hospital ship to off-load the wounded after a nine day voyage that deserves to rank as one of the epics of submarine history. His one regret was the loss of his beloved captain, Baron Spiegel, whom he felt certain had been washed overboard during the duel with *Prize* and it was several weeks before he learned that the Baron was alive and well in a British POW camp.

The Killing Time was now moving to its savage climax. The United States had joined the Allies in April and, during the following month, the first escorted ocean convoy had left Gibraltar for England and arrived safely. These two events were to spell the death-knell of the U-boats although both were long-term developments. Before America could send any substantial aid to the Allies and before the British Admiralty could perfect its convoy organization there was still time for the U-boats to strike a mortal blow at their hated enemies.

In April sinkings had reached a peak of 834,549 tons followed, in May, by a sharp decline to 549,987 tons. But even the loss of half a million tons of valuable shipping was too great a strain on Allied resources and, a month later, Jellicoe warned the War Cabinet that the shortage of shipping was becoming so serious that it would be impossible to continue the war into

23. Two of the Kaiser's sea-wolves, *U-35* and *U-42*, rendezvous to exchange stores and information.

24. A *UC-1* class minelayer returns to base after a Channel patrol.

25. Lt Blacklock RN takes over a surrendered U-boat at Harwich after the Armistice.

26. Kamarad! Kamarad! *U-58* surrenders to the US destroyer *Fanning* in the Bristol Channel on 17 November 1917.

1918 if losses continued at the present rate. And, under the relentless pressure of the U-boat war, morale was beginning to show signs of weakening.

The British Controller of Shipping, Sir Joseph Maclay, told the Prime Minister: 'Statistics prove that what are called areas of concentration (ie the convergence of trade routes) as now managed, have become veritable death traps for our Mercantile Marine and our men are realizing this.' Confidence in the Admiralty's ability to save the situation was fast waning and Lloyd George began a personal probe into the internal workings of the Royal Navy in a sharp search for scapegoats. Yet, despite their success, the German Government was no happier than their enemy. Public opinion was against the war continuing into 1918 and there were sinister portents of revolution from the war-weary population. Questions were asked in the Reichstag and speakers claimed that 'the submarines had not done what the Naval High Command had promised, and ought to be abandoned.'[1] Bethmann-Hollweg's sympathy with the anti-U-boat lobby was well-known and as the mutterings of public opinion mounted in volume the High Command finally succeeded in forcing the Chancellor's resignation. He was succeeded by Georg Michaelis, an almost unknown Prussian bureaucrat, whom the militarists, including the Crown Prince, considered was more likely to follow a strong line. It was, indeed, fortunate that the Allies played their cards so close to their chests during this crucial crisis. Had Germany been aware of the straits to which Britain had been reduced by the 1917 U-boat campaign there can be little doubt that the entire country would have rallied to the support of the Navy in giving the hated enemy the death blow.

At sea, while the politicians struggled for power at home, the war continued without respite. The 'trap ships', as the U-boat captains referred to the decoy Q-ships, were beginning to reach the end of their usefulness. Every submarine commander

[1] *Official History. Naval Operations*, Vol. 5.

knew of their secrets and their effectiveness grew less with every month. On 30 April Ernst Hashagen torpedoed *Tulip* (Q-15) off the Irish coast after his suspicions had been aroused by the Red Ensign at her stern. Few ships carried any sign of identification at this stage of the war, and, a few days later, the decoy ship *Heather* (Q-16) was shelled by a U-boat which came to the surface to fight it out. Her captain, Commander Hallweight, was killed by a shell splinter early in the battle, the ship was badly damaged, and, by the time the guns had been readied for action, the submarine had submerged into the depths and escaped.

2 June, 1917, saw another Q-ship engagement when Gordon Campbell's new decoy, *Pargust*, caught up with Rosenow's *UC-29* south-west of Ireland. It was a typical duel to the death between U-boat and Q-ship and only Campbell's experience and cool nerves won the day. The action began when *Pargust* was torpedoed without warning. Following the standard routine a 'panic party' abandoned ship and took to the boats, while the gun crews remained hidden behind their concealed weapons on the sinking steamer. *UC-29*'s skipper was a cautious man and he waited a full thirty minutes before bringing the submarine to the surface. Then, seeing the 'panic party' beginning to row back to their ship, he opened fire on the lifeboats in an attempt to stop them. Ignoring the shells exploding all around them the men in the boats continued pulling towards the *Pargust* while the unsuspecting U-boat, moving in closer to cut them off, steered herself into the area covered by the Q-ship's hidden guns. Campbell snapped the executive order, the screens fell away, and *UC-29* heeled sharply as the first salvo plunged into the sea a few yards from her exposed beam.

Deception, however, was not a British monopoly and Rosenow replied by sending some of his crew on deck with their hands raised in surrender. Campbell immediately ordered the guns to hold fire but suddenly realized that *UC-29* was trying to escape under cover of the truce. Once again *Pargust*'s guns blazed, and this time no quarter was asked or given. The U-boat rolled over and sank beneath the surface in a pool of oil and bubbles.

But the U-boats could not always blame the British for their misfortunes and on several occasions German submarines were lost as a result of sheer chance or errors of judgement. On 14 May *U-59* missed her navigational fix while outward bound for an Atlantic war patrol and ran into a defensive minefield south east of the Horn Reefs. There was a tremendous explosion and the doomed submarine plunged to the bottom with all hands. Salvage ships were rushed to the spot from Wilhelmshaven but the search was abandoned after several of them met the same fate as *U-59*. Four days earlier the minelayer *UC-76* blew up at Heligoland while being loaded with her lethal cargo and, on the night of 16 May, the destroyer *S.17* sank after striking a German mine while escorting *U-86* out of the Ems River.

German mines were undoubtedly more effective than those of the British and the High Command made considerable use of their submarine minelayers of the UC-type. But it was hazardous work and casualties were exceptionally heavy. Of the first 79 boats of the UC-class only 27 lived to survive the war and the 'sisters of sorrow', as the minelayers were called, were not popular boats with submarine crews. In the main they operated out of Ostend or the other Flanders bases and their usual patrol lines took them along the English coast where shipping concentrations were at their heaviest. Once the mines were successfully laid the UC boat continued to patrol as a conventional submarine ready to attack and sink the enemy with either guns or torpedoes.

UC-26's brief excursion in May was typical of the trials of the coastal minelayers. Although joining the Flanders Flotilla in November, 1916, she had been delayed continually by mechanical trouble and, when these had finally been rectified, she was damaged by a fire which broke out in a steamer anchored close to her moorings. Her first trip had ended in the brush with the *Mona Queen* and she did not leave Ostend again until 30 April when, loaded with mines, her commander, von Schmettow, conned her carefully through the shoals and headed out into the Channel. Penetrating the Dover barrage he laid his mines off Le Havre, Ouistreham, and Cherbourg, and survived an attack by a French seaplane which spotted him on the surface recharging his batteries. After fruitlessly patrolling the main route into Southampton von Schmettow turned east, passed through the Dover defences again, and moved up towards Zeebrugge. By the 9th he had returned westwards to the Calais area where, at dawn, he was sighted by the destroyer *Milne*. *UC-26*, new and untried with a raw and inexperienced crew, took a long time to dive and the delay proved fatal. *Milne* swung towards the U-boat at full speed, her bows sliced into the pressure hull and *UC-26* plunged to the bottom, her end hastened by some skilfully placed depth-charges dropped by two more destroyers which had rushed to the scene on receipt of *Milne*'s signal. Only two members of the crew lived to tell the tale. Eleven days later Seaplane *8663* swooped down on the surfaced *UC-36* off the West Hinder light-vessel and promptly sealed her doom with two well-placed bombs.

The newly built *U-81* was lost on 1 May when she was torpedoed by the British submarine *E-54* while attacking a steamer off Ireland and Kustner's *UB-39* was destroyed by the decoy-ship *Glen* in the vicinity of the Needles on the 17th following a fierce gun battle. Two other U-boats arrived on the scene after *UB-39* had gone down but they quickly slunk away when *Glen* turned to attack them.

But the destruction inflicted on the submarine flotillas was neither sufficient to deter the Germans nor enough to reduce the Allies' shipping losses to a safe margin. In May 580 British merchant seamen lost their lives to U-boat attacks and mines. The Blue Funnel liner *Troilus* went down 140 miles west of

Malin Head on 2 May and the Cunard *Feltria* sank with 45 of her crew three days later when within sight of land. The 7,583 ton *Highland Corrie* fell victim to a prowling U-boat on the 16th and, five days later, the Ellerman liner *City of Corinth* was torpedoed off the Lizard. The more experienced commanders still searched for warships and, occasionally, their luck was in. *UC-75* sank the sloop *Lavender* on 5 May and on the 25th the Armed Merchant Cruiser *Hilary* was struck by three torpedoes from Schwieger's *U-88* while returning to base from duty with the 10th Cruiser Squadron on the Northern Blockade line.

The losses for June rose to 631,895 tons and, despite the belated introduction of a limited convoy organization, the U-boats still appeared to have the upper hand. Twenty-seven boats were operating in the Channel and Western Approaches and the British Admiralty realized that the drop in sinkings during the month of May was only illusory. Germany meant business as this contemporary High Command order made clear:

'The sole aim is that each boat should fire her entire outfit of ammunition as often as possible ... short cruises, short visits to the dockyard, considerable curtailment of practices ... during periods of overhaul only what is absolutely necessary.' Even with minimum numbers, a legacy of the ill-omened first Press Conference, the rapid turn-round of U-boats meant that the German High Command could still obtain the maximum of offensive action and striking power from its submarine raiders. Tactics, too, were being improved. When the British convoy system was instituted Kommodore Bauer organized a special 'target training convoy' at Kiel and U-boat commanders were sent into the Baltic to try their luck in mock attacks. British sailing formations were adopted, the ships zig-zagged in accordance with standard Admiralty practice, and Teutonic thoroughness even led to the ships being painted with Royal Navy dazzle camouflage schemes. The only thing missing was the devastating counter-attack of destroyers with depth-charges.

But perhaps this was asking a little too much even for Prussian perfectionism.

Despite the proved success of the convoy system the British Admiralty continued to hanker after their old methods of standing patrols in areas through which U-boats were known to pass. In June an extensive operation was organized along the Fair Isle Channel involving 31 destroyers and 10 submarines. Over a dozen attacks were made and sightings were numerous yet not a single kill resulted even though at least ten U-boats passed through the area while the operation was in progress. The Admiralty made a further miscalculation by assuming that the Dover Barrage was impenetrable. U-boats used the Channel route with monotonous regularity although they took care to remain submerged until they reached the mouth of the Channel in order to fool the British into believing that the defences were effective.

Fortunately the misconceptions of the Admiralty's top brass did not inhibit the traditional fighting spirit of the Royal Navy and the sailors at sea continued to take a steady if unspectacular toll of Germany's underwater raiders. On 12 June Ober-leutnant Herbert Pustkuchen, the man who had caused a minor international crisis in April 1916 by torpedoing the *Sussex*, was located by the Lizard Hydrophone Division while passing through the Channel in his minelayer *UC-66*. The listeners on shore passed his position to a local patrol group by wireless and armed trawlers were quickly directed to the spot. A well-judged depth-charge attack detonated the U-boat's deadly cargo of mines and the resulting explosion was so violent that, to quote a witness, 'the sea boiled'. It was the first definite success attributable to the new listening devices and this fruitful marriage of seamanship and science was to bode ill for the U-boats in the future.

British surface patrols, too, were increasing in strength almost daily and many submarine commanders began to complain of the 'astounding promptness of the counter-measures.' It was certainly not a happy time for Germany's undersea warriors. *U-57* found 'trawlers everywhere' and *UC-77*, on a mission to shell the Scottish port of Aberdeen, was diverted from her target by destroyers and had to content herself with laying a minefield off the Firth of Forth. This same U-boat also reported that the British were erecting dummy lighthouses in order to lure unwary submarine commanders to their doom in the maze of shoals and mudbanks that fringed the coast of eastern England. *UC-77*, however, bore a charmed life. On the same patrol a depth charge attack by trawlers burst open her oil tanks, she entangled herself in a net from which she escaped by running full speed astern, and, on her way home, she evaded a destroyer which sighted her on the surface.

Losses for July showed a reassuring drop to 492,320 tons and the improved position was maintained when the August figures revealed a further slight fall to 489,806 tons. But the U-boats were not beaten by a long chalk and there were renewed signs that warship targets still interested the more experienced commanders. The destroyer *Itchin* was torpedoed and sunk on 6 July and, fifteen days later, *U-52*'s skipper, Hans, surprised the British *C-34* on the surface in the Shetlands area and sent her to the bottom with a single shot. The following day another ship of the 10th Cruiser Squadron, the Armed merchant cruiser *Otway*, was attacked and sunk by a prowling U-boat just after leaving her Loch Ewe base to take up a patrol line off the Norwegian coast.

July proved a month of horror for both sides. The steamer *Mariston*, torpedoed by *U-66* on the 15th, eighty-two miles out from the Fastnet Rocks, left 18 survivors swimming in the sea after she sank. A shoal of sharks attacked the men, struggling in the water and only one survived. He told his rescuers that von Bothmer, the skipper of *U-66*, had been so sickened by the fate of the unfortunate sailors that he had taken his submarine below the surface to escape the sight.

There were more innocent casualties on 29 July when *UB-20* was caught on the surface by two seaplanes. Her commander, Oberleutnant Hermann Glimpf, known as the Playboy of the Flanders Flotilla, tried to escape retribution by diving but the waters off the Belgian coast were too shallow and he found himself trapped. The bombs scored direct hits which burst open the sides of the U-boat and she sank to the bottom. On this particular cruise Glimpf, true to character, had been taking some army officers and their girlfriends for a brief joy-ride in the submarine and the innocent perished alongside the guilty when the U-boat went down. *UB-27*'s career ended on the same day when she was rammed by the gunboat *Halcyon* off the Smith's Knoll buoy and depth-charged. That these constant attacks were undermining morale became evident later in the month when a much-battered *UB-23* crawled into the Spanish harbour of Corunna where her captain, Oberleutnant Ernst Voigt, accepted voluntary internment rather than face the hazards of the Channel run with his damaged craft.

The last day of the month saw further tragedy when Paul Wagenfuhr's *U-44* encountered the 4,765 ton steamer *Belgian Prince* 175 miles west of Tory Island and sank her without warning. Coming to the surface Wagenfuhr waited until the three lifeboats were clear of the sinking ship and then ordered them to come alongside the U-boat. The steamer's master was seized and taken below as a prisoner of war and the rest of the crew were told to climb aboard *U-44*. One of the survivors, Chief Engineer Thomas Bowman, gave a vivid account of the incident when he arrived back in Britain. 'The officers and crew were ordered aboard, searched, and the life-belts taken off most of the crew and thrown overboard. I may add, during this time, the Germans were very abusive to the crew. After this the German sailors got into the two lifeboats, threw the oars, balers, and gratings overboard, took out the provisions and compasses, and then damaged the lifeboats with an axe.' The third lifeboat was commandeered by the U-boat crew who rowed across to the sinking *Belgian Prince* to search her for loot. 'Then the submarine cast the damaged lifeboats adrift and steamed away from the ship about two miles, after which he stopped. (At) about 9 pm the submarine dived and threw everybody in the water without any means of saving themselves.'[1] Only three men, including Bowman, survived the murderous assault of the *U-44*.

Wagenfuhr's behaviour remains especially puzzling for, on several previous occasions, he had exhibited a natural compassion for his victims. And, on 23 March, 1916, he had actually allowed the giant liner *Mauretania* to pass unscathed, although he had her firmly in his sights. Paul Wagenfuhr never had the opportunity to explain the reasons, if any, for the cold-blooded murder of the *Belgian Prince*'s crew. Twelve days after the killings *U-44* and her captain joined their victims on the floor of the ocean.

The submarine's last hours began with a fierce duel with the Q-ship *Bracondale* and although the U-boat finally succeeded in sinking her adversary with three torpedoes she was seriously damaged by shell-fire. It was dangerous to submerge and Wagenfuhr decided to remain on the surface in the hope of further easy pickings before returning to base at the end of his patrol. On the 12th he sighted the 3rd Light Cruiser Squadron and, as he turned away, the port wing destroyer, *Oracle*, spotted the low grey hull of the U-boat some six miles away. *U-44* dived for cover but the damage wreaked by *Bracondale* quickly forced her to the surface again as tons of water cascaded in through the shell holes in her hull. Wagenfuhr ran for it but it was obvious that the crippled U-boat could not seek refuge beneath the surface for more than a few minutes at a time and *Oracle* built up to maximum speed in close pursuit. Suddenly the submarine's bows surfaced a bare half mile ahead and the destroyer bore down towards her quarry; her

[1] *Submarine and Anti-Submarine*, by Henry Newbolt (Longmans, 1919) p. 175.

bows sliced into the U-boat just behind the conning-tower inflicting 'terrible injuries' and a depth-charge completed the task. *U-44* slid stern-first to the bottom 137 fathoms down taking Wagenfuhr and his crew with her.

The sinking of *UC-44* on 4 August demonstrated that the Royal Navy was not without guile when it came to submarine hunting. British sweepers located a new minefield off Waterford and, to judge by the activity and explosions that followed, they made a good job of clearing it. A few days later there was a violent explosion out to sea and patrol ships rushing to the spot fished a very wet and angry U-boat captain out of the water. Kapitanleutnant Kurt Tebbenjohanns had good cause to be annoyed for he had run full tilt into the selfsame minefield which the British had supposedly swept clear but which, in practice, they had left untouched as a trap for the next minelaying intruder. 'It was a practical joke, admittedly grim, and Tebbenjohanns, perhaps excusably, failed to find any humour in it. Still, his idea that British sweepers toiled unceasingly to keep British waters safe for German submarines exhibits an impudence that approaches the sublime.'[1]

UC-44's hull, when salved, provided the Admiralty with unexpected food for thought. The confidential papers showed conclusively that the Dover Barrage was completely ineffective and that U-boats were passing through it almost daily. The documents containing the commander's operational orders concerning the Dover net defences were clear and unequivocal: 'It is best to pass this on the surface. If forced to dive, go down to 40 metres ... as far as possible pass through the area Hoofden-Cherbourg without being observed and without stopping. On the other hand, the boats which in exceptional cases pass round Scotland are to let themselves be seen as freely as possible *in order to mislead the English*.'[2] (Author's italics.)

The removal of Admiral Sir Reginald Bacon from his post

[1] *The German Submarine War*, p. 196.
[2] *Roger Keyes*, by Cecil Aspinall-Oglander (Hogarth Press, 1951) p. 211.

as C-in-C Dover and the appointment of Rear-Admiral Roger
Keyes, the Senior Officer Submarines during the first year of
the war, came about as a direct result of the *UC-44* episode.
Although the switch did not take place until 29 December,
1917, the matter had been under active consideration for some
months previously and Keyes had been appointed President of
a special committee set up to investigate the problem of the
Dover defences in the late summer, only a few weeks after
Tebbenjohanns' capture. It is an interesting sidelight on the
state of personal relationships in the Admiralty at this crucial
period of the war that, when Jellicoe wrote his book *The Crisis
of the Naval War*, he omitted all mention of Roger Keyes
despite reference to the all-important committee which the
Rear-Admiral headed. Bacon, too, avoided naming Keyes in
his definitive biography of Jellicoe—by no means an easy task
as the careers of the two men had frequently intertwined ever
since the time they had both fought together in the Boxer
campaign of 1900.

Despite the Channel routing of U-boats and the increasing
numbers of boats available, time began to swing against the
Kaiser's sea wolves. American destroyers, which had first
arrived at Queenstown in May, were now playing an ever
increasing part in the patrols covering the Western Approaches
and the convoy system was stemming losses on a scale far
greater than had even been anticipated. October saw the
destruction of 492,147 tons but November's total dropped
dramatically to 259,521 tons and even the upsurge to 353,083
tons in December was not discouraging in the light of sinkings
earlier in the year. The protection offered by the convoy system
was reducing losses nearly ten-fold and, in *The Most Formidable
Thing*, Rear Admiral William Jameson expressed the magnitude of the achievement: 'What this [the convoy system] all
added up to is simply expressed in figures. About one in every
ten ships sailing alone was sunk; for ships in convoy the
proportion was between one and two in a *hundred*.' And, not

only were merchant ship losses falling, the toll being taken of the U-boats indicated that, at long last, the Allies were getting the measure of their underwater foes. Although only three enemy submarines had been sunk during August, no fewer than thirteen were destroyed in the following month.

Not that convoying always provided cast-iron protection. In August Otto Hersing demonstrated that an experienced U-boat skipper could still obtain results provided he pressed his attack home with resolution and determination. *U-21* met up with the convoy south-west of Ireland. It was 'one of those rare sparkling days with hardly a ripple on the sea' and the surface of the water was so glassy that Hersing did not dare to use his periscope for more than a few moments at a time. There were fifteen ships in the formation with six destroyers on either flank and two more, one half-a-mile ahead, the other a similar distance astern. It looked an impregnable defence but Otto was too old a hand to be deterred simply by a show of strength.

Diving between two of the flank destroyers and poking his scope up just long enough to estimate the course and speed of his targets Hersing fired two shots. Then, diving to 40 metres, he waited results. Both torpedoes scored direct hits but retribution followed swiftly. Guided by the bubbling tracks of the torpedoes the destroyers homed on their hidden enemy. A veritable deluge of depth-charges rained down on the lurking submarine and Hersing's crew were shocked and shaken by the violent explosions that followed. 'Every square yard of water was being literally peppered with depth bombs. They were exploding on every side of us, over our heads, even below. The destroyers were timing them for three different depths—ten metres, twenty-five metres, and fifty metres. . . . They were letting us have them at the rate of one every ten seconds.'[1]

A near miss shattered the lights and Hersing was convinced that they were finished. But the reports coming into the control room confirmed that there was no damage and, gritting

[1] *Raiders of the Deep*, p. 219.

his teeth, he twisted *U-21* first one way and then the other to escape his tormentors. 'The sound of propellors followed us wherever we went and the bombs continued their infernal explosions. The *U-21* shivered with each detonation—and so did we.' The hunt continued for five nerve-wracking hours and then, satisfied that they had destroyed the submarine, the destroyers moved off to rejoin the convoy. After such an experience it was small wonder that few U-boat captains tackled an escorted convoy twice.

U-28 had the misfortune to suffer the same fate as her victim when she sank the ammunition carrier *Olive Branch* in the White Sea on 2 September. Schmidt's second shot landed in the ammunition hold and resulted in an explosion so violent that both attacker and victim perished together. According to one story a heavy motor truck lashed to the deck of the *Olive Branch* was blown high into the air by the force of the blast and landed on top of the surfaced U-boat causing such extensive damage that she sank. There was, however, a disturbing shadow over the incident. The merchant ship's crew refused to take the U-boat's survivors into their lifeboats despite the freezing temperature of the Arctic water with the result that *U-28*'s entire complement died. Inhumanity, it seems, is not always restricted to one side.

Hartmann's *U-49* was rammed and sunk by the steamer *British Transport* on the 11th after two torpedoes fired at the merchant ship had missed. Prompt handling of the freighter brought her bows on to the U-boat and the submarine was ripped open and left to sink, her end hastened by two shots from the steamer's 6-in gun on the poop. War was by now fast becoming a matter of the quick and the dead.

Walther Schwieger's *U-88* struck a German mine in the approaches to the Horn Reefs and the resulting explosion was so intense that observers in another U-boat thought his bow torpedoes had been detonated. Schwieger, of course, was the man who had sunk the *Lusitania,* the *Hesperian,* and the *Cymric,* and his death raised little sympathy in Britain. Other submarines to fall victims of mines in September were *UC-21*, *U-50*, and *UB-32*, while Muller's *UC-42* suffered the fate of self-immolation when she ran into her own minefield off Cork on the 10th, a victim to the same trap as Tebbenjohanns' *UC-44* a month earlier.

The British submarine *D-7* caught Sittenfeld's *U-45* on the surface north of Ireland and sent him to the bottom with a single torpedo and Ernst Voigt, another veteran commander, was lost when *UC-72* was bombed and destroyed by Seaplane *8695* off the Sunk Light-Vessel on the 22nd. The growing influence of air power as an anti-submarine weapon was apparent when, a week later, *UC-6* was attacked and sunk by Seaplane *8676*. *UC-55* succumbed to more conventional methods of defence when she was caught minelaying off Lerwick and depth-charged to destruction by two Grand Fleet destroyers.

But, despite these grave losses, the U-boats continued to strike back savagely. The Q-ship *Stonecrop* was torpedoed and sunk on 18 September after fighting a fierce but unsuccessful duel with another submarine the previous day. The crew of the decoy ship drifted on rafts for six days, in addition to the 31 men killed during the gun battle, a further 13 died of thirst during their week-long ordeal on the rafts. In Arctic waters *U-46* caught and sank four ships in October, the *Zillah*, the *Ilderton*, the *Obj*, and the *Baron Balfour* with the loss of eighteen lives while, far to the south in the warm waters around Madeira, the Azores, and the Canaries, the Italian munition ship *Caprera* was blown sky-high by the guns of Kophamel's *U-151*. In October, also, the cruiser *Drake* was torpedoed while on convoy duty in the North Channel and subsequently capsized and sank while at anchor.

Although details of all the losses are too numerous to include mention must be made of one further incident in which the USS *Jacob Jones*, an American destroyer assigned to Queenstown to boost the anti-submarine patrols in the Western Approaches, was torpedoed and sunk by *U-53*. It was a strange coincidence that this same submarine and skipper, Hans Rose, the first to probe the sea lanes of the American coast back in September, 1916, should be the first to sink a United States destroyer just over a year later. Once the warship had sunk, Rose, with his usual humanity, radioed the exact position of the *Jacob Jones'* lifeboats to Queenstown so that they could be rescued without delay. Then, with the satisfaction of a job well done, he submerged and resumed his patrol.

Once again the U-boats demonstrated that they could destroy reputations as easily as they could sink ships. Sir Reginald Bacon was removed from Command of the Dover Patrol on 29 December, but even more shattering was the enforced resignation of Admiral Sir John Jellicoe as First Sea Lord two days earlier. As he wrote to his old friend Admiral Dudley de Chair shortly afterwards: 'I should like you to know that I did not resign but was dismissed very curtly by the First Lord (the political head of the Royal Navy) without any reason at all being given.'[1] The reason, despite Jellicoe's protest, did not need to be stated. It was very simple. The enemy's submarine campaign was still in danger of winning the war for Germany.

Although Reinhold von Scheer's mighty High Seas Fleet had failed to inflict defeat on Britain's greatest admiral since Nelson the U-boats had succeeded.

[1] *The Sea is Strong*, p. 236.

CHAPTER THIRTEEN

'A battleship is enough for one day'

WITH NEARLY HALF a million tons of merchant shipping to his credit Korvettenkapitan Lothar von Arnauld de la Perière stands supreme as the greatest submarine captain of the war. Yet, strangely, this ace of aces regarded the U-boat service as second best, for he had originally set his heart on serving in the Zeppelin branch of the navy and he never forgot the bitter disappointment he experienced when he was rejected for flying duties. Early in 1916, following an intensive training course at the Kiel Periscope School, he was assigned to the Mediterranean where he was to replace Kophamel who, after bringing *U-35* on the long and dangerous voyage through the Gibraltar Straits, had been promoted to command of the Cattaro Flotilla. Von Arnauld's arrival from Berlin was a little less spectacular than that of the man he was to succeed as captain of *U-35*; he came by train.

On his very first cruise in *U-35* he encountered the Q-ship *Margit* and brought her to a halt with a warning shot across the bows. The 'panic party' took to their boats and von Arnauld took the submarine down while he carefully surveyed the abandoned vessel through his periscope. Satisfied that there was no danger he brought *U-35* to the surface and approached the lifeboats which were lying in a huddle some 800 yards astern of the steamer. By keeping close to the boats the ever-cautious U-boat skipper reasoned that no one would dare attack him for fear of hitting their comrades. But he had not allowed for the cold courage of the British sailor. As soon as the U-boat was fully surfaced the hidden guns on the decoy ship sprang into view and a barrage of shells screamed overhead. Von Arnauld did not believe in mock heroics. The safety of his submarine was his paramount consideration and, risking the charge of cowardice, he took *U-35* down fast—so fast, in fact, that the submarine reached 180 feet before her dive could be checked.

For most commanders such an unnerving experience on a first cruise would have quickly determined them to torpedo without warning in the future. But not so von Arnauld. 'I very rarely torpedoed a ship even when it was authorized,' he explained after the war. 'I much preferred the method of giving warning and doing my sinking by gunfire or by placing explosives aboard. In that way I saved torpedoes.' The shrewdness of his French ancestors was more than apparent when he went on to explain that these methods also enabled him to obtain full details of his victim so that his success could be verified and entered on the records. 'Many officers sank more tonnage than appeared on their records because of their inability to produce names and verifications.'

On his second patrol, in February, he sank the French troop transport *Provence II* with the loss of 990 soldiers and, on 1 March, cruising off Port Said, he put a torpedo into the bows of the British sloop *Primula*. 'The torpedo hit her in the bow and her foremast went clattering down. We gaped with wide eyes at what that boat proceeded to do. Her engines reversed and she started to back at full speed, coming at us, and trying to ram us with her stern.' Von Arnauld let go another torpedo but *Primula*'s skipper dodged it and continued his attempt to back into the U-boat. A third torpedo also missed and von Arnauld almost sighed with relief when his fourth shot scored a direct hit and the gallant little sloop sank. 'Four torpedoes for that tiny wasp,' *U-35*'s commander grumbled. 'I didn't want to come up with any more *Primulas*.'

Otto Hersing, still basking in the glory of his battleship sinkings in the Dardanelles a few month's earlier, bagged another major warship on 8 February when he met up with the old French cruiser *Amiral Charner*. A single torpedo sufficed to blow the bottom out of the ancient ironclad and she went down so fast that only one man from a crew of 335 survived. Two month's later, after an unproductive period transporting Turkish military missions to North Africa, he sank the liner *City of Lucknow* off Malta but, from then onwards, his successes in the Mediterranean dwindled and in February of the following year, Otto was recalled to Germany for service in the North Sea and Atlantic where, as noted in the previous chapter, he added more laurels to his already enviable reputation.

Von Arnauld's departure from Cattaro on 26 July was routine; it was just another patrol and few anticipated that *U-35* would set any records. Both the submarine and her commander were already headline material following an impudent mail run into Cartagena harbour on 21 June when Lothar delivered a personally-signed letter from Kaiser Wilhelm to Don Alfonso, the King of Spain, thanking him for looking after German refugees. *U-35* had remained in the Spanish harbour for the legally permitted 24 hours and had been photographed many times over by the world's pressmen who, for some obscure reason, seemed to find the visit of great news value. Once clear of Cartagena von Arnauld turned this particular cruise to good advantage by claiming thirty-nine victims totalling 56,818 tons before returning to Cattaro for fresh fuel and ammunition.

His July patrol, however, made these earlier achievements look meagre by comparison. When he returned to the Adriatic on 20 August he had sunk no fewer than 54 enemy vessels registering 91,150 tons gross. Proof of his unusual methods showed in the submarine's ammunition tally. *U-35* had fired 900 4.1 inch shells from her deck gun but had only expended *four* torpedoes, a remarkable record that has never been equalled.

Yet this same humane and punctiliously correct U-boat captain was the man responsible for one of France's greatest naval disasters when he sighted the 14,966 ton auxiliary cruiser *Gallia* off Sardinia on 4 October. She was steaming hard at 18 knots on a zig-zag course and it took all of von Arnauld's skill to get her in his sights. 'I had only one torpedo left in the stern tube . . . (and) I could not get a good shot, her zig-zagging was so baffling.' Suddenly *Gallia* turned unexpectedly. She was still 900 yards away and at a difficult angle but Lothar took a chance. His last torpedo streaked away and *U-35* angled down in a steep dive. On hearing the fatal boom of the torpedo exploding he came up to periscope depth to observe the final moments of his victim's death-throes. 'The picture of that foundering vessel sticks in my mind with an un-diminished horror,' he recalled afterwards. There were over 2000 troops on board the steamer and 'there was a wild panic on the stricken vessel's crowded deck. Lifeboats were being lowered by men too much in a panic to let them down slowly and safely. Hundreds of soldiers were jumping into the water and swimming around. The sea became a terrible litter of overturned lifeboats, overcrowded and swamped lifeboats, and struggling men.'[1]

When von Arnauld allowed his crew a brief glimpse through the periscope eye-piece they were as shocked as their captain and an atmosphere of gloom settled over the submarine. France lost over 600 trained soldiers when *Gallia* sank but *U-35*'s captain was too sickened by the carnage to jubilate over his success. 'After what I had seen,' he said very simply, 'I did not feel elated.'

At the end of 1915 there had been eight U-boats operating from the Adriatic bases and a further five working from Turkish harbours. By January, 1917, there were no fewer than twenty-five boats based on Cattaro alone and efforts to bottle up the flotilla in the Adriatic by means of a Dover-type barrage across the Straits of Otranto met with little success although *UB-44*, *UB-52*, and *UB-53*, all came to grief while trying to

[1] *Raiders of the Deep*, p. 152.

pass through the minefields and surface patrols as the war progressed.

The Mediterranean U-boats also laid extensive minefields but they failed to claim victims in any substantial numbers although some of the individual losses were, in themselves, grievous. The White Star liner *Britannic*, serving as a hospital ship and, at 48,158 tons the largest casualty of the war, sank after striking mines laid by *U-73* and it was only by good fortune that all but 21 of her 1125 medical staff and crew were saved. Two days later, on 21 November, 1916, the ex-Union Castle liner *Braemar Castle*, also serving as a hospital ship, had to be beached after striking a mine in the Mykoni Channel. *U-73* had also claimed another important victim some months earlier, in April, when the old battleship *Russell* sank after running into a minefield laid by the U-boat in the approaches to Malta.

Submarines were busy, too, in the Black Sea although they failed to achieve any major successes and sank only ten ships during the whole of 1916. Gansser, a former North Sea veteran, was probably the most successful with his *U-33*. He maintained his reputation for callous brutality by torpedoing the hospital ship *Portugal* in March in an attack which cost the lives of 15 nurses, and then sank the steamer *Kiev*. Turning to more difficult targets he managed to bag the Russian destroyer *Pustchin* off Varna in the same month and rounded off his patrol by shelling Toukhoum lighthouse and the little coastal village of Gradant. He was withdrawn from the Mediterranean during 1917 and, on his return to Germany, was given command of the new submarine-cruiser *U-156* whose activities will be described later.

With sinkings in the Mediterranean running at a satisfyingly high level a further group of U-boats were assigned to Cattaro towards the end of 1916 and more famous names joined Kophamel's flotilla in the Adriatic. Hartwig brought Spiegel's old boat *U-32*, Moraht commanded *U-64* which sailed in company with *U-65*, and Walther Hans skippered *U-52*. It was this latter boat which scored the first success. Arriving off Lisbon on the first leg of her long voyage through the Straits of Gibraltar the U-boat sighted the French battleship *Suffren* limping home to Brest, unescorted, for urgently needed repairs. Two torpedoes streaked towards the lumbering old battleship and she vanished in a mighty explosion that took her entire crew to the bottom with her. *U-65*, too, had an early victory when she sank the 9,223 ton liner *Caledonia* off Malta after taking her master, Captain Blaikie, on board as a prisoner.

By the end of 1916 the U-boats were going from strength to strength in the Mediterranean and in the last half of the year a total of 256 ships, of 662,131 tons, were sunk. Another French battleship went down when Steinbauer's *UB-47* torpedoed the *Gaulois* after gallantly penetrating a screen of escorting destroyers on 27 December. And then, only twelve days later, Kurt Hartwig celebrated the New Year and his arrival in the Mediterranean by sending three torpedoes into the British battleship *Cornwallis* a few miles from Malta. According to Lowell Thomas, the American journalist, Hartwig's first two torpedoes brought the battleship to a halt but failed to sink her. Although under depth-charge attack by destroyers *U-32* stayed close and when it became apparent that the British were preparing to take the crippled giant in tow he fired a third torpedo from a range of three quarters of a mile which tipped the ironclad over on her side. A destroyer moved in to pick up survivors and there was a brief but urgent discussion inside the control-room of the submerged U-boat.

'Shall we get the destroyer?' one of the officers asked.

Hartwig stepped back from the periscope and shook his head. 'No,' he replied quietly, 'a battleship is enough for one day.'

After the war he gave his reasons for the decision. 'It would [have been] too inhuman, even for submarine warfare, to torpedo the destroyer crammed with survivors of the battle-ship.' A sentiment that once again showed that not all U-boat captains were cold-blooded murderers.

Valentiner, always a force to be reckoned with, was creating his own hornet's nest at this time. Leaving the sheltered waters of the Mediterranean in December he set out into the Atlantic and, with typical initiative, stopped a Norwegian ship at gunpoint and then forced her to tow him for three days to save fuel. Arriving at Madeira he promptly sank three vessels; the French gunboat *Surprise*, the cable-ship *Dacia*, and the depot-ship *Kanguru*, a very worthwhile bag of valuable naval auxiliaries. And he concluded his raid by shelling the town of Funchal for two hours before finally making his way back, via Gibraltar, to Cattaro.

The continuing successes of Kophamel's flotilla led the High Command to send further reinforcements from Germany and, by the beginning of February 1917, there were 27 U-boats operating in the Mediterranean and Black Sea, supported by 15 Austrian submarines. Even more important than sheer numbers was the calibre of the commanding officers, nearly everyone of whom was an 'ace' in his own right: von Arnauld, the top-scoring U-boat captain of the war; Forstmann, whose final tally of 380,000 tons put him second on the list; Gansser and Max Valentiner, whose forceful and ruthless methods earned them the odium of war criminals; Otto Hersing, probably the most skilful commander of all; Steinbauer, destroyer of the battleship *Gaulois*, and Heino von Heimburg, whose favourite pastime appeared to be sinking other submarines.

Lack of a centralized escort and patrol organization led to one of the year's early casualties when the Italian troopship *Minas* was torpedoed and sunk off Cape Matapan on 15 February with the loss of 870 lives. She had been escorted to the boundary of the Italian control zone by one of her own destroyers but communication problems prevented the Royal Navy from meeting her as she entered the British zone. When the U-boat found her she was unescorted and completely helpless and it needed little skill to plunge a torpedo into her. The French trooper *Athos* was lost in similar circumstances only two days later with a death-roll that topped a thousand.

Battleships, too, seem to have been at a premium in the Mediterranean theatre. Two French and four British had already gone down as a result of U-boat action when, on 19 March, Robert Moraht, in *U-64*, torpedoed and sank the French battleship *Danton* south-west of Sardinia. 'It was all as easy as pie,' he said afterwards. The ironclad's zig-zag course brought her broadside on to the U-boat and two torpedoes from the bow tubes struck home 'blowing two great holes in its side just at the waterline.' But, just at this moment of triumph, *U-64* decided to play tricks. Losing trim she reared and plunged 'like a badly behaved horse' and, to her skipper's horror, broke surface and exposed her conning-tower in full view of the destroyer *Massue*.

Leaving the sinking battleship to find her own salvation the destroyer leapt towards the U-boat at full speed and Moraht just found sufficient time to dive for safety as the depth-charges rained down. Fortunately it was a short-lived attack and when *U-64* returned to periscope depth a few hours later *Massue* was back alongside her sinking charge, taking off survivors.

Unlike some other captains of the Cattaro flotilla Robert Moraht was a humane and kindly officer. When, on the same patrol, he sank the American tanker *Moreni* by gunfire, he passed bandages and medical supplies to the wounded survivors in the lifeboats and then shook hands with the captain. But Admiral Mountevans—Evans of the *Broke*—who had Moraht in his custody as a POW in 1918 had a totally different impression of the U-boat commander. 'I brought home quite a number of German officers and men, prisoners of war from sunken submarines, including Moraht, a very nasty piece of work, arrogant, insolent, and a well-known murderer with a very bad reputation. [He] was on the list of war criminals to be punished by the Germans themselves.'[1] If Lord Mount-evans' strictures were true it seems surprising that the British Government omitted Moraht's name from their own list of War Criminals. The truth, as usual, probably lies halfway between these two extremes.

Throughout the spring and summer of 1917 the Cattaro-based U-boats continued to wreak death and destruction along the crowded shipping lanes of the Mediterranean and, in April, an inter-Allied conference held at Corfu recommended routing all Far East traffic via the Cape. As in other theatres, the U-boats were having a profound influence on the strategy of the naval war. 218,000 tons were sunk during April and the victims included the Italian liner *Ravenna* sunk without warning by Walther Hans in *U-52* off Genoa on the 4th, followed, a few hours later, by the Ellerman liner *City of Paris* south of Nice with the loss of 122 lives. Von Arnauld, too, was busy and in a five week cruise accounting for 65,000 tons he at one time passed through the Straits of Gibraltar to attack shipping in the Atlantic where he sent 17 steamers to the bottom. On returning to the Mediterranean he was attacked by a French seaplane but escaped damage by diving and, after an uneventful voyage around the toe of Italy and up into the narrow Adriatic, he arrived back at Cattaro to a hero's welcome.

For some reason the Allied naval authorities prevaricated over the introduction of convoys and, although defences were strengthened and the Otranto Barrage reinforced, very few successes were obtained. Their problems were not made any easier by a severe shortage of materials and, at one time, Malta was 'defended' by a line of painted oil drums which misled U-boat commanders into assuming they were net defence buoys marking the edges of minefields. In addition, the

---

[1] *My Adventurous Life*, by Admiral Lord Mountevans (Hutchinson, 1947) p. 129.

Mediterranean was fast becoming a hotch-potch of nationalities; British and French patrols were reinforced by Italian and Greek ships while Portuguese naval vessels operated in the western basin. In February, eight Japanese destroyers with supporting craft made an appearance in European waters, one of them, the *Sakaki*, being damaged by a torpedo on 11 June with 55 casualties.

On 26 May Oberleutnant Friedrich Neumann, commanding *UC-67*, made a deliberate attack on the hospital ship *Dover Castle*. He secured two torpedo hits and the vessel sank six hours later with, fortunately, light casualties. This incident was one of the rare occasions where a U-boat captain was brought to justice for his crime. Neumann was tried at Leipzig in 1921, but obtained an acquittal 'on the ground that he was obeying superior orders.'[1] In view of recent developments in the field of international law it is doubtful if such a defence would have sustained an acquittal today.

Von Arnauld restored a semblance of sanity to the situation when, with a gentlemanly respect for law and humanity, he sank another eleven ships west of Gibraltar during his June cruise. But, from then onwards, merchant ship sinkings began to fall off and the hey-day of the U-boats had passed. The strengthening of the Otranto Barrage contributed to this decline in submarine successes and it goaded the Austrian Navy into launching a savage night attack on the line of drifters which kept a constant patrol watch on its complicated system of nets and minefields. The operation was a partial success for, as a direct result of the raid, the drifters were withdrawn from the Straits at night. In addition, *UC-25* managed to torpedo and damage the British cruiser *Dartmouth* as she withdrew from the battle after she had come northwards to support the light craft against the Austrian heavy units.

The belated introduction of a convoy system also had its effect on sinkings and, from the summer of 1917, the U-boats

[1] *The German Submarine War*, p. 250.

had to fight hard for their victories. On the German side there was a drastic reorganization of the Mediterranean submarines and, in June, Kophamel stepped down as Senior Naval Officer at Cattaro. He was succeeded by Pullen who formed two separate flotillas in the Adriatic with Schultze leading the first and Ackermann the second. Kophamel himself was recalled to Germany and given command of the submarine-cruiser *U-151* and before long he was joined by several other leading aces from the old Cattaro flotilla.

In July losses dropped to 85,000 tons although the Allied defences were by no means completely effective, the P & O liner *Mooltan* being torpedoed by a U-boat while under escort from two Japanese destroyers. Wendlandt, too, had a minor field day on 11 November when, in *UC-38*, he probed the naval forces lying off Syria in support of Allenby's advance on Palestine, sinking the destroyer *Staunch* and the monitor *M.15* before returning to Cattaro for fresh fuel and ammunition. Nosing into the Ionian Sea he found the French cruiser *Chateaurenault* on 14 December and sent her to the bottom without ceremony. But it was his last attack. Destroyers escorting the cruiser dashed to the spot where the tracks of his torpedo began and launched a violent depth-charge assault. The severely-damaged *UC-38* was forced to the surface and a hail of gunfire sent her plunging to the depths for the last time. Oberleutnant Hans Wendlandt's moment of triumph had been somewhat shortlived!

1918 found the Adriatic flotilla faced with an unexpected problem. The repair facilities, more than adequate with the small force of U-boats originally assigned to the Mediterranean in 1915, were clogging up under the persistent demands of the grossly inflated flotillas now serving in the theatre. Matters were at their worst in January when, of 33 operational submarines, only five were at sea, while the remaining 28 were undergoing repairs and refitting. The logistics situation, in fact, became so bad that boats requiring extensive overhaul were being sailed back 4,000 miles to German yards. Their difficulties were in no way lessened when, after two years of argument, the Allies finally appointed Vice-Admiral Sir S. A. Gough-Calthorpe as supreme commander to centralize and co-ordinate anti-submarine operations in the Inland Sea.

Moraht, at sea in *U-64* early in January, achieved only sparse success in comparison with earlier cruises. He sank a total of five ships, including the 13,528 ton American freighter *Minnetonka*, but these were very meagre pickings for such an experienced commander. Trouble, too, in the Austro-Hungarian fleet, including an abortive mutiny at Cattaro, also left U-boat commanders constantly looking back over their shoulders and worrying about the security of their bases while they were away on patrol. There can be little doubt that von Arnauld experienced a sense of relief when he received a recall signal from Berlin to take over the newly commissioned submarine-cruiser *U-139*, and, with a typical lack of flamboyance, he returned to Germany in the same way as he had left, by passenger train.

The convoy system developed by Gough-Calthorpe brought swift returns and, at long last, life in the Mediterranean began to be dangerous for the submarines which had dominated it for so long. On 9 January the escort sloop *Cyclamen* snagged *UB-69* with an explosive paravane and, nine days later, another Flower class sloop, *Campanula*, depth-charged Wernicke's *UB-66* to death while on convoy duty off Cape Bon. Later, in April, a small motor launch operating out of Gibraltar caught *UB-71* on the surface at night, forced her to dive, and then blew her out of the water with two depth-charges. It was learned that the submarine, one of three, had been en route from Germany to reinforce the Cattaro Flotillas.

The merry month of May proved a decided misnomer so far as the U-boat commanders were concerned. Of the sixteen boats on combat patrol no fewer than five were lost. *UB-70* was depth-charged by convoy escorts on the 8th while *U-32* went down under the gunfire from the sloop *Wallflower* while attacking an Alexandria convoy the same day. *UC-35* was shelled and sunk by the French on the 25th while *U-39* was towed into Cartagena by another submarine following damage sustained from a bombing attack by six seaplanes and was interned by order of the Spanish Government. The fifth submarine to be lost was Launburg's *UB-52* which was surprised on the surface by the British submarine *H-4* who sank her opponent with two nicely judged torpedoes.

But despite these successes May was not entirely one-sided and during an attack on a troop convoy en route from Alexandria to Marseilles with much needed reinforcements for the Western Front the Orient liner *Omrah* and the Union Castle liner *Leasowe Castle* both went down following wolf-pack assaults by three U-boats. Yet, in comparison with earlier months, losses were relatively small and it was becoming apparent, at last, that the Allied navies in the Mediterranean had the measure of the submarine menace.

Robert Moraht's sparkling career came to an end in June during a fight with a convoy near Sicily. Having dived underneath a large freighter after an abortive torpedo attack he successfully sank another steamer but suffered an almost direct hit from a depth-charge as he tried to run clear. There was water in the stern compartment, the steering-gear had gone wrong and, worse still, the U-boat was rising to the surface completely out of control. She came up smack in the middle of the convoy and was immediately heavily fired upon by the escorts. *U-64* plunged beneath the waves but, at 60 feet, the diving gear again misbehaved and she shot back to the surface.

'I threw open the conning-tower hatch for a good look round,' Moraht said after the war. 'A destroyer was bearing down on us at full speed to ram us. I gave a frantic order to dive. No use. She would not dive. There was a rending crash. The ram hit the conning-tower. The boat lurched and began to sink.'

U-64 dropped to the bottom like a stone and, with no diving gear working, Moraht had to decide between coming up to face certain death at the guns of the escorts or of sinking to the depths where the U-boat would be crushed to pulp by the pressure of the sea. He gave the order to blow all tanks, closed up the gun crew ready to fight his way out of trouble, and held on tight as the submarine angled to the surface for the last time. It was a desperate fight. *U-64*'s guns fired as the avenging escorts closed in but, against such odds, there could only be one result. An exploding shell wiped out the forward gun crew, another smashed into the conning-tower, while more shattered the pressure hull. Suddenly Moraht found himself standing knee-deep in water as the gallant *U-64* sank beneath his feet. The wireless aerial snagged his legs dragging him down with the sinking boat but he managed to struggle free and, after a short interval in the water, was dragged to safety by a boat from one of the British destroyers. He ended the war in the safety of a POW camp near Ripon but 38 members of *U-64*'s crew were lost.

The famed Otranto Barrage claimed its last victim on 1 August when *UB-53* was seriously damaged on mine nets and was scuttled by her commander to enable his crew to escape. There was a sense of double revenge in the officers' mess at Cattaro a few days later when they learned that *U-47* had torpedoed the French submarine *Circe*. Not only did it redress the balance for *UB-53* it also avenged the loss of the *UC-24* which *Circe* had sunk in the Spring of 1917.

Allied losses for August dropped to 49,000 tons and it seemed that it was all over bar the shouting. But the U-boats kept fighting to the bitter end. The *War Arabis* was torpedoed and sunk off Cape Sigli on 9 September, the *Wellington* and *Tasman* both went down on the 16th, and the 3,309 ton steamer *Bylands* met her end north-west of Cape Villano on 1 October. Successful attacks on submerged U-boats were continually being reported by over-optimistic escort ships but, somehow, their victims always survived. As Vice-Admiral C. V. Usborne commented: 'The war-scarred and wily Germans were a hardy race and many a "certainty" limped [back] into Cattaro. We cannot withhold from these seamen our ungrudging admiration.'[1] High praise indeed from an enemy flag-officer.

One of the last attacks in the central Mediterranean came from a relative newcomer, Oberleutnant Karl Dönitz, who brought his *UB-68* in on the surface for a determined assault on a Malta-bound convoy. Unfortunately for the U-boat the escorts were wide awake and the sloop *Snapdragon*, far more lethal than her name suggested, blasted the submarine with her guns to such effect that Dönitz had to scuttle his boat and surrender.

The end of the war in the Mediterranean, when it finally came, was sudden and disastrous. On 30 October the Ottoman Empire surrendered and the following day Hungary proclaimed her independence from Austria who, in turn, asked for an armistice. But, although her allies were crumbling, Germany was still fighting and Pullen, the flotilla commander at Cattaro, had a difficult decision to make. The four U-boats based on Constantinople had little choice but to surrender and they gave themselves up to the Russians at Sevastopol. The other commanders were ordered to re-fuel and make their way back to Kiel or, should this prove impossible, to sail to Spain and seek internment. The small *UB* and *UC* boats, incapable of the long voyage back to Germany, were scuttled or destroyed, five at Pola and one at Trieste on 28 October; two minelayers, also at Pola, on the 30th; and, the following day, *UB-129* was demolished at Fiume. The remaining fifteen submarines, leaving harbour in ones and twos, set course south and then west for their last great adventure.

Yet, faced with the certainty of defeat, they kept fighting. The *Mercia* and *Suruda* were both torpedoed and sunk without

[1] *Smoke on the Horizon*, by Vice-Admiral C. V. Usborne (Hodder & Stoughton, 1933) p. 266.

warning on 2 November, 1918, and, even as late as the 7th, the Blue Funnel liner *Sarpedon* was attacked by an unknown submarine, but succeeded in avoiding its torpedoes. Moving west the homeless U-boats found the British waiting in the Straits of Gibraltar and each commander was told to try and negotiate the defences independently.

Hartwig, in *U-63*, narrowly avoided being rammed by a destroyer when he surfaced to fix his position and he had to endure a heavy depth-charge attack for his temerity. 'The very closeness of our danger saved us. The depth-bombs were exploding directly below us. They had been set for ninety feet, the depth at which we should normally take refuge. But the enemy was on top of us so fast that we had not the time to get any deeper than thirty feet,'[1] Hartwig explained later. The speed of the attack saved his life and, when things had quietened down, he made his way out into the Atlantic to rendezvous with his colleagues.

U-35, von Arnauld's former boat, was one that failed to make and she limped quietly into Barcelona to accept the humiliation of internment. Johannes Klasing was not so fortunate. His *U-34* was spotted by a motor-launch north of Ceuta and he took the submarine down rapidly as Very lights illuminated the sea. A depth-charge forced him to the surface and the Q-ship *Privet*, now refitted after her fight with *U-85* in March, 1917, was waiting. Her guns opened fire and *U-34* crash-dived as the third shell tore her conning-tower open. Depth-charges were dropped from the stern of the decoy ship and *U-34* went to her final resting place on the bottom, the last U-boat of the war to be sunk in action.

Yet the submarines still had the will and the ability to strike back. Within hours of *U-34*'s final plunge Oberleutnant Kukat, driving his little *UB-50* northwards in a desperate run for home sighted a British battleship in the darkness. The two ships met off Cape Trafalgar, a none-too-propitious location

---

[1] *Raiders of the Deep*, p. 344.

for an enemy of the Royal Navy, but the young U-boat officer
cared nothing for the lessons of history. He turned the submarine towards his opponent and let go two torpedoes. Both
scored direct hits and *Britannia* settled slowly in the water as
the sea poured in. She took more than three hours to sink and,
when Kukat impatiently raised his periscope to check progress,
the battleship's secondary armament opened up with such
venom that the U-boat had to duck quickly beneath the waves.
With only two days of war left both sides could still demonstrate that fighting to the last was a tradition inbred into both
their navies.

Having safely negotiated the Straits of Gibraltar the remaining thirteen submarines of the Cattaro flotilla grouped
themselves together far out into the Atlantic and, in a single
formation, turned north for home. They rounded the tip of
Scotland with the lightness of heart of men returning to their
loved ones after months, and in some cases years, of dangers
and hardships and it was only when they put into a Norwegian
fjord for a brief rest that they learned the horrifying news of
Germany's collapse and the mutiny of the High Seas Fleet.
But Gustav Siess, senior officer and temporary leader of the
homeless flotilla, had not travelled so far to be thwarted. Like
most dedicated career officers of the old Imperial German Navy
duty came first.

'The red flag of revolution floated over Kiel,' he recalled
after the war. 'Mutiny reigned aboard the ships in harbour and
the red flag flew from mastheads. [But] the thirteen U-boats
of the Cattaro base came into harbour in war formation [and]
with war flags fluttering in the breeze.'

It was an appropriate homecoming for a group of gallant
men who had, on the whole, fought cleanly and honourably
to the very last.

CHAPTER FOURTEEN

'One of the luckiest decisions I ever made'

WHEN THE GIANT mercantile submarine *Deutschland* first arrived in American home waters in July, 1916, she came on a peaceful mission and was greeted, deservedly, with congratulations and good wishes on her enterprising success in breaking the British blockade. No one in the United States at the time saw any inherent menace in her huge bulk or in her long range and few stopped to consider that their Atlantic coastline was now open to attack should Germany make naval use of her capacity to construct such submarines for operational purposes.

But the busy unprotected shipping routes along the Atlantic seaboard of the United States exercised a magnetic lure for the tonnage-hungry High Command and, soon after Hans Rose returned to Germany with *U-53* after his pioneer raid in American waters in October, 1916, plans were put in hand to convert the mercantile submarines (there were seven built and building) into long-range U-boats capable of waging war on America's front doorstep. At the same time two more submarine cruisers, designed from the keel up as war vessels, were nearing completion on the building slips of the Krupp's Germaniawerft at Kiel. These latter boats, originally named after the U-boat heroes Schwieger and Weddigen but later numbered *U-139* and *U-140*, were larger even than the *Deutschland* class. Displacing a massive 2,483 tons submerged, they were 311 feet long, and carried six torpedo tubes plus two 5.9 inch deck guns—an armament heavy enough to discourage any ship smaller than a cruiser. They were the largest U-boats completed and commissioned during the war and, appropriately enough, were assigned to two of

225

Germany's leading aces; Lothar von Arnauld de la Perière taking *U-139* and Waldemar Kophamel, former commander of the Cattaro Flotilla, *U-140*. These two submarines, plus the seven ex-mercantile *Deutschlands*, now numbered from *U-151* to *U-157*, were to spearhead a new underwater offensive which would extend the battle against commerce westwards to the Atlantic coast of the United States and beyond the equator, almost to the Cape of Good Hope, in the south. And it was an offensive that promised a rewardingly fruitful harvest.

U-155, the converted ex-*Deutschland*, was first to leave and she made her way slowly out of Kiel harbour on the morning of 24 May, 1917, under the command of Kapitanleutnant Meusel. The Channel passage was far too hazardous for a submarine the size of *U-155* and course was set towards Norway with the intention of turning westwards to skirt the northern tip of Scotland before sailing south. Her new career as a sea-wolf nearly came to a dramatic end when she was only three days out. Passing through an area where British submarines often lay in wait for U-boats returning from patrol she was sighted on the surface by Johann Spiess who was running submerged in his *U-19* scouting for enemy submarines. Failing to recognize the boat through his periscope he sent his crew to action stations and moved in for an attack. It was only when he switched to his high-magnification attack lens that he realized the mysterious submarine had a number of detailed features which were peculiar to German-built boats. Keeping his fingers crossed that he had not encountered a new form of Q-ship, Spiess came to the surface and flashed a challenge. Meusel's reply was correct and the two U-boats saluted each other as they passed by on their respective ways. It had been a near thing.

By July, *U-155* was off the Azores in calm seas and bright sun. With no targets in sight Meusel considered the problem carefully. One important aim of the cruise was psychological, to show the Allies that the U-boats were now capable of

striking far out into mid-Atlantic—but if they encountered no
ships on the vast empty wastes of the ocean their presence
would remain unreported and, therefore, useless. Meusel solved
the problem with typical teutonic thoroughness. Turning
east he made straight for the Azores and, on the morning of
4 July, his two 5.9-in deck guns opened up on the peaceful
town of San Miguel on the island of Punta Delgada. Then,
satisfied that the world now knew where he was, he moved
south towards the shipping lanes running down to the Cape of
Good Hope.

U-155 covered 10,220 miles on this first pioneer cruise and
remained at sea for 105 days before finally returning to
Germany on 4 September. Even more remarkable was the
fact that Meusel only ran submerged for a total of 620 miles,
a sure indication that Allied defences in mid-Atlantic were
woefully deficient. But it was not a tremendously successful
patrol in terms of losses inflicted on the enemy. Only 19 ships
were sunk and, of these, ten were innocent neutrals.

Twenty-four hours before *U-155* tied up to her mooring-
buoy in Kiel harbour at the end of the marathon cruise
Waldemar Kophamel eased *U-151* out of the crowded road-
stead, dipped his flag in salute to the flagship *Baden*, and set the
bows of the U-boat into the choppy seas of the Baltic on the
northward run through the Kattegat and Skagerrak into the
North Sea. Beating against the fierce arctic gales around
the tip of Scotland seemed a far cry from the tranquil waters of
the Aegean where he had been cruising with *U-35* some
twelve months earlier but Kophamel was too old a U-boat
hand to be disturbed by weather. One of the longest-serving
officers in the submarine branch, he had been First Lieutenant
of *U-1* when she made her maiden voyage in 1906, and
had then moved on to command Germany's second submarine,
U-2. *U-151* could certainly not have been in better hands for
her long voyage to the Azores.

Meusel, now transferred to command *U-152*, and Gansser in

U-156, followed a short distance behind Kophamel and the three boats spent part of the time hunting in a pack. According to *The Times* all three submarines entered the harbour of Funchal on 3 December and shelled the town unmercifully, killing many civilians, and destroying the ancient church of Santa Clara. Gibson and Prendergast in their standard work *The German Submarine War*, however, give the date of the Funchal bombardment as 12 December and credit it solely to Gansser's *U-156*. Judging by this particular officer's notorious record of brutality it seems likely that the shelling was, in fact, the work of his U-boat alone and that the other two commanders were not implicated.

In the course of his 12,000 mile cruise Kophamel accounted for 13 vessels totalling 30,000 tons, including one of the toughest opponents he had ever encountered, the Italian steamer *Caprera* sailing from the United States to Genoa. Kophamel attacked on the surface and the Italian crew put up a desperate fight with their stern gun as the little ship crammed on full speed and ran for it. But *U-151*'s surface speed of 12 knots was more than adequate and, slowly, the range closed until, after a three-hour chase, the U-boat scored a hit on the steamer's stern. Suddenly the entire situation changed. The ammunition began exploding in all directions and, in a trice, the Italian crew were taking to the boats and rowing as hard as they could away from the steamer.

With a healthy respect for the exploding ammunition Kophamel stood off some distance and leisurely finished off his victim with the deck guns. Suddenly the reason for the Italian sailors' hurried departure became evident. 'A shell hit the steamer squarely amidships (and) I thought the end of the world had come,' Kophamel recalled later. 'Our eardrums almost burst. Where the steamer had been was now a vast billowing cloud of smoke. The sky darkened and the air became thick and grey . . . the ship had been blown to atoms.' It was only after the dust and fury had settled down that

U-151's skipper learned from the steamer's crew that she had been carrying 1,000 tons of dynamite. As he confessed after the war, his decision to keep his distance from the *Caprera* 'was one of the luckiest decisions I ever made.'

Kophamel rounded off his cruise with a visit to the harbour at St Vincent where he removed a vital cargo of copper from a Norwegian steamer and sank two Brazilian ships. Then, well satisfied, he headed for home. Meusel, too, was back with a tally of 40,000 tons to *U-152*'s credit, leaving only Gansser, with his *U-156*, to prowl the area for more victims.

Having completed an unusual sabotage operation—cutting the five trans-Atlantic telegraph cables which were routed through the Azores—Gansser launched a vicious offensive against everything that crossed his path. The British steamer *Britannia* and the Portuguese lugger *Briziela* were despatched on 8 December and four more luckless ships were torpedoed off Portugal on 4 January. The attacks on the British sailing-vessel *W. C. M'Kay* and the steamer *Artesia* were sufficiently brutal in the execution to warrant Gansser's inclusion on the British government's official list of war criminals and there seems little doubt that *U-156*'s commander carried out a deliberate terror campaign in an attempt to scare shipping from the area.

Despite the submarine-cruiser's ability to cross the Atlantic the High Command, for some reason, continued to send them south. Kolbe in *U-152* was away from 23 December, 1917, until 19 April, 1918, in a cruise that took him as far as the Canary Islands and resulted in a bag of 30,000 tons. Meusel's old command, *U-155*, passed to Eckelmann who left Kiel on 14 January on an arduous patrol that lasted until early May. Luckier than Kolbe, Eckelmann chalked up a tally of 50,000 tons which included not only the Spanish liner *Giralda* but also the Italian fleet collier *Sterope* from whom he thoughtfully re-fuelled before sending her to the bottom. Max Valentiner, already notorious for his ruthlessness, also carried out several attacks off the Spanish and Portuguese coasts during March in his new *U-157* but his luck, on this occasion, was out and he only secured a meagre bag of victims before returning to Germany.

By April Gerke's *U-154* was probing even further south into the tropics and, on the 9th, he surfaced and bombarded the wireless station at Monrovia in Liberia. The next day he shelled the Elder Dempster liner *Burutu* after missing her with a torpedo. The liner's master, Captain Yardley, made a run for it and, after a chase that lasted until nightfall, the liner succeeded in giving Gerke the slip although she had been hit twice and had lost one man killed.

Joined by *U-153* Gerke prowled the sea lanes off West Africa for fresh victims and, on 25 April, the two submarines sighted the Q-ship *Willow Branch* off Cape Blanco. Faced by a brace of cruiser-submarines the British warship fought gallantly for nearly three hours but against such odds there could be but one result and, with their ship blazing from end to end, the crew took to the boats. Even then their cruel ordeal was not over. One lifeboat disappeared and was never seen again. The other drifted helplessly under a blazing sun for nine days. Eleven of the sailors went mad after drinking sea water and twelve more died from exposure and exhaustion after making landfall near the mouth of the Senegal river. Of the total crew of 53 only three men survived, the third officer who had been taken on board one of the submarines as a prisoner-of-war, and two sailors who were picked up by friendly Arabs when they reached the shore. The two U-boats had not escaped scot-free either and they left the field of battle with one dead and seven wounded.

Remaining together, the two submarines turned north for the long run back to Kiel. But fate had not yet dealt them its last blow. Approaching Cape St Vincent on 11 May they fell foul of the British submarine *E-35* commanded by the Dardanelles hero, Guy D'Oyly Hughes. He first sighted *U-154* at 4 pm. She was quartering the surface and apparently waiting to rendezvous with a companion but the constant alterations in her course made it difficult for D'Oyly Hughes to get the enemy square in his sights. After more than two hours of patient stalking he finally manouvered E-35 into an attacking position but, by now, the range was down to 200 yards—almost too close for comfort for British torpedoes took all of that distance to pick up their correct running depth. At 6.18 pm he fired a single shot from his bow tubes. It missed and U-154 moved slowly south-west, apparently unaware that she was under attack. D'Oyly Hughes reacted quickly. Turning to port he began to close on his victim again and when Gerke unexpectedly swung on to a westerly course E-35 found herself in a copy-book position. At 6.25 pm a second torpedo streaked away, followed, a fraction later, by a third. This time there was no mistake. One struck U-154 beneath her forward gun, the other exploded directly under the stern gun. There were two explosions, almost simultaneous, and the giant U-boat vanished from sight leaving a large patch of oil in which three survivors were struggling.

Hughes surfaced immediately and, with the sub-lieutenant, the coxwain, and a seaman up in the bows with life-lines, E-35 ploughed into the oil on her errand of mercy. But it was not to be. Someone in the conning-tower, probably Hughes himself, suddenly spotted the slender stalk of another periscope approaching and, with a mad scramble, the men dashed through the hatch as the submarine submerged. They were none too soon. Three minutes later U-153 fired a torpedo but, fortunately for E-35, it missed and the two submarines, after groping blindly for each other under the water for nearly an hour, lost contact and did not meet up again. Thanks to the intervention of their comrades in U-153 the three survivors from the sunken U-boat were never picked up.

Having apparently tested the temperature by their raids in the mid-Atlantic the High Command decided it was time to try their U-cruisers in American waters and, on 14 April, 1918,

U-151, the former mercantile submarine *Oldenburg*, set out from Kiel under the command of Korvettenkapitan von Nostitz und Jackendorff. The full story of this cruise has survived[1] and the details throw an interesting light on the problems of operating a large submarine many thousands of miles from its home base.

Although under strict orders not to molest any shipping while outward bound on his mission, von Nostitz could not restrain his instincts when, on 2 May, he sighted the steamer *Port Said*. A torpedo was fired but it missed and *U-151* surfaced to destroy her victim with gunfire. But the British steamer managed to run clear and there were anxious faces in the U-boat's control room when they heard her wireless transmitting details of the encounter. 'Violating official instructions is sometimes glorious when you score a brilliant victory,' an officer admitted later, 'but not when all you achieve is failure.'

They reached the Azores safely and the giant U-boat changed course as she headed out into mid-ocean. For the crew the magic of tropical waters was a new experience. 'Flying fish went darting over our bow. Spearfish rushed at our iron sides, struck vainly against the metal, and then went diving away. At night ... the sky was full of stars and a tropical moon beamed down. The sea was alight too. It was aglow with millions of tiny phosphorescent organisms. It seemed as though we were travelling through an ocean of glistening molten metal. The waves were silvery, and a silver mist sparkled over our bow.'

On 13 May they sighted the British India *Huntress* but, again, *U-151*'s torpedo missed and their second erstwhile victim escaped over the rim of the horizon with her wireless screaming the news that an enemy submarine had been sighted. Having been made to look foolish twice von Nostitz now moved with the utmost caution and, for the rest of the voyage, he took care to avoid being seen by any of the various

[1] *Raiders of the Deep.*

ships he met up with. On 21 May, just over a month after leaving Kiel, they made landfall off Cape Hatteras and immediately began preparing for the minelaying operations which formed an important part of their mission.

As they proceeded north they passed a number of ships including an American cruiser returning from target practice, but nothing was allowed to detract from their primary task. Surfacing at night U-151 began laying her deadly cargo off the busy port of Baltimore while von Nostitz made good use of the various coastal navigational lights, which the Americans had thoughtfully left switched on, to fix their exact position. A passing armoured cruiser gave them a momentary scare but her sleepy lookouts apparently failed to see the submarine and she passed by in stately majesty with all lights burning. The U-boat men shrugged in disbelief at America's lack of preparedness and then returned to their duties.

On its way up the coast to Delaware Bay U-151 fell in with three sailing vessels. All were stopped, and their crews were taken on board the submarine as prisoners, before being sunk with explosive charges. Their victims were only small fry but, of more immediate importance, they carried fresh provisions which the U-boat men joyfully looted after weeks of living on canned and dried food. Arriving off New York on 28 May they cut two telegraph cables, one to Europe and the other to South America, and then moved on to Delaware Bay to unload the rest of their mines. There was another sudden scare when the submarine inexplicably went out of control but the trouble did not take long to trace and rectify and U-151 submerged to finish off her second minelaying operation under-water. On returning to the surface von Nostitz found himself in thick fog surrounded by the bellow of fog horns from other ships in the area. With admirable impudence the U-boat skipper remained on the surface and used the submarine's high-pitched siren to clear a passage down the main shipping lane into the open sea.

Bad weather forced them to run south after leaving Delaware Bay and, on 2 June, they despatched yet another sailing-vessel, the *Isabel B. Wiley*, and the steamer *Winneconne*, using the opportunity to off-load their twenty-six prisoners into lifeboats which, equipped with engines, would ensure their safe return to the coast only a few miles away over the horizon. Two more schooners were destroyed after lunch, followed by the steamer *Texel* carrying a cargo of sugar from Puerto Rico to New York and a very busy day ended in the early evening when the passenger ship *Carolina* was stopped for examination. After safely disembarking her passengers and crew she was sunk by gunfire. A total of 14,518 tons of shipping sent to the bottom of the sea in twelve hours left von Nostitz with a warm glow of satisfaction enhanced, no doubt, by the knowledge that not a single person had been killed or injured during the attacks.

The minefields left behind off Baltimore and in the Delaware Bay had, by now, claimed their first victims and a wild panic ensued on shore. German U-boats were reported everywhere, ships were hurriedly recalled to harbour by their owners, freight rates began to rise, and marine insurance premiums soared. While US Navy ships and seaplanes scoured the coast the crew of the *U-151*, now safely many miles away out to sea, exchanged grins as the various messages picked up by the submarine's wireless officer were relayed to their messes.

The U-boat continued her cruise south claiming more victims as she went. On one occasion they picked up a decrepit old sailing-vessel crewed by poor whites and negroes. Their captain explained they were off to Greenland on a whaling expedition and that the boat was owned by a number of poverty-stricken families in Mississippi whose livelihood depended on them. Once again von Nostitz showed genuine compassion and, after a brief hesitation, he agreed to let them continue their voyage unharmed.

The Norwegian ship *Vindeggen*, however, presented a

different problem. One of the steamer's crew was found to have his wife and baby on board and the seas were too rough to contemplate them being placed in the lifeboats. In addition the ship carried a cargo of 2,000 tons of copper which *U-151*'s captain knew was desperately needed by German industry. Von Nostitz considered the matter carefully and decided to hi-jack the copper at the earliest opportunity and then take the woman and child on board the submarine for safety. The *Vindeggen*'s master was given a course to steer and, with *U-151* trailing behind, the Norwegian ship steamed towards an empty quarter of the ocean which von Nostitz had chosen as a rendezvous. One hundred and fifty miles out, the two vessels stopped, and for the next two days the copper was laboriously transhipped to the submarine, much of it being stored in place of the iron ballast she normally carried. Then, with the hi-jack completed, the *Vindeggen* was blown up, her crew placed safely in the lifeboats, and the woman and child taken on board the U-boat where the cook had prepared a special meal for the little girl of cakes, candies, fresh fruits, and whipped cream, and she 'became the ship's darling.'

With the destruction of the *Heinrich Lund* that same evening *U-151*'s tally rose to 14 ships sunk and, as she sailed into the deepening dusk, she towed a string of lifeboats behind her which were later cast off within sight of a patrol boat which took all the survivors aboard. With her errand of mercy accomplished *U-151* turned northwards again in search of more victims. But her mission was now nearly over. Fuel was running short and, after two days without sighting a thing, von Nostitz turned his back on the American coast, set course to the east, and began the long run back to Germany.

The schooner *Samoa* and the sailing-ship *Kringsia* were both sent to the bottom the following day and, on 18 June, the U-boat torpedoed the British steamer *Dvinsk* without warning. As the ship was defensively armed von Nostitz had some excuse for the attack and, in any case, the steamer's crew got away in their boats before the ship actually sank. But they were 400 miles from land and their chances of survival were slim. Only two boats were ever found, one after drifting for eight days, the other after ten days. It was the only black mark against von Nostitz in the whole of the long cruise but it was enough to have him branded as a war criminal by the British Government.

An abortive attack on the ex-German liner *Kronprinz Wilhelm* on the return leg of the cruise led to an unusual reversal of roles. Having dodged the torpedo which von Nostitz had fired the liner steamed hard in the direction of its source and began dropping depth-charges. *U-151* went deep and her crew stared at each other 'pale as death' as explosions rocked and buffeted the submarine. *U-151* went deeper and then, suddenly, she was out of control. Soon the depth gauges were registering 180 feet and she was still dropping. The submarine had only been tested to a depth of 150 feet and the hull seemed certain to cave in under the crushing pressure of the sea and, unconsciously, all eyes went to the erect bearded figure of the captain as he struggled to save them. They dropped to 273 feet and, in a last desperate attempt to save his boat, von Nostitz ordered all tanks to be blown under high pressure. The extra power worked. She steadied and stopped falling. Gradually, rising faster and faster, she shot to the surface. There was a wild scramble for the guns but, this time, fortune was on their side. The *Kronprinz Wilhelm* had long since passed over the horizon, well satisfied that her depth-charges had destroyed another U-boat and, when *U-151*'s crew rushed out on deck, they found only the emptiness of the sea waiting for them.

The remainder of the voyage back to Germany passed without incident although, while running through fog one day, the Cunard liner *Mauretania* enjoyed her second escape from destruction at the hands of a U-boat when von Nostitz allowed her to pass unharmed. Kiel was reached at 9.30 am on the morning of 20 July, 1918, and *U-151*'s log registered a total of 10,915 miles, a tremendous distance for a single patrol in those days. Twenty-three ships amounting to 61,000 tons had been sunk and a further four had met their end after striking the mines she had scattered in her path. Prophetically one of the officers, Frederick Körner, remarked at the end of the cruise: 'To those who can see into the future surely this is a warning of what later wars may bring. For the day will come when submarines will think no more of a voyage across the Atlantic than they do now of a raid across the North Sea . . . America's isolation is now a thing of the past.'

The undoubted success of *U-151*'s cruise encouraged the High Command to send more of their giant U-boats to the American coast and, even before von Nostitz had returned, both Kophamel, in *U-140*, and Richard Feldt, in *U-156*, left Kiel on similar missions. Kophamel had an uneventful patrol which kept him at sea until October but, for such an experienced commander, his pickings were meagre and he returned with a disappointing bag of 30,000 tons. Feldt was even more unfortunate. Having laid several minefields along the American coast his boat was sunk on 25 September in the newly-completed Northern Barrage when he was 130 miles off Bergen. There were no survivors. The great mine barrier across the top of the North Sea had been laid by units of the United States Navy and, in the circumstances, there was an element of poetic justice in the fact that the 13,680 ton American cruiser *San Diego* should have fallen victim to one of the mines which Feldt himself had laid off Fire Island, New York. The coincidences of war can, indeed, be ironic.

Eckelmann in *U-155* and Franz in *U-152*, Meusel's old boat, both left Kiel in August for further raids on the New England coast but were both recalled during October before commencing serious operations and did not finally arrive back in Germany until after the Armistice. Max Valentiner, who was also at sea in *U-157* when the war ended, put in to Trondheim on 11 November rather than return to the revolutionary chaos of the German dockyards and his colourful career ended in a Norwegian internment camp. It was probably a wise choice for Max knew that he would be facing war crime charges if Britain or one of the other Allies could have got their hands on him. Droescher, in *U-117*, was also recalled from the American coast during October but there are no records available of his patrol or of his final fate.

The great assault on the coastal shipping routes of the United States was over, dying with a whimper rather than a snarl.

It was left to the irrepressible Lothar von Arnauld to end the saga of the U-cruisers on a note of excitement. Patrolling in the vicinity of Cape Finisterre at the entrance to the Bay of Biscay with his new *U-139* he ran into a ten-ship convoy escorted by two armed merchant cruisers. The ships were following an intricate zig-zag course and Lothar's first torpedo missed its target. He dived deep as a precaution against depth-charges but, when no attack developed, he decided to fight it out on the surface. It was a risky decision to take but, as we have noted earlier, Germany's leading U-boat ace always preferred using his guns to his torpedoes.

The submarine surfaced in the centre of the convoy and every ship opened fire as the U-boat appeared. Von Arnauld's men fought back gallantly but things were too hot even for Lothar and he thrust *U-139* below the surface again in a crash dive. They were only just in time. As the U-boat dipped beneath the waves one of the British guns sent a shell crashing into the sea right on top of the submarine and the crew could hear the fragments of hot steel thudding against the hull plates. A depth-charge attack followed but *U-139* was too deep to be caught and, as the noise of the explosions died away, von Arnauld came up for another attack. The convoy was, by now, steaming hard for the horizon but the submarine's powerful MAN diesels were more than a match for the British coal-burners and, running on the surface, U-139 soon came within striking distance again. On this occasion the U-boat managed to damage two of the merchant ships with gunfire before, under the threat of a determined ram attack by the escorts, she was forced to dive for cover a third time. Another depth-charge attack followed and, when this had died away, the unshaken and imperturbable von Arnauld climbed to periscope depth to spy out the situation once more.

One of the steamers was listing badly and, anxious to complete the kill, U-139 prepared to finish her victim off with a torpedo. But the patrol boats spotted the stalk of the submarine's periscope and Lothar had to seek safety in the depths yet again. It was pitch dark the next time he tried and, anxious to escape from the hornet's nest he had stirred up, von Arnauld took a snap shot with the bow tubes. There was a satisfying explosion and it was patently clear to everyone on board the U-boat that their victim had been hit, finally and fatally. But then came a terrifying sequel!

'Less than a minute later there was a terrible crash overhead and our boat shook from stem to stern as if it had been cracked open by the giant blow. The lights went out. Water rushed in from above. The boat listed to one side.'

The chance in a million had happened. With her bottom blown out by the exploding torpedo the steamer had settled immediately and was sinking directly on top of them!

U-139 plummetted down like a stone, her victim carrying her to the sea bottom in a morbid death grapple that could only end 3,000 feet below on the ocean floor with both vessels crushed to pulp by the inexorable pressure of the sea. Von Arnauld seemed unperturbed. He passed instructions to the other officers in the control room and the crew moved quickly through the boat, checking leaks, shutting off power circuits, and setting the pumps in motion.

'Air pressure all tanks,' Lothar commanded quietly and there was a high pitched hiss of air as the valves were turned. The submarine's wild descent eased. She lurched under the immense strain and there were loud bangs as various pieces of deck equipment snapped under the strain and then, suddenly, U-139 broke clear. The sinking ship slid away while the U-boat shot upwards with all three periscopes broken. Even now her troubles were not over. The convoy escorts were waiting and von Arnauld was forced to dive again as yet another deluge of depth-charges showered down. But respite was near at last. Under Lothar's expert guidance U-139 gave her pursuers the slip and crawled quietly away on her electric motors—the sounds of the exploding depth-charges slowly receding into the distance as they ran clear. When, an hour later, von Arnauld rose to the surface the sea was black and empty. Only the beams of the searchlights far to the north indicated that the British were still looking for him. Grasping the conning-tower rail in silence for a few moments he stared into the darkness as if recapturing some forgotten moment from his memory. Then, with a last quick glance at the search-lights, he hurried below and set course in the opposite direction while his crew began the tedious task of patching the damaged hull with cement.

The convoy action was von Arnauld's final brush with the enemy he had fought so fiercely for two years. As the sub-marine approached the Azores the High Command's general recall signal was received and U-139 swung north in a wide circle. Blue diesel smoke belched from her exhausts as she increased speed and the Imperial ensign at her stern seemed to droop disconsolately with the humiliation of defeat. Germany's greatest U-boat ace had completed his last patrol.

CHAPTER FIFTEEN

'We must and we will succeed'

THE FINAL DEFEAT of Imperial Russia, completed by the
Treaty of Brest-Litovsk signed by the Bolsheviks in December
1917, released Germany's entire potential for an assault in the
west and, for the first time since the failure of their offensive
against Paris in August, 1914, the possibility of victory looked
bright to the military pundits in Berlin. To strike fast and hard
before the Americans could arrive on the Western front in any
worthwhile numbers was the only solution which the Kaiser
and his army advisers could now foresee. And no one had any
doubts that the German army could do it.

With the High Seas Fleet bottled up in its bases the Navy
looked to the U-boats as its strongest weapon and, to ensure
that it was wielded with maximum efficiency, the operational
direction, training, and construction of submarines, was
centralized under a newly formed U-boat Office with Kommodore Andreas Michelsen in command. 1917 had already seen
the ordering of 273 more submarines ranging in size from
giant U-cruisers to twenty 360 ton *UF*-type coastal defence
boats. But even more important than these paper programmes
was the fact that a total of 103 new submarines had been
commissioned and put into service—the largest number for
any year of the war. And, as the news filtered back to the
British admirals in Whitehall, it became more than apparent
that the German Navy had selected the U-boat arm as its
main striking force and was relying on the premise that
success could only be achieved by sheer weight of numbers.

These drastic reorganizations had little effect on the day-to-
day routine of the war and submarine captains and their

crews still faced the same problems and dangers as before. Aggressive commanders of the Flanders Flotilla continued to hazard all on a quick dash through the Dover defences at night and Losz, skipper of *UB-57*, always gave his comrades the same advice: 'Go through on the surface. The patrol boats are blind. They can't see a thing. I go through under their very noses.' And so he did, again and again, with an impunity that gave strength to his boast until, on 14 August, he met up with a blind unseeing mine that blew him and his submarine to atoms.

But where physical defences often failed the psychology of silence achieved more powerful results. Acting on Jellicoe's advice the British Admiralty made a point of never indicating how or where their U-boat victims perished. The intention was to demoralize submarine crews and make them prey to rumours each time one of their flotilla mates disappeared while on patrol. The policy, however, brought unexpected strategic results. In January, 1918, four U-boats were sunk, all well outside the area of the main Channel defences. *U-87*, actually lost on Christmas Day although this was not known to the U-boat Office at the time, had been rammed and sunk in the Irish Sea; *U-93*, the boat which Ziegner had brought back to Germany after the fight with *Prize*, was accidentally run down by a merchant ship off the Lizard; *U-84* went to the bottom after a savage fight with *PC-62* in the St George's Channel; and *U-95* just disappeared somewhere down-channel, a victim of the unknown hazards of the sea. With no glimmer of information from enemy sources the U-boat Office concluded that all four submarines had been destroyed in the Dover defences and, as a precautionary measure, all U-boat captains were ordered to proceed north about Scotland in future patrols. Michelsen's cautious attitude was partially justified by events for, during January, both *UB-35* and *U-109* were lost in action with ships of the Dover Patrol.

But, even in the north, a new threat was growing. Grinding away quietly and efficiently in the chill mists and gale-swept wastes of the area between Norway and the Shetlands the American Navy were progressing mile by mile with their vast project to lay a mine barrier across the top of the North Sea. And, once completed, the U-boats faced yet another hazard each time they set out on patrol.

Hospital ships, too, after a long period of immunity, came under attack again with the dawning of the New Year. The 7,308 ton *Rewa*, on passage from Malta with 279 patients on board, was torpedoed on the night of 4 January by Werner's *U-55*. The mercy ship was running fully lighted and carrying all the obligatory recognition signals but even this was not enough to deter Wilhelm Werner who, it will be remembered, was the officer responsible for the *Torrington* atrocity almost exactly a year earlier. He repeated the attack on 10 March in similar circumstances when he sent a torpedo into the side of another hospital ship, the *Guildford Castle*, as she steamed up the Bristol Channel carrying 438 patients which she had brought back to 'Blighty' from Cape Town. On this occasion Werner's blood-lust went unsated. The torpedo failed to explode and the hospital ship docked at Avonmouth a few hours later none the worse for her experience. When her hull was examined later experts found a series of dents and abrasions down her port side where the torpedo had struck her before passing harmlessly astern.

But even Werner's brutality paled into insignificance beside the actions of Kapitanleutnant Patzig, commander of the 946 ton *U-86*. He, too, selected a hospital ship as his victim although, by good fortune, she was not carrying any patients at the time. At 9.30 pm on the night of 27 June the 11,423 ton *Llandovery Castle* was 116 miles from the Fastnet Rocks and, in accordance with International Law, she was fully lighted with large red crosses on her funnels and her hull brilliantly illuminated by powerful lamps. *U-86* fired a single torpedo which struck her No 4 hold and, within ten minutes, the ex-liner had disappeared.

Patzig brought *U-86* up and watched the cluster of lifeboats silently for a few minutes before calling the master's boat alongside. The U-boat commander then alleged that there were eight American aviators on board but Captain Sylvester, the *Llandovery Castle*'s master, quickly refuted the claim. He explained that the vessel had been a hospital ship and pointed out that, in the lifeboat with him, were seven Canadian medical officers. He did not add, as he might have done, that there were fourteen nurses in the other boats.

U-86 turned away from Captain Sylvester's lifeboat and glided slowly towards the others. Blue smoke belched from the exhausts as Patzig put on speed and then, according to Sir Henry Newbolt, he 'took his U-boat on a smashing-up cruise among the survivors and by hurling it hither and thither he succeeded in ramming and sinking all the boats and rafts except one (the master's boat) which escaped. The survivors in this boat heard the sound of gunfire behind them for some time (and) it can only be conjectured that the murderers were finishing their work with shrapnel.'[1]

It was, beyond doubt, the most cold-blooded and atrocious crime of the entire war for there could be neither rhyme nor reason for Patzig's brutal murder of the 14 nurses and the rest of the crew. The master's boat, with 24 survivors aboard, was eventually picked up 50 miles from the shore by a destroyer but, of the remaining 234 souls on the hospital ship, no trace was ever found. *U-86* had done her killing very thoroughly.

After the war Patzig and his lieutenants, Boldt and Ditmar, were indicted for trial but the U-boat commander succeeded in escaping to Danzig before the court was actually convened. When the trial took place at Leipzig in July, 1921, it was revealed by the prosecution that only Patzig, the two officers, and the gunner, were on deck during the shelling and that these four men were solely responsible for what had happened. Boldt and Dittmar each received a four year sentence for their

[1] *Submarine and Anti-Submarine*, p. 176.

part in the incident but Patzig, the instigator of the crime, was never brought to justice.

Despite the strengthened defences and the increased number of ships available for anti-submarine patrol, losses continued at a high rate and, in February, 1918, sixty-eight British merchant ships were sunk by U-boats with the loss of 697 lives. In terms of tonnage 224,501 went to the bottom—a reduction on the 1917 figures but still too much for comfort. Among the victims was another hospital ship, the *Glenart Castle*, torpedoed and sunk by *UC-56* on the 26th. Heavy seas had been running when the ship went down but Kiesewetter, the U-boat's captain, ignored the cries for help from the survivors and by morning only thirty were left alive. It was, like the *Llandovery Castle*, an appalling tragedy. Eight nurses, fifty RAMC staff, and ninety-five of the crew were lost and Kiesewetter's name joined those of Patzig, Werner, Neumann, and the other killers of the sea on the British list of War Criminals.

The increasingly heavy toll of U-boats which was now being taken by mines, net defences, surface patrols, and sea-planes, began to have its effect on the quality of the crews. By January, 1918, the old volunteer system had broken down and both officers and men were drafted into the submarine service as further boats were commissioned. In his history of the Queenstown Command, Keble Chatterton records that when *U-110* was sunk in a fierce fight with the destroyers *Moresby* and *Michael* on 15 March the survivors from her crew 'were found, as had long been expected, to be very young and inexperienced. Clearly Germany was getting to the end of her resources as regards submarine personnel.'[1] But, even if this was true, they had certainly put up a tough fight.

U-110 had been caught submerged at 130 feet after torpedoing the 10,037 ton *Amazon* off Malin Head. Six depth-charges shook the submarine badly and her diving-gear was seriously damaged by the explosions. Seeking safety in the depths

[1] *Danger Zone*, by E. Keble Chatterton (Rich & Cowan, 1934) p. 331,

Korvettenkapitan Karl Kroll took her down to 300 feet but the tremendous pressure of the sea caused numerous leaks in the hull and he was forced to bring the U-boat to the surface to avoid disaster. *Michael* was five miles away when the submarine appeared but she opened fire immediately and Leutnant zur See Busch was killed as he led the gun's crew out on deck for a last desperate stand. More hits were scored and Kroll, assembling his men on deck in their life-jackets, ordered them to jump into the sea. *U-110* was by now half awash and, after being rammed by one of the destroyers, she sank rapidly leaving only ten survivors swimming in the water. Karl Kroll, like the rest of the crew, went down with his boat.

But not all U-boat men fought so hard and the inexperience noted by Keble Chatterton was beginning to tell. On 30 April a small armed drifter, *Coreopsis*, spotted *UB-85* on the surface near the notorious Maiden Rocks. It was 2.45 in the morning and, although it was still dark, it seemed too good a chance to miss. The drifter crammed on full speed, headed towards the shadowy shape of the submarine, and opened fire. Two of the first three shots scored direct hits and the drifter's crew prepared themselves for a stern battle. The U-boat carried double the weight of armament and, handled even moderately well, could blow the impudent little fishing vessel out of the water with ease. But Gunther Kresch, her captain, had no stomach for a fight even when the odds were soundly in his favour. A Very light soared up from the submarine's conning-tower and, across the dark waters, the men on *Coreopsis* could hear the U-boat crew shouting in well-trained teutonic unison: 'I will surrender—we are your prisoners.'

Watched cautiously by the drifter the German sailors jumped into the water one by one where they were quickly picked up by the fishing-vessel's dinghy. At the last minute, when it seemed likely that the U-boat would fall into the enemy's hands in one piece, Krech opened the valves and scuttled her—much to the disappointment of the drifter's skipper, Lieutenant Peat, RNR. When asked why he had surrendered with so little resistance the young U-boat commander explained: 'I had been down two days. My crew were all ill with gas; I could not submerge as my conning-tower was damaged, and as I saw you still firing, and saw other ships, what was the use?'[1] What, indeed, from a man who, like so many of his comrades, had lost the will to win?

The U-boat service as a whole, however, had not yet admitted defeat and many officers still displayed a dogged determination to win that compared well with the verve and elan seen during the early days of the war. Spiess, a submarine veteran with an equally veteran boat, *U-19* which dated back to 1913, attacked the 17,515 ton Armed Merchant Cruiser *Calgarian* early in March and put a torpedo into her from a range of 200 yards. She was a well-built ship and, with her crew reacting quickly to the emergency by closing all watertight doors, she remained comfortably afloat for some time. Other vessels hurried to help and within hours she was protected by a screen of seven destroyers, eleven trawlers, and three sloops—more protection, in fact, than was usually found in a full-scale convoy. Spiess refused to be deterred and, determined not to be cheated of his victim, he penetrated the screen and put two more torpedoes into the unfortunate *Calgarian* to seal her fate. Faced by such formidable opposition *U-19*'s captain certainly displayed more than usual gallantry by his persistent efforts to secure a kill.

The Killing Time flourished for both sides as the winter of 1918 passed into spring. February saw a world tonnage of 318,900 tons sunk by U-boats or mines. The total for March rose to 342,500 tons, fell in April to 278,700 tons, and increased slightly again for May to 295,500 tons. But the submarines suffered heavily too; three destroyed in February, seven in March, including *UB-106* lost accidentally in the Baltic and

[1] *Danger Zone*, p. 334.

UC-48 interned by Spain following battle-damage sustained while fighting off British patrols, and a further seven in April.

May was a black month for the U-boat Office with sixteen submarines destroyed including Claus Rucker's *U-103* which was rammed and sunk by the luxury liner *Olympic*. Once again the inexperience of the crew contributed to the loss of a veteran commander. Rucker had already seen much service in the Mediterranean with *U-34* and he had been switched to command the new *U-103* with orders to hunt the troop-carriers bringing the American Expeditionary Force to France. He found the *Olympic* coming up-Channel escorted by four US destroyers and, with experienced skill, he placed his boat in the exact position necessary for a successful attack. But, at the last moment, the crew failed to bring the after-torpedo tubes ready for action and Rucker had to break off his interception and find another attack position. While passing alongside the liner with his periscope poking above the surface, further incompetence by the men controlling the diving trim caused the submarine to break surface and she was quickly spotted by the troopship's look-outs. A shot rang out but the range was so close that the shell passed harmlessly over the top of the conning-tower. *Olympic's* helm went hard over and she swung towards the U-boat which was desperately attempting to turn inside the liner's turning circle. But it was too late. The bows of the former White Star liner ripped into *U-103's* hull and, as the submarine bounced and jolted down the length of the liner, the tip of *Olympic's* port propeller cut her victim open. The U-boat's bows swung up, pointed to the sky for a few seconds, and then slid back on her last dive to the bottom. Rucker and sixteen of his crew were picked up by the destroyer *David*, a gesture of mercy that contrasted vividly with Rucker's own treatment of the trawler *Victoria* in June, 1915, when he had mercilessly shelled her crew to death.

Two other incidents from May, 1918, deserve mention. On

the 24th Wilhelm Kiesewetter, the man who had sunk the hospital ship *Glenart Castle*, crawled into the Spanish port of Santander for internment with his *UC-56* crippled and, on the last day of the month, *UC-75* was rammed so hard by the old destroyer *Fairy* during a convoy battle that both submarine and attacker sank together.

There was a certain callousness about *The Times'* report of *UB-74*'s demise following a spirited fight with the armed yacht *Lorna* off Portland Bill: 'So decisive was the result that only one German prisoner was picked up and he died from his injuries within three hours.' Sir Henry Newbolt's account of the action throws a vivid light on the horrors facing the U-boat crews when the cards were down. Having dropped two depth-charges the crew of the *Lorna* suddenly spotted four objects in the water bobbing about in the disturbance caused by the explosions.

'The next moment was a terrible one. As *Lorna*'s third depth-charge dropped into this seething cauldron, cries of "*Kamarad*!" were heard and those on the yacht's deck, looking back as she raced over, saw the new explosion hurl into the air the bodies of four men, who for a brief instant had been survivors from the sunken U-boat.'[1] When *Lorna* returned to pick them up 'one was found still crying "Help" and "*Kamarad*" but the other three were already dead.'

The writing was on the wall in other ways. In the spring of 1917 the U-boats had been destroying one ship for every two days spent on patrol. By the early summer of 1918 the average had dropped to one ship for every *fourteen* days of patrolling. Yet the German High Command continued to pin their hopes of victory on the submarines and, even as late as June, a further 124 U-boats were placed on order, none of which could possibly be ready for service before January, 1919. Admiral Scheer, still doggedly optimistic despite the shattering losses of the previous month, continued to claim that victory was

[1] *Submarine and Anti-Submarine*, p. 225.

possible. 'We could achieve it by this means [the U-boats] alone . . . *we must and we will succeed.*'[1]

The June losses dropped to 255,500 tons but rose fractionally to 260,900 tons in July. In exchange Germany lost another nine U-boats; one, *UB-65*, suffering a mysterious fate while under attack by the American submarine *AL-2*. Apparently before *AL-2* had fired her torpedoes there was a tremendous explosion and *UB-65* blew up of her own accord. No one quite knows what happened but it seems likely that a magnetic pistol in the snout of a German torpedo detonated prematurely, blowing the submarine up as it exploded in the tube. An alternative theory claims that a second U-boat, known to be in the vicinity at the time, torpedoed her flotilla mate by accident.

In Berlin hopes were raised when the August sinkings rose to 283,800 tons but were quickly dashed by a dramatic fall to 187,800 tons in September. Could the promise of April, 1917, ever be fulfilled?

Gone were the halycon days when a U-boat could meet up with, and sink, as many as four ships in a single afternoon. Oberleutnant Schtiendorff, the unfortunate skipper of *UB-74*, sank only three ships during seven days on patrol before he was sunk by *Lorna*. And Kresch, the commander of *UB-85* fared even worse. In the fourteen-day patrol that culminated in his surrender to the drifter *Coreopsis* he had sighted only six ships, and had missed every one with his torpedoes. In June the *U-98*, one of Germany's most modern submarines, sank only one small neutral ship during an entire twenty-three day patrol but even more revealing were the numerous counter-attacks she was forced to endure in that time.

Three days out from Emden a British submarine, lurking in ambush, attempted to torpedo the U-boat but missed and, as *U-98* entered the Irish Sea, a second submarine also made an abortive attack. On the tenth day of the patrol she was depth-charged by destroyers escorting a large merchant ship and,

[1] *The Most Formidable Thing*, p. 244.

later the same day, escorts from another convoy forced her to make an emergency crash dive. Having been attacked both from the surface and underneath the unfortunate U-boat was next assaulted from above the surface when a British airship straddled her with bombs while she was manoeuvering into position to attack a third convoy. In Cardigan Bay a pattern of twelve depth-charges exploded in *U-98*'s vicinity after a hydrophone flotilla picked up the hum of her electric motors below the surface and, shortly after this escape, the U-boat had to evade a determined torpedo attack from yet another British submarine. Her final frustration came when, having located a large convoy escorted by destroyers, airships, and a kite balloon, she was forced to break off her attack by anti-submarine patrol ships which had picked her up on their hydrophones.

With such experiences fresh in their minds it is not surprising that U-boat captains looked red-eyed, grey faced, and haggard when they brought their rust-streaked sea wolves back to harbour. Constant counter-attacks were bad enough but when the success of victory also eluded them the strain became, suddenly, too much.

Yet the tried and tested veteran commanders would still snatch a prize where their less experienced comrades failed. Ernst Hashagen, a U-boat skipper who had taken part in the first unrestricted campaign of 1915 and who had eight combat patrols to his credit, found the French cruiser *Dupetit-Thouars* steaming hard to rendezvous with a convoy which she was to escort into Brest. It was sunset and the deep red of the sky made a dramatic back-cloth as *U-62* steered a converging course with her intended victim. Two torpedoes leapt from the bow tubes and a billowing cloud of smoke was proof enough that both had hit. The cruiser sank in twenty minutes and Hashagen turned his boat away to avoid the inevitable retribution which would follow when a pack of avenging destroyers arrived on the scene.

Although the rate of sinkings was falling with every passing day the U-boats were still grabbing victims when opportunity presented itself. On 12 September *U-82* sent the *Galway Castle* to the bottom south-west of Ireland. The sea was extremely rough and many of the lifeboats were swamped by the waves. 143 men went to their death as a result. On the 14th the steamer *Gibel-Haman* sank in the Channel with the loss of 21 lives, and another 43 merchant seamen went down in *Polesley* in the same area seven days later. It was estimated that one U-boat alone, operating off south-west England in September, sank no fewer than nine different ships with a loss of 202 innocent lives.

The notorious Flanders Flotilla had long been a thorn in the flesh of the British and numerous attempts had been made to stop the little *UB* and *UC* boats operating from their inland bases around Bruges. As the war progressed air raids on the submarine pens became almost continuous and ships of the Dover Patrol also assisted with bombardments of the Belgian coast on more than one occasion. Finally, in a desperate effort to seal the sea wolves in their lair, a gallant and memorable blocking operation had been carried out by volunteer units of the Royal Navy on St George's Day, 1918. The submarines, snugly secure in their concrete-roofed pens well inland from the coast, usually made their way out into the North Sea by means of the Belgian canal system. One exit was situated at Zeebrugge, the other at Ostend. Based on a plan prepared by Vice-Admiral Roger Keyes, simultaneous operations were mounted against both exits but, unfortunately, only one, at Zeebrugge, succeeded. The heroic raids cost the British Navy 635 casualties but, with their Ostend bolt-hole still clear, the U-boats continued to use their inland bases with impunity and it was only when the advances of the Allied armies along the coast threatened to overrun the vast complex of repair docks, torpedo stores, and barracks, at Bruges, that the order to evacuate was reluctantly approved by the High Command.

All available submarines escaped north to German harbours except for four, caught in dry-dock under repair, which had to be scuttled by their fleeing crews. For once the 'poor bloody infantry' had succeeded where the Royal Navy had failed.

September, too, saw the loss of Beitzen, the man who had laid the minefield on which Lord Kitchener had perished in 1916, when his new submarine *U-102* struck a mine in the Northern Barrage and went down with all hands. There was a certain irony in the fact that he should have died by the same blind instrument of destruction as his illustrious victim.

Even Scheer was showing signs of despair by now. 'Many a U-boat with a splendid and experienced crew did not return,' he lamented in his memoirs. 'The results of the last months had shown that the successes of individual boats had steadily decreased.' The lure of victory which had continued to burn bright in his eyes even in these final desperate weeks was, at last, growing dim. Lowering his sights to the realities of the situation he no longer sought victory, only 'a tolerable peace.'

Fighting back like cornered dogs the U-boats could still send a shudder of horror through the world by their misdeeds. On 4 October the Japanese liner *Hirano Maru* was sunk in the Irish Sea during a violent storm and a large number of children were amongst the toll of 292. And, just a few days later, the Irish mail-boat *Leinster* went down in thirteen minutes after being struck by two torpedoes taking a further 176 men, women, and children, to the bottom with her.

'Brutes they were when they began the war,' Arthur Balfour, the British Foreign Secretary, exclaimed on hearing the news, 'and, as far as I can judge, brutes they remain at the present moment ... it was pure barbarism, it was pure frightfulness, deliberately carried out.'[1] It was also a worthy epitaph to the U-boat war that had raged for four years and which was, at last, reaching its bloody end.

Despite Scheer's failing optimism, plans were still being laid

[1] *The German Submarine War*, p. 322.

for a continuation of the war into 1919. While GHQ was meeting at Cologne to discuss the possibilities of obtaining an armistice, senior officers of the U-boat Office were conferring with ship-builders about the construction of more submarines authorized by the Hindenburg Submarine Building Programme the previous month. If all else failed the U-boat arm of the Navy remained determined to fight to the bitter end.

By 20 October Ostend, Zeebrugge, Bruges, and the other Flanders bases had been evacuated and the work of the U-boats rendered more difficult by the increased passage time to the trade routes of the Channel. Life was becoming increasingly dangerous and it was estimated that, by October, boats of the Flanders Flotilla only made an average of six patrols before being destroyed.

British submarines succeeded in bagging two of the last U-boats to be destroyed in action. On 16 October Meyer's *UB-90*, completed only a few month's earlier, was caught on the surface in the Skagerrak recharging her batteries and was torpedoed by *L.12* and, on the 28th, *G.2* sent Bolbrecht's *U-78* to the bottom of the North Sea in similar circumstances. Another October victim was *UB-123* who fell foul of the Northern Barrage minefields and blew up with all hands. Yet they still fought on and, with defeat in sight, one U-boat commander made a valiant last attempt to salvage his own, and the Imperial Navy's honour.

UB-116 headed north in the true spirit of the Valkyrie of ancient Teutonic legend. All had been lost, the Kaiser's empire was crumbling, and the invincible German army was retreating. But even now honour could still be saved in a last and glorious exploit. The submarine's bows plunged through the waves, a damp autumnal mist hung over the sea and Kapitanleutnant Emsmann peered up hopelessly for a sight of the sun with which to fix his position with certainty. With a last despairing glance at the grey October sky he turned to Leutnant Schutz standing watch at his side.

'No chance of a fix with all this fog and cloud about,' he grumbled. 'Let's hope the pilot's navigation is as good as he says it is. We'll have to go in on dead reckoning. Prepare to submerge.'

Schutz ducked down into the control room and his clipped orders sent the crew hurrying to their diving positions. A moment later Emsmann followed him down into the interior of the submarine, slamming and dogging the hatch behind him.

'Stand by to dive.'

'All vents open. Clutches out. All switches on. Depth twenty metres. Dive!'

UB-116 slid under the waves and Emsmann, studying the pilot's plot on the chart, passed a series of new course directions to the helmsman. Ten miles ahead, shrouded in the mist, lay the dreadnoughts of the Grand Fleet, anchored at Scapa Flow. Once, at the beginning of the war, von Hennig had tried to penetrate the anchorage and failed. He was now a prisoner of war while his boat, *U-18*, lay a shattered wreck on the bottom of the sea. Since then not a single U-boat captain had dared to challenge the giants in their lair. Such an attack could only have one of two results, success or suicide. Emsmann was prepared to take the gamble.

It is a fine tribute to the U-boat service that *UB-116* was manned by her own regular crew despite the hazardous nature of her mission. Only one man, Leutnant Schutz, was a volunteer and even he had served in the submarine on a previous patrol. They were just a group of men doing their duty according to their own lights. Not heroes and not daredevils. Just ordinary sailors obeying the commands of a trusted captain.

As *UB-116* closed the vast anchorage her presence beneath the surface was located by the shore detection devices of the outer Hoxa defences. With narrowed eyes and racing pulses the British officers allowed her to continue deeper into the trap. They waited until she was in the centre of a controlled minefield and then an anonymous hand came down on a switch. Suddenly *UB-116*, Emsmann, Schutz, and the rest of the submarine's crew were no more. The mines, detonated by an electrical circuit controlled from a shore station, exploded and the U-boat settled for her last rest on the bottom of the sea, the final U-boat to be sunk by enemy action in the waters surrounding the British Isles.

For Emsmann it had been a wasted journey. Many months before the Grand Fleet had moved its main base to the Firth of Forth and the great expanse of land-locked water was empty. But whether Emsmann had discovered the futility of his mission before the mines exploded will never be known.

CHAPTER SIXTEEN

'Are you absolutely sure
of your crew?'

THE EVENTS OF October, 1918, moved with startling swift-
ness. At the beginning of the month the British army smashed
through the vaunted Hindenburg line north of St Quentin
following the battles of Bellecourt and Le Catelat and, with
over 2,000,000 casualties during the previous six months of
fighting, the German military position collapsed.

On 5 October the new Chancellor, Prince Max of Baden,
appealed for an armistice in the hope of obtaining honourable
terms from the Allies. President Wilson informed him that all
occupied territory must be given up first and added, a few
days later, that 'all inhuman acts' must cease. The Chancellor
read this further condition as a reference to the U-boat campaign and the Kaiser, convinced that the Navy was his trump
card, travelled to Berlin to beg Prince Max to continue the war
at sea. Backed by Admiral Scheer, whose faith in submarine
warfare was by now almost fanatical, Wilhelm claimed that
the U-boats and the High Seas Fleet were Germany's most
valuable bargaining counters in any negotiations for peace on
reasonable terms, and that to suspend operations at sea was
tantamount to committing national suicide.

But the politicians, many of whom had opposed unrestricted
submarine warfare from the very beginning, were, by now,
heartily sick of the Kaiser and his militarists. Anxious to
placate the American President, and no longer fearing the
power of the All Highest, they refused to accept his arguments
and a reluctant Scheer was ordered to send a signal to the
U-boats informing them that attacks on passenger ships must
cease from 21 October. The order was transmitted by wireless

and, one by one, the U-boats abandoned their patrol areas and turned towards home. For one British steamer the message was received too late. During the final day of the campaign the *St Barchan* was torpedoed without warning four miles off the coast of Ireland with the loss of eight seamen. Although only a small coasting vessel of 362 tons she has her place in naval history as the last merchant ship sunk in British home waters by a U-boat's torpedoes in the 1914–1918 war, the very last to be sunk in the campaign were the *Surada* and *Mercia* both torpedoed off Port Said on 2 November.

Scheer, however, refused to give up hope. Wilson's conditions had not forbidden U-boat attacks on warships and, in addition, the High Seas Fleet was still intact. In consultation with Admiral von Hipper, the Chief of Naval Staff began to plan a vast operation which involved the use of both surface ships and submarines in an ambitious two-pronged attack. One, a raid on the Flemish coast, was to be undertaken by cruisers and destroyers with the battle fleet in support; the other, a powerful strike by the Second Scouting Group, was to be launched on shipping in the Thames estuary backed up by the battle-cruisers. In anticipation of Beatty's Grand Fleet coming south from its Scottish bases the U-boats were allocated ambush positions athwart the enemy's probable line of advance.

Had such a clash taken place it would have undoubtedly outranked Jutland as the greatest sea battle ever fought. But, as with so many of Scheer's plans, it never came to fruition.

Cooped up in harbour for nearly two years, with its best officers and petty-officers withdrawn for service with the U-boats, the High Seas Fleet was a hotbed of discontent. Revolutionary agitators ashore had been working on the demoralized sailors for many months, inflammatory pamphlets circulated the mess decks of every ship and, with little to do, the sailors spent fruitless hours discussing politics and grievances.

'The men did not now trouble to hold their meetings in secret, before the very eyes of their officers they flaunted their revolutionary opinions . . . No one worried any longer about keeping a look-out . . . every duty was carried out merely as a matter of form [and] carried out slowly and grudgingly.'[1]

In such a seething atmosphere it needed little to ignite the smouldering embers of mutiny and Scheer's grandiose plan acted as the spark. When the signal was hoisted by the flagship to raise steam in readiness for the operation the crews of the battleships *Ostfriesland* and *Thuringen* came out in open mutiny. Stokers drew fires, and sailors smashed the capstan to prevent the anchors being raised. Then on both ships the mutineers barricaded themselves into the forward battery, defying all efforts by the officers to dislodge them.

There is a bitter irony in the fact that the date of the Navy's betrayal was 28 October, the same day on which Emsmann and the crew of *UB-116* had sacrificed their lives in the gallant but suicidal attack on Scapa Flow for the honour of Germany.

Johann Spiess, the veteran commander of the U-boat war who we last saw attacking the auxiliary cruiser *Calgarian* in *U-19*, was waiting to take his new *U-135* to sea when the mutiny erupted and he was immediately ordered to report to Kommodore Michelsen's office. The first question Michelsen put was a clear indication of what the authorities had in mind.

'Are you absolutely sure of your crew?'

Spiess, surprised at the question but half-suspecting what was to follow, confirmed that he was. Michelsen did not enlighten him further but told him to report to the fleet commander. On arrival the Admiral repeated the question and, once again, Spiess assured him that he was absolutely sure of his men. The proposition was then put to him—*U-135* was to accompany two harbour boats full of armed sailors into the Schillig Roads where the mutinous ships lay at anchor and, it was implicit in

[1] *Fifty Mutinies, Rebellions and Revolutions*, by Alastair Maclean (Odhams Press) p. 108.

the instructions, the U-boat was to torpedo one or both battleships if the mutineers refused to surrender. Spiess asked Admiral von Trotha for written orders but his request was ignored. Clearly, with the possibility of widespread revolution at the dockyard gates, no one intended to take responsibility. What had happened to the Admirals and officers of the Imperial Russian Navy was only too fresh in everyone's mind. Even Hipper, when asked, avoided giving the U-boat commander a direct order and there is little doubt that the flag officers were exploiting Spiess's loyalty and patriotism with the intention of keeping their own skins intact.

U-135 carried out her distasteful task without argument and Spiess placed his submarine 'between the two mutinous battleships, ready to torpedo one or the other with bow or stern tubes.' In the event force was not required—the threat was enough. The men on both ships surrendered, the mutiny was quelled and, although disaffection remained rife, no further trouble was anticipated. The loyalty of the U-boat crews had proved unshakeable even in the face of mutiny.

It was an unfortunate decision by the new Social Democrat Government that rekindled the flames. Matters were taken out of the hands of the naval authorities and instructions were given that the mutineers were to be freed from prison and, even more disastrous, the fleet was to be dispersed to its individual bases. Although the Naval Staff, with surprising indiscipline, disobeyed the first part of the Government's order they acquiesced in the second and the various squadrons made their way to their home ports.

The ships dispersed to Kiel were rapidly coerced by the revolutionaries in the dockyards and a mass meeting was scheduled for 2 November at which inflammatory speeches were made demanding the abolition of the monarchy and the officer class, and the release of the imprisoned mutineers from the *Ostfriesland* and *Thuringen*. A further meeting was called for the following Sunday and, by this time, the authorities were seriously alarmed by the incipient revolt. A general recall signal was made while the meeting was in progress but the sailors ignored it and, when armed shore patrols were sent to round them up, they were disarmed and, in many cases, persuaded to join the rebels.

Anticipating an attack on the naval prison where the mutineers were being held, the authorities needed a loyal section of the Navy who could be relied upon to defend it against the mob. Once again they picked the U-boat men and, when the mutineers, carrying red flags and shouting 'All power to the soviets', began their march on the prison they found their way barred by a line of men from the *Deutsche Unterseeboots Flotille* drawn up with fixed bayonets. The leutnant in charge ordered the rebel sailors to halt. They ignored him. 'Turn about,' he shouted. But they came on.

When they were within twenty yards of the defenders an order was given and a volley of shots was fired over the marcher's heads. The mob hesitated but, forced on by the momentum of the crowds in the rear, they began to advance again. This time the U-boat men fired straight into the oncoming mass. Two ring-leaders fell dead and forty mutineers were wounded. There was a sudden panic and the enormous mass of marching sailors broke up in disorder, fleeing wildly in all directions, 4,000 routed by a handful of stalwart submarine men.

But the damage had been done. Ship after ship joined the mutineers until every single battleship at Kiel had the red flag flying from its masthead to signify that it was under the control of a Sailor's Council. The sailors, too, began organizing themselves into armed raiding parties which spread the revolutionary gospel out into the surrounding countryside far beyond the gates of the naval dockyard. The Government issued orders strictly forbidding the authorities to open fire on the rebels again and lurid newspaper reports of the shootings at the naval prison inflamed the rest of the fleet into joining what was, by now, a full-blooded bolshevik-inspired revolt. The squadron at Brunsbuttel threw down their arms and joined the rebels on 5 November and, shortly afterwards, the men at Wilhelmshaven added their strength to the revolutionary struggle. Soon Hamburg and Bremen came under the control of the Sailor's Councils and, by the 7th, Hanover, Brunswick, and Cologne, were also in the hands of the mutineers.

Kommodore Michelsen gathered his U-boats together and took them to sea in a vain search for a refuge uninfected by the red fever that was seizing the nation. By now all the main fleet bases were controlled by the mutineers and it was felt that even Heligoland, Borkum, and Sylt—islands off the coast and thus cut off from the mainstream of the revolution—were no longer safe havens in which to hide. In desperation the U-boat commanders were summoned to a Council of War on the cruiser *Graudenz* where the men who had brought terror and death to the seven seas sought comfort from each other and anxiously discussed where they could run for safety. In the end the bitter truth had to be faced. There was nowhere they *could* go, except to return to Germany and accept the humiliation of surrendering to the Soldiers' and Sailors' Councils which were now in complete control of the naval bases.

By common consent *U-135* was excepted from the *Graudenz* decision because it was feared that Spiess and his men would be victimized, and probably shot, for their part in crushing the October mutiny in Schillig Roads and Michelsen agreed that the U-boat could head east into the Baltic in the hope of escaping to Memel. But Spiess never made it. A wireless message warning that British destroyers had broken into the Heligoland Bight with orders for all U-boats to take up their war stations immediately made him reverse course. But the signals were false. Realizing that there could be no escape from the nemesis that had overtaken his beloved country, and disregarding his own personal safety, Spiess obeyed orders, returned to Wilhelmshaven, and surrendered his boat to the mutineers.

Battered by the tempests of the Atlantic, beaten by the anti-submarine defences of the Royal Navy, and betrayed by their own comrades serving in the surface warships, the U-boat flotillas had come to the end of their careers. Fighting to the last and unaffected by the fever of revolution gripping the rest of the armed forces they were finally forced to surrender in circumstances against which further resistance was impossible.

The Naval Terms of the Armistice, signed on 11 November, 1918, laid down that the German fleet was to be handed over to the Allies for internment pending the signing of the Peace Treaty. The U-boats, however, those hated underwater killers, were to be ignominiously surrendered. It was a bitter blow to the men who had manned the submarines throughout the war. As the captain of *U-152*, Franz, remarked: ' . . . the submarines have been doing all the work in the war. The battleships and cruisers of the High Seas Fleet have been doing next to nothing.' Franz, unwittingly, had hit the nail on the head. The battleship crews, demoralized and mutinous, constituted no viable threat to the dominance of the Royal Navy. But the U-boats, which in 1917 had brought Britain to the brink of defeat, were crewed by men full of fight and spirit. *They* remained an ever present threat and Britain was not prepared to take chances.

Paragraph 22 of the Armistice spelled out the doom of the U-boats in phrases that brooked no misunderstanding:

[Germany is] to surrender at the ports specified by the Allies and the United States all submarines at present in existence (including all submarine-cruisers and minelayers) with armament and equipment complete. Those that cannot put to sea shall be deprived of armament and equipment and shall remain under the control of the Allies and the United States. Submarines ready to put to sea shall be prepared to leave German ports immediately on receipt of wireless orders to sail to the port of surrender, the remainder to follow as soon as possible. The conditions of this article shall be completed within 14 days of the signing of the Armistice.

The sad procession of defeated U-boats began on 20 November when the first twenty submarines arrived at Harwich, the White Ensign flying proudly above the German Imperial flag to symbolize their abject surrender. And any thoughts which the officers may have had about scuttling their boats in Germany were quickly dispelled when the Allies made it known that, in such an eventuality, they would occupy the island fortress of Heligoland.

Commander Stephen King-Hall revealed the human side of the surrender in his autobiography. As one of the Royal Navy officers deputed to supervise the surrender he met several German captains and mentions one, Kapitanleutnant Oelricher, who had brought over *U-98*. After the routine paper work had been completed King-Hall queried whether the Zeiss binoculars slung around Oelricher's neck were his own or Government property. The German admitted they were naval issue 'and solemnly placed them round my neck. He then held out his hand rather shyly. We were strictly enjoined to have no intercourse with the German captains but I shook him by the hand; he looked so miserable with the White Ensign flying over the German ensign. He brushed aside a tear and muttered a "thank you" as he stepped off his ship on his way back to Germany.'[1]

Other commanders chose different courses. Von Schrader, skipper of *U-53*, the boat which Hans Rose had made famous, acted on his own initiative and took his command to Sweden for internment. Franz, captain of the submarine-cruiser *U-152*, taking a democratic line, put the matter to his crew and took a a vote. Ten were in favour of going to Sweden for internment but seventy favoured returning to Kiel and surrendering. Their

---

[1] *My Naval Life*, p. 161

decision was carried out faithfully and, on 24 November, *U-152* joined the other disconsolate submarines at Harwich— her final trip across the North Sea being made under a young leutnant who had been elected to act as captain by the crew.

Others, like the irrepressible Otto Hersing, took their own measures to salve their honour. His *U-21* was ordered to surrender but, quite fortuitously, she sprang a leak and sank while in the tow of a British ship. It was not difficult to guess from Hersing's sardonic smile when he told the story that the leak was more inspired than providential. *UB-89*, *UC-40*, *UC-71*, *UC-91*, *U-16*, and *U-97*, all foundered while on passage to England which suggests that Hersing was not the only one to continue his struggle to the very last.

Von Arnauld's *U-139* arrived back at Kiel three days after the Armistice was signed and she ended her days serving under the French tricolour as the *Halbronn*. To add to the bitterness of defeat, Germany's ace of aces had to leave his boat in the command of a young leutnant and walk ashore in plain clothes to avoid recognition by the revolutionary sailors in control of the base. He remained in the service of the German Navy throughout the inter-war years and met his death in a flying accident shortly after the French surrender in 1940, while acting as an intermediary in secret negotiations with Admiral Darlan and the Vichy Government.

Many other leading commanders survived the war including Kurt Hartwig, Ernst Hashagen, Heino von Heimburg, Otto Hersing, and Waldemar Kophamel. But others were not so fortunate and, in all, 515 officers and 4,894 sailors of the U-boat service lost their lives in action. On the material side 178 German submarines had been destroyed by enemy action or accident, a further 14 scuttled in the Adriatic or in Flanders, and by 1 December 122 U-boats had been surrendered at Harwich. To balance these German losses 6,692,000 tons of British shipping had been sent to the bottom by direct submarine attack and, according to the most reliable statistics available, a world total of 5,708 ships were destroyed by the U-boats, representing the almost incredible total of 11,018,865 tons capacity. In terms of civilian lives the toll was even greater. 13,333 non-combatants, including women and children, perished in British ships sunk or damaged by U-boat attack and a further 1,620 were lost through mines. The world figures have never been revealed but, based on tonnages sunk, the casualty figures are probably at least double these totals. It was, in every way, the Killing Time.

It is small wonder that Admiral Sims, the United States C-in-C, observed: 'Could Germany have kept fifty submarines constantly at work on the great shipping routes in the winter and spring of 1917 *nothing could have prevented her from winning the war.*'

*   *   *

Sitting behind the barbed wire of his prison camp the commander of *UB-68* speculated on the future. His boat, as narrated in Chapter 14, had been sunk during a surface attack on a convoy near Malta on 4 October, 1918. As a prisoner of war his prospects were bleak but, unlike many of his comrades, he had at least survived the war. Night after night he sat alone in his wooden hut deep in thought as he considered ideas on the correct tactics which should have been adopted by the U-boats. Just over thirty years later his theories were put to the test and, once again, the U-boats nearly won a war for Germany. 785 U-boats were destroyed in this second attempt to change world history and more than 14,500,000 tons of merchant shipping went to the bottom. One man more than anyone was responsible for their successes, the former commander of *UB-68*. His name was Karl Dönitz.

APPENDIX ONE

EQUIVALENT RANKS

Imperial German Navy	Royal Navy
Grossadmiral	Admiral of the Fleet
Admiral	Admiral
Vizeadmiral	Vice-Admiral
Konteradmiral	Rear-Admiral
Kommodore	Commodore
Kapitän zur See	Captain
Fregattenkapitän*	Commander
Korvettenkapitän*	Commander
Kapitänleutnant	Lieutenant-Commander
Oberleutnant zur See	Lieutenant
Leutnant zur See	Sub-Lieutenant

* The ranks of Fregattenkapitän and Korvettenkapitän have no precise equivalent in the Royal Navy.

APPENDIX TWO

GERMAN SUBMARINE ACES

Officer	Patrols	Tonnage sunk
K/K Lothar von Arnauld de la Perière. (*U-35* & *U-139*)	10	400,000
K/L Walther Forstmann. (*U-12* & *U-39*)	16	380,000
★ K/K Max Valentiner. (*U-38* & *U-157*)	17	300,000
K/L Hans Rose. (*U-53*)	12	210,000
K/L Otto Steinbrinck. (*UB-10*, *UB-18*, *UB-57*, *UC-65*)	24	210,000
K/L Waldemar Kophamel. (*U-35*, *U-151*, *U-140*)	10	190,000
★ K/L Walther Schwieger. (*U-20* & *U-88*)	12	190,000
K/L Hans von Mellenthin. (*UB-43* & *UB-49*)	11	170,000
★ K/L Claus Rücker. (*U-34* & *U-103*)	14	170,000
K/L Wünsche. (*U-25*, *U-70*, *U-97*)	12	160,000
O/L Reinhold Salzwedel. (*UB-10*, *UB-81*, *UC-21*, *UC-71*)	12	150,000
O/L Steinbauer. (*UB-47* & *UB-48*)	10	140,000
★ K/L Gansser. (*U-33* & *U-156*)	8	140,000
K/L Robert Moraht. (*U-64*)	9	130,000
★ K/L Wilhelm Werner. (*U-55*)	10	130,000
K/L Leo Hillebrand. (*U-16* & *U-46*)	12	130,000
K/L Otto Schultze. (*U-63*)	6	130,000
K/L Rudolf Schneider. (*U-24* & *U-87*)	10	130,000
K/L Ernest Hashagen. (*UB-21* & *U-62*)	8	130,000
K/L Kurt Hartwig. (*U-32* & *U-63*)	10	130,000

★ Listed as War Criminals by the British Government.

APPENDIX THREE

DISTRIBUTION OF OPERATIONAL U-BOATS

	North Sea*	Baltic	Flanders	Adriatic	Constantinople
Sept 1914	19†	4	–	–	–
Sept 1915	10	4	15	9	5
Feb 1917	49	2	33	24	3
May 1918	98†	–	34	33	4

* Based on North Sea harbours but operating in North Sea, Atlantic, United States and African coasts.

† Approximate numbers.

Note: A varying number of obsolescent submarines were attached to the Periscope School at Kiel throughout the war including, at one time, Weddigen's *U-9*.

APPENDIX FOUR

REPRESENTATIVE U-BOAT CLASS DETAILS

Class	U-1	U-9	U-27	U-51	U-71
Submerged displacement	283	611	867	902	832
Surface displacement	238	493	675	712	755
Length	139'	188'	212'	214'	186'
Prototype launch date	4-8-06	1910	1913	1915	1915
Surface speed	10.8	14	16.75	17	10.6
Submerged speed	8.7	8	9.8	9	7.9
Torpedo tubes	1-18"	4-18"	4-20"	4-20"	2-20"
Guns	–	1-37mm	2-3.4"	2-3.4"	1-3.4"
Complement	22	29	35	35	32
Builders	G	D	D	G	V
					(38 mines)

Class	U-81	U-99	U-105	U-139	U-151
Submerged displacement	946	952	1000	2483	1875
Surface displacement	808	750	798	1930	1512
Length	230	221'	235'	311'	213'
Prototype launch date	1916	1917	1917	1917	1916
Surface speed	16.8	16.5	16.4	15.8	12.4
Submerged speed	9.1	8.8	8.4	7.6	5.2
Torpedo tubes	6-20"	4-20"	6-20"	6-20"	2-20"
Guns	1-4.1"	2-3.4"	1-4.1"	2-5.9"	2-5.9"
			1-3.4"	2-3.4"	2-3.4"
Complement	35	36	36	62	56
Builders	G	W	G	G	G

APPENDIX FOUR (*cont.*)

Class	UB-1	UB-30	UB-103	UC-1	UC-55
Submerged displacement	142	303	649	183	498
Surface displacement	127	274	519	168	415
Length	92′	121′	182′	111′	165′
Prototype launch dates	1915	1915	1917	1915	1916
Surface speed	6.5	9.5	13.6	6.25	11.6
Submerged speed	5.5	5.7	8	5.25	7.3
Torpedo tubes	2–18″	2–20″	5–20″	–	3–20″
Guns	–	1–3.4″	1–3.4″	1–mg	1–3.4″
Complement	14	23	34	14	26
Builders	G	BV	BV	V	D
				(12 mines)	(18 mines)

Notes on tables:

(a) Displacement stated in tons
(b) Length stated in feet
(c) Speed stated in knots
(d) Gun calibres and torpedo diameters converted to nearest equivalents
     in inches
(e) Builders: G: Germaniawerft, Kiel
                D: Danzig Dockyard
                W: A. G. Weser, Bremen
                V: A. G. Vulcan, Stettin and Hamburg
               BV: Blohm & Voss, Hamburg

272

BIBLIOGRAPHY AND SOURCES

The author would like to acknowledge his debt to the following published works which have provided much of the source material for this book. For the reader who wishes to learn more about the naval history of the First World War and the role played by the U-boats this will also provide a useful bibliography.

The German Submarine War by R. H. Gibson and Maurice Prendergast (Constable, 1931)
Smoke on the Horizon by Vice Admiral C. V. Usborne (Hodder & Stoughton)
Raiders of the Deep by Lowell Thomas (Heinemann, 1929)
Subs and Submariners by Arch Whitehouse (Muller, 1961)
The Most Formidable Thing by Rear-Admiral William Jameson (Rupert Hart-Davis, 1965)
A Damned Un-English Weapon by Edwyn Gray (Seeley Service & Co, 1971)
Official History of the War. Naval Operations (Volumes 1 to 5) by Sir Julian S. Corbett and Sir Henry Newbolt (Longmans, 1923)
My Naval Life by Commander Stephen King-Hall (Faber & Faber, 1952)
Sea Fights of the Great War by W. L. Wyllie and M. F. Wren (Cassells, 1918)
Der Krieg zur See, 1914–1918, Der Handelskrieg mit U-Booten edited by Rear-Admiral Arno Spindler. (No English edition available)
War Memoirs of David Lloyd George (Nicholson & Watson, 1933)
My Memoirs by Grand Admiral von Tirpitz (Hurst & Blackett, 1919)
Warships of World War 1 by H. M. Le Fleming (Ian Allan)
Germany's High Seas Fleet in the World War by Admiral Scheer (Cassell, 1920)
The Times History of the Great War (Volumes 1–22)
The Grand Fleet by Admiral of the Fleet Earl Jellicoe (Cassells, 1919)
Fear God and Dread Nought edited by Arthur J. Marder (Jonathan Cape, 1952–1959)
By Guess and By God by William Guy Carr (Hutchinson, 1930)
The Life of John Rushworth Earl Jellicoe by Admiral Sir Reginald Bacon (Cassell, 1936)
The Crisis of the Naval War by Admiral of the Fleet Earl Jellicoe (Cassell, 1920)

BIBLIOGRAPHY AND SOURCES (*cont.*)

The Navy and Defence by Admiral of the Fleet Lord Chatfield (Heinemann, 1942)
My Adventurous Life by Admiral Lord Mountevans (Hutchinson, 1947)
The Dark Invader by Kapitan von Rintelen von Kleist (Lovat Dickson, 1933)
British Sea Power by Vice Admiral B. B. Schofield (Batsford, 1967)
Submarine and Anti-Submarine by Henry Newbolt (Longmans, Green & Co, 1919)
German Warships of World War I by John C. Taylor (Ian Allan, 1969)
The Approaches are Mined by Captain Kenneth Langmaid (Jarrolds, 1965)
Q-Ships and their Story by E. Keble Chatterton (Sidgwick & Jackson, 1922)
Danger Zone by E. Keble Chatterton (Rich & Cowan, 1934)
The Dover Patrol by Admiral Sir Reginald Bacon (Hutchinson)
Q-boat Adventures by Lt-Commander Harold Auton, VC (Herbert Jenkins, 1919)
My Mystery Ships by Rear Admiral Gordon Campbell, VC (Hodder & Stoughton, 1928)
Strange Intelligence by H. C. Bywater & H. C. Ferraby (Constable, 1931)
Fifty Mutinies, Rebellions and Revolutions (*Mutiny of Despair*, Page 106), by Alastair Maclean (Odhams Press)
Sub-Sunk by Captain W. O. Shelford (Harrap, 1960)
Pull Together The Memoirs of Admiral Sir Lewis Bayly (Harrap, 1939)
The Eyes of the Navy by Admiral Sir William James (Methuen, 1955)
The Far and the Deep by Edward P. Stafford (Arthur Barker, 1968)
The Sea is Strong by Admiral Sir Dudley de Chair (Harrap, 1961)
Keeping The Seas by Captain E. R. G. R. Evans (Sampson Low, 1919)
Roger Keyes by Cecil Aspinall-Oglander (Hogarth Press, 1951)
Victory at Sea by Rear-Admiral W. Sims (Murray, 1921)
Aim Straight by Peter Padfield (Hodder & Stoughton, 1966)
Russians at Sea by David Woodward (Kimber, 1965)
Records by Lord Fisher (Hodder & Stoughton, 1919)
Jutland—An Eye-Witness Account by Stuart Legg (Rupert Hart-Davis, 1966)

INDEX

Abosso, 181
Aboukir, HMS, 50–1, 61
Ackermann, K/L, 218
Aden-Wen, 94
Ajax, HMS, 42
Alarm, HMS, 62
Alfonso, King Don, 210
Alnwick Castle, 180
Amalfi, 124
Amazon, 245
Amiral Charner, 210
Amiral Ganteaume, 66–7
Anna Maria, 176
Arabic, 105, 110–12, 146
Ariel, HMS, 94
Arnauld de la Perière, Leut. Friedrich
    von, 94
Arnauld de la Perière, K/K Lothar von,
    208–11, 214, 216–17, 219, 226, 238–
    240, 265
Arrogant, HMS, 123
Artesia, 229
Askold, 123
Athos, 215
Attentive, HMS, 59–60
Auguste Conseil, 94

Bachmann, Admiral, 84, 111–12
Bacon, Admiral Sir Reginald, 202–3, 207
Baden, Prince Max of, 257
Baden, 227
Balfour, Rt. Hon. Arthur, 171, 253
Baron Balfour, 206
Bauer, Kommodore, 60, 65, 71, 77, 157–
    158, 197
Bauer, Wilhelm, 25–8, 31, 50
Bay, Petty-Officer, 190–1
Bayly, Vice-Ad. Sir Lewis, 72–4
Beagle, 183
Beatty, Admiral Sir David, 63, 80, 102,
    157–8, 258
Behncke, Admiral, 22
Beitzen, K/L Kurt, 153–5, 253
Belgian Prince, 200–1
Bell, Capt. John, 92–3
Belridge, 89

Ben Cruachan, 78
Ben Rinnes, 61
Berckheim, K/L Egewolf, von, 60
Birmingham, HMS, 43, 49
Blackwood, Comdr., 168–9
Blaikie, Capt., 213
Blanche, HMS, 95
Boadicea, HMS, 158
Bolbrecht, K/L, 254
Boldt, Leut., 244
Bothmer, K/L von, 159, 199
Bowman, Ch.Eng. Thomas, 200–1
Branlebas, 114
Britannia, HMS, 224
Britannia, SS, 229
British Transport, 205
Briziela, 229
Buruto, 230
Busche, Leut. z See, 246
Bylands, 221

Caledonia, 213
Calgarian, 247, 259
Calley, Lt. William L., 86
Calthorpe, Vice Ad. Sir S. A. Gough-,
    219
Cambrank, 90
Campanula, HMS, 219
Campbell, VC, Capt. Gordon, 177–8,
    194
Capelle, Admiral von, 139
Caprera, 206, 228–9
Carolina, 234
Carson, Sir Edward, 171
Carthage, 127
Casement, Sir Roger, 147
Caucasian, 109
Chair, Ad. Sir Dudley de, 59, 207
Chateaurenault, 218
Chatfield, Capt. A. S. M., 63
Churchill, Winston S., 20, 37, 42
City of Birmingham, 165
City of Corinth, 197
City of Lucknow, 210
City of Paris, 216
Clan Macleod, 131

Coreopsis, HMS, 246, 250
Cornwallis, HMS, 213
Cressey, HMS, 50, 52, 61
Cyclamen, HMS, 219
Cymric, 205

Dacia, 214
Danton, 215
Dartmouth, HMS, 217
David, HMS, 248
Deppe, Machinest, 186, 189
d'Equevilley, R., 30–1
Ditmar, Leut., 244
Dönitz, O/L Karl, 87, 222, 266
Dorothy Gray, 68
Downshire, 90
Drake, HMS, 45, 206
Dreadnought, HMS, 95
Drina, 180
Droescher, K/L, 63–4, 79, 91, 238
Dublin, HMS, 158
Duff, Captain, 43
Duff, Douglas, 172
Duff, Rear Admiral A. L., 171, 182
Dulwich, 89
Dupetit-Thouars, 251
Durward, 77
Dvinsk, 235

Eagle, 25
Eckelmann, K/K, 229, 237
Eemdijk, 145
Ehrentrant, O/L Otto, 179
Eichmann, Adolf, 86
Emsmann, K/L, 254–6, 259
Endymion, HMS, 61

Fairy, HMS, 249
Falaba, 98
Falkenhayn, General von, 136–7
Falmouth, HMS, 45, 159
Feldkirchner, K/L, 61, 64–6
Feldt, K/L Richard, 237
Feltria, 197
Firedrake, HMS, 161
Fisher, Ad. of Fleet, Lord, 20, 39, 182
Fjeldi, 175
Flora, 52
Forelji, 30
Formidable, HMS, 73
Forstmann, K/L Walther, 94, 109, 130, 214
Forstner, K/L Freiherr von, 97
Franz, K/K, 237, 263–4
Fritzoe, 140
Fulton, Robert, 25
Furbinger, K/L Gerhardt, 103

Gallia, 211
Galway Castle, 252
Gansser, K/L, 130–2, 212, 214, 227–9
Garrett, Rev. G. W., 29
Garry, HMS, 69
Gaulois, 213–14
Gentian, HMS, 152
Georg, K/L Karl von, 139–41
Gerke, K/L, 230–1
Gibel-Haman, 252
Giralda, 229
Glimpf, O/L Hermann, 200
Glitra, 64–6
Gloucester Castle, 183
Goschen, Lord, 64
Graeff, K/L Ernest, 107
Graudenz, 262
Green, Capt. J. R., 99
Grey, Sir Edward, 39, 58
Gröning, Leut., 184
Gross, O/L Karl, 108
Grosserkurfurst, 167
Gulflight, 98, 100
Gunther, Torpedoman, 119
Gurkha, HMS, 93

Halcyon, 200
Hall, Stephen King-, 169, 264
Hall, Adm. Sir Reginald, 187
Hallweight, Comdr., 194
Hampshire, HMS, 154
Hanna, 98
Hanna Larsen, 179
Hans, K/L Walther, 157, 199, 213, 216
Hansen, K/L Klaus, 113
Hartmann, K/L Richard, 205
Hartwig, K/L Kurt, 212–13, 223, 265
Hashagen, K/L Ernst, 140–1, 149–50, 187, 194, 251, 265
Hawke, HMS, 61
Heimburg, K/K Heino von, 124–5, 128–129, 130, 133, 214, 265
Heinrich Lund, 235
Hela, 46, 54
Helfferich, 162
Hennig, K/L Heinrich von, 59, 68–9, 109–10, 166
Herbert, Comdr. Godfrey, 105–6
Hermes, HMS, 67
Hersing, K/L Otto, 13, 44, 46, 55, 67–8, 78–9, 118–24, 126–8, 129, 133, 204, 209, 214, 265
Hesperian, 112, 205
Highland Corrie, 197
Hilary, 197
Hindenburg, Marshal Paul von, 162–3
Hipper, Admiral von, 258, 260

Hirano Maru, 253
Hogue, HMS, 50-1, 61
Holland, John Phillip, 28-9, 31
Holtzendorff, Admiral von, 112, 136-8, 146, 162, 171
Hollweg, Chancellor Bethmann, 66, 70, 77, 111, 138-9, 146, 171, 193
Hoppe, K/L Bruno, 75-7, 149-50, 178
Hornsey, 179
Horsa, 187
Horton, Cmdr. Max, 46, 54
Hospital Ships:
    Anglia, 114
    Asturias, 79, 183
    Britannic, 212
    Dover Castle, 217
    Glenart Castle, 245
    Guildford Castle, 243
    Llandovery Castle, 243-5
    Portugal, 212
    Rewa, 243
    Triumph, 119-20, 122
Housatonic (Federal), 28
Hroptotz, 166
Hughes, Lt. Comdr. Guy D'Oyly, 230-1
Huntress, 232

Ilderton, 206
Ingenohl, Admiral von, 65, 80
Inverlyon, 108
Iron Duke, HMS, 42, 158
Isabel B. Wiley, 234
Itchin, 199

Jacob Jones, USS, 206-7
Jacobsen, Isak, 174
Jagow, Herr von, 162
Jellicoe, Admiral Sir John, 26, 42, 45, 62-64, 75, 96, 151-2, 154, 158-60, 170-171, 182, 192, 203, 207, 242
Johnson, Capt., 60
Jupiter, 173-4

Kanguru, 214
Karnak, 183
Kerry Range, 177
Keyes, Vice Admiral Sir Roger, 53, 94, 203, 252
Kieswetter, K/L Wilhelm, 245, 249
Kiev, 212
Kilcuan, 79
Kirchner, O/L, 130
Kitchener, Field Marshal Lord, 154-5, 253
Klasing, K/L Johannes, 223
Knappe, Seaman, 189
Koenig, K/L Georg, 76

Kolbe, O/L Walther, 229
Konig, Kapitan Paul, 151
Kophamel, F/K Waldemar, 92, 130-1, 133, 206, 208, 212, 214, 218, 226, 227-9, 237, 265
Korner, Leut. Frederich, 237
Kresch, K/L Gunther, 246
Kringsia, 235
Kroll, K/L Karl, 246
Kronprinz, 167
Kronprinz Wilhelm, 236
Kukat, O/L, 223-4
Kustner, K/L Heinrich, 196

La Belle France, 141
Laertes, 77-8
Lanfranc, 183
Launburg, O/L Otto, 220
Laurence, Lt. Com. Noel, 166
Lavender, HMS, 197
Leasowe Castle, 220
Leinster, 253
Leo, 109
Lepsius, O/L Reinhold, 92-3, 108
Liberty, HMS, 179
Lightning, HMS, 114
Linda Blanche, 79
Lloyd George, Rt. Hon. David, 171, 182, 193
Lorna, 249-50
Losz, O/L, 242
Loxley, Capt., 74
Ludendorff, Field Marshal von, 162
Lusitania, 18-23, 71, 100, 109, 111, 146, 166-7, 169, 205

Maclay, Sir Joseph, 193
Majestic, HMS, 123, 126
Mallachite, 67-8
Maori, HMS, 93, 114
Mariston, 199
Marquette, 130
Marzala, 121
Massue, 215
Mauretania, 147, 201, 236
Medea, 97, 145
Mercia, 222, 258
Meusel, K/L, 226-7, 229, 237
Meyer, O/L, 254
Michael, HMS, 245-6
Michaelis, Chancellor Georg, 193
Michelsen, Kom. Andreas, 241-2, 259, 262
Milne, HMS, 196
Minas, 214
Minotaur, HMS, 158
Minnetonka, 219

Moecke, O/L Fritz, 179
Mohawk, HMS, 114
Mona Queen, 180, 196
Monarch, HMS, 42
Mooltan, 218
Moraht, K/L Robert, 212, 215-16, 219-221
Moreni, 215
Mountevans, Admiral Lord, 215-16
Muller, O/L Hans, 206
Muller, Admiral von, 64, 80, 84, 111-112, 136, 156-7
My Lai Massacre trial, 86

Naesborg, 166
Narragansett, 180
Neptune, HMS, 95
Neumann, O/L Friedrich, 217, 245
Nicosian, 104-6
Nor, 98
Nordenfelt, Thorsten, 29-31, 101
Nostitz und Jackendorff, K/K von, 232-237
Nottingham, HMS, 157-8
Nuremburg Trials, 86-7
Nymphe, HMS, 62

Obj, 206
Oelricher, K/L, 264
Olive Branch, 205
Olympic, 248
Omrah, 220
Oracle, HMS, 201
Orion, HMS, 42
Ostfriesland, 259-60
Otway, HMS, 199

Palembang, 145
Pallada, 61
Panteleiman, 129
Pass of Balmaha, 107
Patagonia, 129
Pathfinder, HMS, 46, 54, 78, 120
Patzig, K/L, 243-5
PC-62, HMS, 242
Peat, RNR, Lieut., 247
Pelican, HMS, 159
Pennewell, Capt., 174
Persia, 132
Piercy, Lt-Comdr., 95
Pohl, Vice Ad. Hugo von, 64-5, 70-1, 80-1, 83-4, 89, 97, 111-12, 138
Polesley, 252
Porpoise, HMS, 159
Port Said, 232
Powhatan, 181
Primo, 68

Primula, HMS, 209
Princess Louise, HMS, 107
Propert, Capt. W. H., 77-8
Provence II, 209
Pullen, 218
Pustchin, 212
Pustkuchen, O/L Herbert, 144-6, 198

Q-Ships:
   Baralong, 105-6, 113
   Bracondale, 201
   Farnborough (Q-5), 177-9
   Glen, 196
   Heather (Q-16), 194
   Margit, 208
   Pargust, 194-5
   Pearl, 113
   Penshurst, 179
   Prince Charles, 107
   Privet (Q-19), 179, 223
   Prize, 185-7, 189, 192, 242
   Q-18, 179
   Stonecrop, 168-9, 206
   Tulip (Q-15), 177, 194

Rappahannock, 165
Ravenna, 216
Regin, 98
Rintelen, Kapt. Franz von, 145
Robinson, Capt., 109
Roburn, HMS, 93
Rohr, K/L Walther, 179
Rose, K/L Hans, 158, 163-4, 176, 207, 225, 264
Rosenow, K/L Ernst, 194
Royal Edward, 130
Rucker, K/L Claus, 130, 248
Russell, HMS, 212

S-17, 195
Sakaki, 217
Salybia, 145
Samoa, 235
Sanders, Lieut. W. E., 186-7
San Diego, USS, 237
Sarpedon, 223
Saturnia, 176
Savill, Capt., 154
Scheer, Admiral Reinhold von, 138, 146-147, 151-3, 156-9, 162-4, 167, 207, 249, 253, 257-9
Schmettow, K/L Graf von, 196
Schneider, K/L Rudolf, 67, 72-4, 105, 110-12
Schrader, K/L von, 264
Schtiendorff, O/L, 250
Schulthess, K/L, 107

Schulze, K/L Otto, 159, 218
Schwieger, K/L/Walther, 13–21, 23, 71,
  86, 91–100, 109, 111–12, 147, 167–9,
  197, 205, 225
Seaplane 204 (German), 94
Seaplane 8663 (British), 196
Seaplane 8676 (British), 206
Seaplane 8695 (British), 206
Sebelin, O/L, 180
Siess, K/K Gustav, 224
Sims, Vice Admiral W. S., 182, 266
Sittenfeld, K/L Erich, 174, 176
Snapdragon, HMS, 222
Southland, 130
Spiegel, K/L Baron Adolf, 75–7, 173–4,
  180, 184–7, 189–90, 192, 212
Spiess, K/L Johann, 36, 41, 47–50, 52,
  62, 80, 91, 226, 247, 259, 260, 262
Staunch, HMS, 218
Steinbauer, K/L, 188, 213–14
Steinbrinck, K/L Otto, 139, 147–9
Sterope, 229
Stoss, K/L Alfred, 91, 93
St Barchan, 258
Submarines:
  (American)
  AL-2, 250
  (British)
  A-13, 33
  C-24, 102
  C-27, 108
  C-34, 199
  D-7, 206
  E-3, 64
  E-7, 125, 129
  E-9, 46
  E-16, 108
  E-20, 129
  E-22, 148
  E-35, 230–1
  E-54, 162, 196
  G-2, 254
  G-13, 151
  H-4, 220
  J-1, 167
  L-12, 254
  (French)
  Circe, 221
  Turquoise, 129
  (German) See under U-boats
  (Pioneer)
  Der Brandtacher, 25–7, 31
  Diable-Marin, 27
  Forelj, 30
  Gymnote, 29
  Holland I, 29
  Holland V, 29

Holland IX, 31
Hunley, 28
Karp class, 30–1
Le Plongeur, 28
Nautilus, 25
Nordenfelt types, 29–30
Resurgam, 29
Turtle, 29
Suffren, 213
Surprise, 214
Suruda, 222, 258
Sussex, 144, 146, 198
Sylvester, Capt., 244

Tara, 131
Taranaki, HMS, 102–3
Tasman, 221
Taylor, Lieut., 102
Tebbenjohanns, K/L Kurt, 202–3, 206
Texel, 234
Theseus, HMS, 61
Thor II, 174
Thordis, 92
Thracia, 172–4
Thrasher, Leon C., 98
Thrasher, HMS, 179
Thuringen, 259–60
Tirpitz, Grand Admiral von, 19, 24, 31,
  34, 84, 96, 111–12, 137–8
Toro, 181
Torpedo-boat 95, 130
Torrington, 181, 243
Tresillian, 176
Trident, HMS, 152
Troilus, 196
Trotha, Admiral von, 260
Turbantia, 145–6
Turner, Captain, 16–17, 22

U-boats:
  U-1, 31–2, 227
  U-2, 32, 227
  U-3, 32
  U-4, 32
  U-5, 69
  U-6, 91–3, 108
  U-7, 76–7, 149
  U-8, 91, 93–4
  U-9, 33, 35–6, 40–2, 46–53, 61–2, 80,
    91, 94, 161
  U-10, 161
  U-11, 69
  U-12, 93–4
  U-13, 42
  U-14, 90, 108
  U-15, 42–3
  U-16, 68, 89, 265

U-17, 61, 64–5
U-18, 59, 68–9, 109, 166, 255
U-19, 33–4, 44, 77, 147, 226, 247, 259
U-20, 13–15, 17–19, 45, 63–4, 71, 79, 91, 100, 113, 166–8
U-21, 44–6, 67, 78–9, 118–24, 126–29, 133, 204–5, 265
U-22, 44, 75–7, 99, 149–50
U-23, 107–8
U-24, 66, 72–3, 110
U-26, 60
U-27, 64, 67, 91–2, 104–8, 113
U-28, 97–8, 205
U-29, 91, 94–6
U-30, 89–90, 98, 100, 166–7
U-31, 75–6
U-32, 75–7, 96, 152, 184, 212, 213, 219
U-33, 130–1, 212
U-34, 130, 223, 248
U-35, 96, 130–1, 208–11, 223, 227
U-36, 107–8
U-37, 96
U-38, 109, 130, 132
U-39, 109, 130, 175, 220
U-40, 102–3, 108
U-41, 113
U-43, 177
U-44, 147, 200–2
U-45, 174, 176, 206
U-46, 206
U-47, 221
U-49, 159, 165, 205
U-50, 165, 206
U-51, 162
U-52, 157–8, 199, 213, 216
U-53, 158–9, 163, 165, 176, 207, 225, 264
U-55, 181, 243
U-56, 165
U-57, 139–40, 199
U-59, 195
U-60, 177
U-62, 187, 251
U-63, 159, 223
U-64, 212, 215, 219, 220–1
U-65, 213
U-66, 147, 152, 159, 199
U-67, 177
U-68, 160
U-69, 147
U-73, 212
U-74, 161
U-75, 153–5
U-77, 162
U-78, 254
U-80, 177
U-81, 196

U-82, 252
U-83, 177–8
U-84, 179, 242
U-85, 179, 223
U-86, 195, 243–4
U-87, 242
U-88, 168–9, 197, 205
U-91, 265
U-93, 173, 184–6, 188–91, 242
U-95, 242
U-98, 250–1, 264
U-102, 255
U-103, 248
U-109, 242
U-110, 245–6
U-117, 238
U-135, 259–60, 262
U-139, 219, 225–6, 238–40, 265
U-140, 225–6, 237
U-151 (Ex Oldenburg), 206, 218, 227–229, 232–7
U-152, 227, 229, 237, 263–5
U-153, 230–1
U-154, 230–1
U-155 (Ex Deutschland), 226–7, 229, 237
U-156, 212, 228 –9, 237
U-157, 203, 237
UB-4, 108
UB-6, 180
UB-7, 129–30
UB-8, 129
UB-13, 160
UB-14, 124, 128–9
UB-15, 124
UB-17, 114
UB-18, 139, 147–8
UB-20, 200
UB-21, 140–1, 149
UB-23, 200
UB-24, 221
UB-25, 180
UB-26, 160
UB-27, 200
UB-28, 145
UB-29, 144
UB-30, 179–80
UB-32, 206
UB-35, 242
UB-39, 196
UB-44, 211
UB-45, 130
UB-47, 213
UB-48, 188
UB-50, 223
UB-52, 211, 221
UB-53, 211, 221

U-boats: *cont.*
  UB-55, 143
  UB-57, 242
  UB-65, 250
  UB-66, 219
  UB-68, 222, 266
  UB-69, 219
  UB-70, 219
  UB-71, 219
  UB-74, 249–50
  UB-85, 246
  UB-89, 265
  UB-90, 254
  UB-106, 247
  UB-116, 254–6, 259
  UB-123, 254
  UB-129, 222
  UC-2, 108–14
  UC-3, 161
  UC-5, 114, 160–1
  UC-6, 206
  UC-7, 162
  UC-8, 112
  UC-9, 112
  UC-10, 162
  UC-13, 129–30
  UC-14, 129
  UC-15, 129–30
  UC-18, 179–80
  UC-21, 206
  UC-25, 217
  UC-26, 180, 195–6
  UC-29, 194
  UC-32, 179
  UC-35, 220
  UC-36, 196
  UC-38, 218
  UC-39, 179
  UC-40, 265
  UC-42, 206
  UC-43, 180
  UC-44, 202–3, 206
  UC-46, 179
  UC-48, 248
  UC-55, 206
  UC-56, 245, 249
  UC-66, 198
  UC-67, 217
  UC-71, 265
  UC-72, 206
  UC-75, 197, 249
  UC-76, 195
  UC-77, 199
  UC-91, 265
  UF type, 241

W-1 & W-2, 30
Bremen, 151
Deutschland, 150–1, 163, 225–6
Oldenburg, 232

Urbino, 113
Use of neutral flags, 81–3, 85, 97–8, 100, 105, 113, 133
Usedom, Leut., 189–90

V-26, 180
Valentiner, K/K Max, 13, 109–10, 130, 132, 214, 119, 237–8
Vanguard, HMS, 45
Velox, HMS, 114
Vernon, HMS, 169
Victoria, 248
Viking, HMS, 93
Vindeggen, 234
Vine Branch, 181
Voigt, O/L Ernst, 200, 206
Vosges, 99

Wachendorff, O/L Siegfried, 75
Wagenfuhr, K/L Paul, 147, 200–2
Wallflower, HMS, 220
War Arabis, 221
War Diary of U-202, The, 184, 187
W. C. M'Kay, 239
Weddigen, K/L Otto, 13, 33, 35–6, 40–2, 46–55, 61–3, 80, 91, 94–6, 161, 225
Wegener, K/L Bernhard, 64, 104–6, 113
Weisbach, K/L, 147
Wellington, 221
Wendlandt, O/L Hans, 218
Wenniger, K/L Ralph, 142–3
Wernicke, K/L, 219
Werner, K/L Wilhelm, 129, 181, 243, 245
Wilhelm II, Kaiser, 19, 23, 35, 59–60, 65–66, 70–1, 77, 80–1, 83–4, 86, 111–12, 131, 136, 138–9, 144, 156–7, 163, 167–8, 171, 172, 210, 241, 257
Willow Branch, 230
Wilson, President Woodrow, 146, 164, 171, 257–8
Winneconne, 234

Yardley, Capt., 230
Yasaka Maru, 132

Zalinski, Edmund, 29
Zede, Gustav, 29
Zentner, Leut. Rudolf, 23, 71, 86
Ziegner, Leut. Wilhelm, 189–92, 242
Zillah, 206